# We as Self

# We as Self

## *Ouri*, Intersubjectivity, and Presubjectivity

Hye Young Kim

LEXINGTON BOOKS
*Lanham • Boulder • New York • London*

Published by Lexington Books
An imprint of The Rowman & Littlefield Publishing Group, Inc.
4501 Forbes Boulevard, Suite 200, Lanham, Maryland 20706
www.rowman.com

6 Tinworth Street, London SE11 5AL, United Kingdom

Copyright © 2021 by The Rowman & Littlefield Publishing Group, Inc

Cover illustration: *(Learning) The Grammar of the Act*. Liat Grayver. 2019. Interactive Robotic Room Installation with the e-David Project and Casa Paganini/InfoMus. This site-specific work is based on the movement and location of the visitors at the library of the University of Konstanz during the month of May 2019. The movement is extracted using a surveillance camera, translating each individual first into a digital trajectory then into brushstrokes painted by a robotic arm on a 100-meter long rice paper roll. At the end of each day, the roll is fully painted with different calligraphic lines describing the movement of visitors throughout the space.

*All rights reserved.* No part of this book may be reproduced in any form or by any electronic or mechanical means, including information storage and retrieval systems, without written permission from the publisher, except by a reviewer who may quote passages in a review.

British Library Cataloguing in Publication Information Available

**Library of Congress Cataloging-in-Publication Data**

Names: Kim, Hye Young, author.
Title: We as self : ouri, intersubjectivity, and presubjectivity / Hye Young Kim.
Description: Lanham : Lexington Books, [2020] | Includes bibliographical references and index.
Identifiers: LCCN 2020039739 (print) | LCCN 2020039740 (ebook) | ISBN 9781498554657 (cloth) | ISBN 9781498554671 (pbk) | ISBN 9781498554664 (epub)
Subjects: LCSH: Self (Philosophy) | Intersubjectivity. | Belonging (Social psychology)
Classification: LCC BD438.5 .K56 2020 (print) | LCC BD438.5 (ebook) | DDC 128—dc23
LC record available at https://lccn.loc.gov/2020039739
LC ebook record available at https://lccn.loc.gov/2020039740

*For Pascal Johann Deutsch*

Dasein

Zwischen den Orten begegnen wir uns
ein Lächeln, ein Stolpern, ein Blick
Im gestuften Stein tragen Schritte Namen
Alle Reisen zwischen Hoffnung und Neugier
glücklich, wer den falschen Zug verpasst
Auf den Treppen singt Licht uns von Liebe
Der Ewigkeit ist es egal wie schnell die Zeit vergeht.

*Auguste von Blau*

*"Poesie und Alltag"*
　*Das erste von 21 Exponaten aus der Ausstellung*
　*im öffentlichen Raum, „Zwischen Gleisen"*
　*von Auguste von Blau und Thomas Klingberg*
　*am alten S-Bahnhof Berlin Schöneberg*

# Contents

| | | |
|---|---|---|
| Preface | | xi |
| Acknowledgments | | xiii |
| 1 | We in Korean? Why? | 1 |
| 2 | We in Korean | 19 |
| 3 | Self in Korean | 49 |
| 4 | Self as Subject | 61 |
| 5 | Self in Pre-subjective Relation | 87 |
| 6 | Self-in-Relation and Pre-subjective We: Mathematical Representation | 99 |
| 7 | We in Diagrams | 121 |
| 8 | Primacy of We? | 135 |
| 9 | Notion of Relation | 153 |
| 10 | Feelings and Corporeality | 165 |
| 11 | Collective Memory: Boundary, Place, and Home | 181 |
| 12 | Epilogue: Violence of the We | 195 |
| Bibliography | | 199 |
| Index | | 209 |
| About the Author | | 215 |

# Preface

### OURI

*Ouri* is a Korean word that means 'we,' 'our,' or 'us.' It is pronounced as *oo-rie*.

Korean is written using *Hangeul* (한글, the Korean alphabet) invented by King Sejong the Great in 1443. *Hangeul* consists of twenty-four basic letters with fourteen consonants (ㄱ ㄴ ㄷ ㄹ ㅁ ㅂ ㅅ ㅇ ㅈ ㅊ ㅋ ㅌ ㅍ ㅎ) and ten vowels (ㅏ ㅑ ㅓ ㅕ ㅗ ㅛ ㅜ ㅠ ㅡ ㅣ), each of which is designed after the shape of the articulator and phonetic feature of its pronunciation. These letters are written in syllabic blocks arranged in two dimensions. Ironically, though, the fact that Korean has its own alphabetic writing system that designates its phonetic information, and which is also relatively easy to learn, has been one of the factors—among many others—that the Romanization of Korean has been confusing and inconsistent.

The old McCune-Reischauer (M-R) System of Romanization for the Korean language was developed in 1939. About half a decade later, the Yale Romanization of Korean, which is the standard Romanization of the Korean language in linguistics, was developed at Yale University. In 2000, the Ministry of Culture and Tourism of Korea released the Revised Romanization System (RR) in attempts to streamline the vowels and consonants of the Korean language, so that they could be readily identifiable. North Korea uses the New Korean Orthography System. The M-R and RR are the most commonly used systems for writing Korean in Latin letters.

However, the biggest problem of the M-R System is that it is hard to type on a standard computer keyboard because of the extra breves. In terms of the phonetic sounds being transliterated into Latin letters, the pronunciations of the Romanized words in the M-R System are closer to their Korean counterparts, even though the Korean vowels and consonants are more easily identifiable in the RR System, not only but especially for those who can read *Hangeul*.

The Romanization of the Korean words was one of the biggest challenges for this research, because most of the readers are not expected to speak or read Korean. I wanted to make sure that any reader who reads this book can have clear (at least, not confusing) phonetic information attached to the words that are being investigated, even if they do not speak Korean, and the readers should be able to read the words in Latin letters without having extra background information (the Romanization table) in order to understand what the breves and the apostrophes sound like. For that reason, despite its merit in reproducing the phonetic sounds, I decided to use the RR System over the M-R. However, there is still the problem that Romanized words under the RR System do not provide accurate pronunciation information.

A compromise that I found was to write the Romanized words using the RR System in *italic* and to add the pronunciation next to words when they are introduced for the first time in the text. However, instead of the phonetic alphabet, I used the regular English alphabet to provide information for sounding-out Korean words that are close to the actual Korean pronunciation for English-speaking readers. I then wrote the words or sentences in *Hangeul* in the footnotes. For example, the word that matches 'we,' 'our,' and 'us' in English:

*Uri* (Romanization)—[oo-rie] (Pronunciation)—footnote: 우리 (*Hangeul*)

However, exceptionally (and this is the only exception in the entire text), I write this word as *ouri* instead of *uri* in the text. This is done to increase the intuitive comprehension of the word through visuality. I assume that one could have a better sense of the word in connection with the English word 'our' when it is written as *ouri*. The French pronunciation matches this spelling: *ou* pronounced as *ou* in French. Therefore,

*Ouri* [oo-rie]—우리

This is the main word and the very topic of investigation which appears in the title of the book as well. Therefore, I wanted the readers, including potential readers who only see the cover of the book and do not speak Korean, to be able to feel some connection, instead of feeling totally estranged by an unexpected encounter with a completely foreign word. Of course, we should not judge a book by its cover, but the cover says so much to us already.

More detailed information about the Romanization table for the Korean language and the Korean alphabet can be found on the website of the National Institute of Korean Language: https://www.korean.go.kr/.

# Acknowledgments

First of all, I would like to thank my friends and colleagues who have accompanied me for the last few years as I was working on this project in Berlin and Paris.

I would like to express my gratitude for David Carr who became a very important friend to me in the last few years. I thank David for always reading all my first drafts and giving me insightful feedback and the warmest support, and for being such a faithful and loving friend.

Louis Kauffman opened the huge door to the world of mathematics for me. I thank Lou for his openness and generosity, for taking his time to discuss with me literally anytime, even during the holiday seasons. Discussions with Lou led me to develop the most crucial ideas of this project.

I would also like to thank Steven Davis for helping me to sharpen the discussion on the language use of the 'we' with his delicate and sharp commentary on my papers. I am very grateful also for his trust in me as a person and a philosopher and for his friendship.

Had I not moved to Paris and had all these people and experiences that only Paris could give, I must not have been able to finish this book. Dominique Pradelle and Uriah Kriegel made it possible for me to live and continue my research in Paris. Spontaneous discussions and conversations with Uriah were always inspiring. I thank Dominique for his generous acceptance. The well-thumbed couch at the old library in rue d'Ulm was my soothing reading spot. I am also very appreciative of my friend Michel Puech for his generosity, inspiration, and trust.

Eric Nelson and Jason Wirth have encouraged and supported me to pursue this project from the very beginning on. I am very grateful for their genuine friendship, ceaseless support, and unwavering trust. I thank Andreas Falck very much for his time to read my papers and discuss over many critical points, providing crucial reference information in related fields outside of philosophy.

I would like to thank Hilge Landweer, David Haekwon Kim, Josette Rapiera, Marisa and Luis Rabanaque, Arturo Romero, Carlos Lobo, and Soyoung Kim for hosting me to present my work in progress as I was developing the ideas for this project, and for the inspiring discussions and the thoughtful feedback.

In summer 2019, while the manuscript was slowly falling into place, my friend Ágnes Heller never returned from Lake Balaton. Ági was a brave and loving person. She was down-to-earth and loved jokes but was also a surprisingly well-read and insightful scholar. When I was in doubt and despair, she trusted and remembered me. She was a thoughtful friend, generous *Oma*, and a wise teacher to me. Our discussions were never dull. We laughed a lot together. We enjoyed our meals; afternoon liquor; little strolls in Berlin, Budapest, and Paris; and our countless stories. It was an unusually bright moment in life to run into someone with such a laugh and a great mind. I celebrate and remember our time together that won't be lost in time. I thank her for her love, for sharing her love for philosophy, people, and life.

I thank my Budapest friends David Weberman, Csaba Olay, and Mihály Vajda for their continuous support and caring friendship. I was able to see Ági off, thanks to these friends.

Shortly after the first draft was ready, I was invited to take part in the last journey of a special person as he was having his very conscious and thoughtful closure with his own life and everyone in it. I remember Grandpa Arthur Anderson, who lived in such a complete way. He was a humble person, a farmer who always saw himself in the field. But I saw, through him, how one person's genuine gratitude for life and compassion for people fill the life of his own and many others. I could have a glance at the meaning (*Sinn*) of a person's life, the life of the one who knew and accepted his end, just as he knew and accepted his life fully. It was the moment that the *Entschlossenheit* (resoluteness) truly unfolded itself in the present, without losing itself by taking its anxious risk in the future. As we had our last family Thanksgiving meal with Grandpa near the *día de muertos* (the day of the dead), the old farmhouse and its giant yellow trees were fully covered with Christmas snow, as if the strings of *our time* were curved in the *web* of our relation.

I would like to thank Jana Hodges-Kluck and the other staff from Lexington Books and the reviewer of my manuscript as well for their engagement and support that made the publication of this book possible.

The last but not the least: this project was thoroughly supported and fully funded by 'our' husband, Stephen Deutsch. I would like to thank Stephen, the most careful reader and the biggest supporter of my work, for his trust, patience, and devotion. I also remember and thank our son Pascal Johann, whose time with us was short but who taught us what it really means to "be with."

October 2020<br>
Les Récollets, Paris<br>
A.

*Chapter 1*

# We in Korean? Why?

### 1. WE

"Der Schulleiter und sein Team fördern das Wir-Gefühl" (the principal and his team promote the we-feeling) was the title of an article in *Berliner Morgenpost* on December 7, 2015, that introduced the story of how a primary school in Berlin, where nobody had wanted to send their kids anymore, was able to revive. The key was the we-feeling that saved the school. In recent years, we-ness and empathy have often been highlighted as a remedy for multiple issues of our current society, and sometimes tangible results were witnessed. But why is it that now we have to work to rediscover it? What do we understand by it, and what does it do when we belong to "the we?"

This research aims to find a way to start a new conversation in philosophy, whereby we might be able to open up and navigate our thoughts and beliefs more fully. This research is designed to strive toward a fuller intersubjectivity through which the understanding of 'I,' 'we' and 'the other' can be enriched and modified so that we can understand what it means to coexist and how we can do so. What I insist upon here is that traditional philosophy needs to reach out more in order to have not only a wider but also deeper insight into our understanding about ourselves and the world. I would like to pose a different perspective to understand selfhood: I argue that the 'we' is pre-subjective as well as intersubjective.

The question of subjectivity and intersubjectivity is crucial not only for philosophy but also for understanding the self and the world in various scientific fields, not only within the scope of humanities but also in the fields of natural sciences and the arts. In effect, not only within the realm of sciences but also in reality, the understanding of self and other has been affecting the way the history and the politics of the world have been shaped. The world has continually faced problems such as conflicts between cultures, nations, ethnic groups, classes, genders, and more. For instance, in recent decades and the present day, we have observed and experienced the rise of fascist nationalism and racial supremacism. These issues are closely and necessarily related to philosophy because philosophy provides the ideology and worldview for how we understand the self and the world. An understanding of subjectivity, in other words, to understand 'who I am as I,' is the beginning of thinking. As Descartes articulated in his famous proposition *cogito ergo sum*, the realization of my existence as a thinking subject has been considered to be the very beginning of our thinking. This has been presented as the starting point of understanding not only the self but also everything else that is not the self.

There has long been a doubt about 'the idea of social subject' in philosophy, namely that it has really only been discussed within the realm of the idea of an individual subject and has not overcome the limits of this 'self-centered' discourse of the 'we' to some extent. As Carr writes, "Other individuals are analogues of myself; but the idea of a social subject seems at best a *façon de parler*, at worst pure myth or construction."[1] This forms the core problem of the other in a philosophical work based on the system of I-subjectivity: How can the other exist as other subjects, and what is the relation between my perception of the other and their existence? How does the self have access to other minds? A debate has thus ceaselessly raged around the relation of the individual subject and intersubjectivity. In the system evolved around 'I' as the subject, however, the risk of solipsism has always been present.

A discussion of the 'we' cannot escape this problem as long as the 'we' is conceived of only as an intersubjective concept made up of the combination of the 'I' and other I's. When either the 'you' stands as the precondition of the 'I' or the 'I' stands as the precondition of the 'you,' 'I' or 'you' must come first for the 'we' to be there. Then the 'we' comes by combining them together, 'I' and 'you.' But we still need more than this to understand the we-ness; a simple aggregation of 'I' and 'you' doesn't seem to say enough for a lot of the we-experiences we have.

Social cognition, intersubjectivity, and empathy are highly demanded and researched topics currently in humanities. There are views in cognitive science and psychology that insist and try to prove that the individual cognition of self is necessarily based on an irreducible social cognition. In other words, the 'we' as a group is not something that individuals build together, but it is a co-minded group that primes and causes one's irreducible collective behavior, assuming that one's potential for social understanding and action is enlarged by cognizing in a dedicated collective mode.[2] This research starts with this idea of the we-mode: that the 'we' is more than a group of minds formed by individuals through their separate state of being and action. I attempt to show that our subjective self-consciousness and self-cognition are bound with the pre-subjective notion of the 'we.'

## 2. LANGUAGE

Why does language matter? There are many different manners of communication, and it is not only through language that we think and communicate, but language does represent and construct our way of interpreting the world and expressing our interpretation. Despite the various ways of communication, there is sound consent that language is the most powerful and versatile medium of communication, and all known human groups possess language.[3] Images and sounds express our interpretation and thought, enabling communication, and I discuss incorporeal communication and its significance in this book as well. However, through language, we can construct the way we perceive the world and ourselves, transfer information to others or into other forms, pass on that knowledge, or influence the way the world is performed and acknowledged.

I would neither declare, however, that this is linguistic research, nor does it point at the linguistic turn. Rather, it is to study how we understand the self and the other, through which I want to show that collective intentionality or social cognition as the 'we' is more than a collection of individuals, or in other words, that the group of 'we' is "minds in the we-mode" rather than "groups with minds."[4] The debates on shared intentionality in cognitive science and psychology have enlightened the interactive turn in social cognition, in which its proponents explain that the shared, collective, or we-intention is an irreducible collective mode that remains latent until individuals become engaged in particular interactive contexts.[5] The collective mode of we-intention is present when more than two agents come together and act as a group in achieving a collective goal intentionally, and the statement of their doing something together suggests that no member of the group does it 'on her own.'[6] The collective mode is expressed and read through the language we use ordinarily. For example, when my brother and I baked cookies and said "we baked these cookies," this could mean that my brother baked a few batches and I did the rest, or my brother made the dough and I baked them in the oven, or this 'we' in this sentence could express the collective mode of we-intention by inferring that we baked all of the cookies jointly.

Through language we can conceive the question of how to conceptualize the specific attitude that underpins collective intentional behavior.[7] Gallotti and Frith claim that the collective reading of what is expressed in the above sentence characterizes the irreducibility of group behavior as a feature of the bearer holding the relevant attitude. This 'we' with a joint action ascribes a 'we-as-a-group' attitude that implies that there is a minded group as a plural subject, rather than the individuals forming the relevant group.[8] Our perception of others (even in the mere presence of others) in the we-frame is not a matter of rational choice, but the we-mode might work as an "implicit and automatic mechanism of mentalizing."[9] Other studies show that our social perception of others shapes one's own multisensory peripersonal space.[10] The intuition of collective intentionality, which suggests that the mind is not only a product of a social environment but rather that is social all the way through, could be manifested through linguistic expressions. Human cognition is enriched with resources for cognizing in an irreducibly collective mode.[11] Cognitive scientists have demonstrated this irreducible we-mode in their theory of interaction in the we-mode.

I would say that the core of this research is to study how the we-mode and collective intentionality are *expressed, read, interpreted, felt, and suggested* in our practices of language. Language might or might not form the way we think, but it guides the direction of our point of view and suggests the structure of the framework. Considering this, however, the vast fields of the humanities have developed their scope of research mostly based on the tradition of Indo-European languages, especially in philosophy. Here we have one of the main questions of the research: What about in other languages? The way in which the 'we' is used and expressed in different languages with different social and cultural contexts should be reexamined. In fact, there is already a wide gamut of literature on this issue, in terms of language and social relations,[12] or signs in society,[13] and in linguistic or semiotic anthropology, not to mention the studies on imposters and pronouns in different languages in linguistics.[14] However, these studies do not exactly make their approach from a philosophical viewpoint. In other words, these languages and cultures were approached as foreign objects that exist outside of the scope of the canonical references, that is, the norms that serve as the source of metaphysical and existential thinking. These foreign subjects are often taken as exotic objects implied as exceptions.

## 3. ALTERNATIVE REFERENCE POINTS

One of the problems of taking foreign cultures and languages as the subjects of studies in humanities is grounded in the fact that there exists a tacit agreement on the authority of certain references. Some might find Niranjana's criticism of classical anthropology too radical, but it also speaks to philosophy related to the question of the authority of scholarship. According to Niranjana, in classical anthropology, the unspoken purpose of the studies was "to produce a self-understanding of the West" in which "the centrality of

Western civilization" is assumed.[15] The twist reveals itself when the investigator from the so-called third world is subjected to the questioning of the "subject-position."[16] As she asks, "Who writes, and for whom? What might be the possible differences between metropolitan and third-world representations of third-world contexts?"[17]

The purpose of anthropological projects was to translate one culture into terms that are intelligible to another,[18] and the ethnographers, the workers in literature, function as a translator.[19] Traditionally, the task was basically to translate *the other* cultures to the "Euro-American language" and compare it to the investigator's Western one, and in doing so, "a humanity" is "uncovered."[20] Niranjana argues that the bases of comparative study, as well as philosophy and all the other fields of humanities, have been "a humanism and a universalism that presumed a common human nature: in spite of their superficial differences, all people in the world were thought to be ultimately the same, or in the process of becoming like one another."[21] Although I believe in the universality of humanism and philosophy as the core of human existence over the ineffability of differences in us, Niranjana has a point as she remarks that the universal truth of humanities is "made from above, as it were."[22] In this general atmosphere, she describes that even so-called third-world intellectuals undertake their comparative work with the viewpoint of the West, "comparing their cultural products with metropolitan ones,"[23] to live up to "the label," whether it be that of philosophy or literature, "to find something that is ours which *deserves the dignity.*"[24]

When investigators, whose "subject-positions and location are in the third-world,"[25] study and compare cultures and spaces other than their own, the following questions are aroused: "In the third-world, how do we read one another so that we do not appear simply as footnotes to Western history?[26] How do we learn to question the epistemological structures through which knowledge about third-world peoples are produced?"[27] In his book *Black Skin, White Masks*, Franz Fanon analyzes the situation of the black person in the white world who ought to live as a white man.[28] Can a 'man of color' see another man of the same color not through a 'white' man's eye? Fanon talks about this based upon his own personal experiences. He was and is not alone. As Niranjana claims, it is indeed time to start seeing through 'our' own eyes.[29] We need to find a new perspective concerning "how one's location helps critique one's complicity with metropolitan systems of knowledge and representation."[30]

How can different cultures communicate and understand each other? The documentary *Qallunaat! Why White People Are Funny*[31] by Mark Sandiford touches this issue, poking at the sore reality with sarcastic humor. There are multiple documentaries about the 'exotic' Inuit people that take the Inuit lifestyle, habits, language, and even their physiological condition as the subject of observation. 'We,' in the Western metropolitan system, whether 'white' or not, are so used to acting as an observer of these exotic people through these documentaries that exhibit them as the other—'we' forget that 'we' are the strange 'other' to the Inuit. This documentary by Sandiford, however, presents the reversed view. It is not about the Inuit but about the exotic 'Qallunaat,' which is the Inuit word for 'white people.' This does not necessarily refer to their skin color but instead refers to a certain state of mind: "their odd dating habits, unsuccessful attempts at Arctic exploration, overbearing bureaucrats and police, and obsession with owning property."[32] The documentary examines their odd way of greeting each other, repressing natural bodily functions, complaining about being cold, and wanting to dominate the world.[33] It always has caused me an uncomfortable, or maybe rather, *un-homey* feeling to face the reality that the culture and history where I come from is treated as an 'exotic' subject of research. It is exotic to whom? As a person, I have always felt like one side of my self was suppressed, while as a researcher in philosophy, I have always asked myself, if it could be believed that I could be more than a translator. This is why it was so unnerving to face what the film is poking at in a reversed situation, where the Inuit scholars gauge the features and the behaviors of the 'white' people who are the subject of their observation.

As Niranjana says, we need to question the "norming of the comparative axis"[34] by addressing:

> the question of how these different regions have been discursively constructed as objects of knowledge, to examine closely the technologies and theories that have enabled their emergence, and to understand the extent to which our readings of each other in the present are informed by those discursive grids,[35]

and ponder upon the meaning of "the development of alternative frames of reference, so that Western modernity is no longer seen as the sole point of legitimization or comparison."[36] Surely, the character, the methodology, the subject, and the objective of philosophy are differentiated from that of anthropology, which was the major target of the above criticism. However, I question whether philosophy or, at least, the tendency of today's philosophy research and education can be fully exempted from this criticism.

For instance, the goal of this particular research is to investigate the 'we.' How can an investigator gain access to the 'we?' For a philosophical investigation, a philological investigation is also crucial. It is important to understand what previous thinkers have already thought about the subject so that one doesn't have to reinvent the wheel all over again. However, a philological investigation comprises only a part of a philosophical investigation. When it comes to researching the 'we,' I want to start to investigate what I mean and understand when I say 'we' and how I say it. This investigation starts from my practice of saying 'we.' In *Soi-même comme un autre*, for example, Ricoeur starts his analysis of 'self' by comparing *le soi*, self in French to other European languages that have a more or less the same or similar word to *le soi*, whereby he explains the crucial differences which result from the different viewpoints and ways of comprehension of the 'self.'[37] It is not only perfectly reasonable and understandable but also not exceptional to do so, because Ricoeur's mother tongue is French, which reflects his way of understanding the world not only as a philosopher but also as a person with his own native language. Nobody in philosophy would think that this approach is exceptional, exotic, or peculiar for a philosophical investigation of the 'self'—unless the language used for the investigation is Korean, Malagasy, or any other marginalized one.

Bernasconi's description of the distinctiveness of phenomenology is not exclusive to phenomenology, but it is right to claim that the distinctiveness of philosophical research, in general, lies in its sensitivity to the question of how the investigator gains access to that which is to be investigated.[38] However, where does this sensitivity lie? And how can an investigator gain and maintain this sensitivity? If a philosophical investigator whose native language is not one of the European languages is required to switch off their mother tongue, in part because the language and the system of philosophy are considered to be founded in European languages, where can this investigator acquire the sensitivity needed for this investigation? This absurd situation is comparable to the situation of the philosophy of religion. Can a philosopher investigate a religion completely unrelated to one's own religious background? Here what is meant by religion also includes the case of the investigator having an atheist or nonreligious stance. The irony of learning about other religions in philosophy lies in that the investigator has to revert to the testimony of other investigators and draw parallels that assume what is to be established, argues Bernasconi, which restricts the range of phenomena available for investigation exactly at the place and time when a philosophical investigation is supposed to be the most open.[39] As for precisely which religions are open to the individual investigator, they are determined in advance by the investigator's personal life story,[40] and similarly, precisely which languages are accessible to the individual investigator, whose research depends largely on linguistic practices—including their expressions and implications—are also determined in advance by the investigator's personal background.

The investigator has to constantly ask herself how she can retain her sensitivity and her philosophical method with the utmost degree of openness. Each investigator's personal life story starts with her language. The action of 'saying' in our saying 'we' is grounded in the language(s) that *I* use. But when *I* say 'we,' *wir*, *nous*, *ouri*, or *jeohi* [jaw-hee],[41] do I always mean the same thing? Do these words come with the exact same schema and signification? Can an investigator of the 'we' think of the 'we' detached from the practices of saying 'we' in her mother tongue?

Hamid Dabashi's radical question "Can non-Europeans think?" points at the core of the question, "Why is European philosophy 'philosophy,' but African philosophy 'ethnophilosophy'?"[42] What makes African philosophy not simply philosophy but ethnophilosophy? It is the culture and the language. It is because African languages and cultures, for example, are taken as subjects of regional or cultural studies rather than the subjects of disciplines that seek after 'universal' truth based on 'scientific' and 'objective' sources of research. In the case of the study of subjectivity, what is the objective and rational (as if it were opposed to cultural) source of research? Is there a standard language for this investigation that serves as the reference that *better* represents the universality of the human mind?

Human language is universal to human beings. Language is a crucial means of communication, which is a social process. In verbal interaction, utterances are selected in accordance with socially recognized norms and expectations.[43] The interaction between the social organization of behavior and the use of language as human behavior has been heavily examined in the sociology of language[44] because the communication of social information is believed to presuppose the existence of regular relationships between language usage and social structure.[45]

From this point of view, communication, either everyday talk or formal dialogues, never takes place in isolation, but rather every communication is an ongoing discourse through a verbal exchange which is situationally oriented and inextricably connected with a relevant context. This context is not objective but intersubjectively interpreted.[46] Disciplines such as linguistic sociology, ethnography, and anthropology have been engaged with the study of everyday talk and analysis of dialogue to investigate language because of the belief that language reflects the social structure and that talk is systematically localized within its sociocultural context.[47] Language reflects the diversity of human life and understanding based on its diverse human cultures and societies.

Even if the most valuable contribution of ethnography is the detailed description of communicative events in their full complexity,[48] we need more than just collecting ethnographic facts about language forms and variation in cultures and communities for a comparison of language. The sociocultural structure in which we find ourselves influences the way we think, behave, and understand ourselves. The study of language in different social and cultural contexts deserves and requires a philosophical investigation, not to search for and present the similarities and differences between the diverse forms of languages and societies but to study our 'way of thinking' and 'viewing the world,' including our own being as human beings, which also reflects the diversity of the society, language, and culture that we are in. We need to do more than describing the 'other' languages and comparing them to the reference language, whichever that language is, that is considered to be the standard language of investigation.

This is the sore truth of the current situation of academic philosophy—we might be playing the same old game within the same framework as that of traditional anthropology. If someone believes that women cannot think philosophically, just as birds can fly, but human beings cannot, or as women can give birth, but men cannot, it would also be possible to believe that only some languages are suitable for philosophy and some are not. By this I do not mean translating philosophical texts to other languages—certainly one can read Kant and present papers in Korean, for example, and Korean native speakers can publish papers on Kant in German—but philosophically investigating and posing questions in one's own linguistic and cultural world.

Trying to read another language and culture is similar to trying to understand another person. It is a world that is mostly inaccessible. It is not only the other, but even within oneself, it is hard to see, know, and understand what is going on. However, somehow, we figure it out. We communicate and understand. Probably never fully, yet communication and understanding are possible. Philosophical investigations and classical literature say something about us, touch us, move us, in whatever kind of 'we' that we belong to, in whichever language they are written. They are able to communicate. In this sense, as Hannah Arendt claims, philosophy can be "a mediator between many truths."[49] This is not because philosophy holds the only truth that is valid for all but because what each person may believe in their isolation from all others can humanly and actually become true only in reasoned communication, that is, philosophy.[50]

## 4. IN KOREAN

Is it *really* true that the first step to understand the problem of being is not to tell stories (μῦθόν τινα διηγεῖσθαι)?[51] This is supposed to mean that one should take being as being itself, but not as a character of an entity, in order to understand it. But can we really grasp even a blurry corner of it without understanding the stories of our own? Why does the problem of being even matter to us human entities? It is because we are there. We are there, but the starting point of this understanding is not the same for each one of us, despite the fact that we all are there. There is no philosopher whose philosophical questions and discourses are completely detached from the time and place in which they live. Our thinking is nestled in our personal life, our identity attached to some cultural memory, the zeitgeist of our time, whether we are aware or unaware of these connections.

How about I tell you a story (μῦθόν τινα διηγεῖσθαι)? I had heard the myth (μῦθός) about the languages that contain no word that matches the 'to be' verb. Derrida also attracted attention when he brought up this issue. This discovery was indeed fascinating, but I am not sure if the impact of this discovery had been much more significant on my study of being than the discovery of the fact that "dolphins lament over the sudden death of their kin for several days." It was only toward the end of my lecture in Antananarivo, Madagascar, during the discussion session when the Malagasy philosophers mentioned that the 'to be' verb does not exist in Malagasy. They were there, even if they did not have the word 'to be' to say that they were there. I posed a naive but inevitable question back to the audience: How does one say that 'I am here' in Malagasy, meaning 'I exist here'? They answered, 'I live here.' When a man exists, that man exists by living their life. We live instead of just being there as a table is there. The existence of the 'to be' verb may not be a necessary linguistic condition for the understanding of human existence. For a person whose understanding is rooted in a language with the 'to be' verb, it requires a change of paradigm to question whether the 'to be' verb is not the primary unit for bringing any existent into language. One is challenged to think about the frame of thinking this verb builds for the understanding of entities, especially human existence. In effect, it is as hard as trying to envision oneself living with a different gender.

I posed another naive but inevitable question: How does a native Malagasy speaker understand and accept the structure or, so to speak, the system of the problem of being, which is based on European languages? Madagascar was a French colony between 1897 and 1958, yet I was not fully aware of what exactly it meant. Not only but especially in higher education, the French language is still recognized and utilized officially. The philosophers responded to my naive question with their brutally realistic response, which was unexpected but, in fact, expected: "But we philosophize in French."

It is not common—or maybe it is rather a taboo—to share a personal story in academic writing, because academic writing must maintain its objectivity—as opposed to being subjective. Instead of telling the story of encountering the language that has no 'to be' verb, it would not only be more professional but also safer to cite Derrida's testimony of knowing of a language without the 'to be' verb. The irony of learning about other languages and cultures whereby the investigator has to revert to the testimony of other investigators while rejecting one's own stories is mine, even if the investigator herself is from the 'other' culture and language, and her lifeworld is still on the other side.

## 5. TRANSLATION OF PHILOSOPHY

What does it do to someone's philosophizing when the person is a native Korean speaker? For example, one could read Aristotle's *Categories*[52] in Korean, and it would be read as Aristotle's *Categories* applied to the universal human mind, and not particularly as the categories only in ancient Greek. Aristotle's categories give us guidelines to categorize existing things so that we can comprehend what is there. In other words, the categories are the categories to understand τί ἐστι (being; sein) of τόδε τι (this one; dieses da). In the following paragraphs, I would like to briefly explain the problem of language in philosophy, its terminologies, translation, and relation to daily language with the example of Aristotle's *Categories*.[53]

There are translated words in Korean for the names of categories that Aristotle came up with in ancient Greek. The names of these categories in German are also translated from ancient Greek. However, even in a translation that is supposed to be almost a word-to-word direct translation or one that utilizes artificially invented words for interpretation from the Greek, terminologies already have different spectra of meanings and a different schema of ideas in a translated language. The translated terminologies reflect the culture, the place, and the time of the translating language.

Table 1.1 shows the translated names of the categories from Greek in Latin, German, English, Chinese, and Korean. The second Korean version is a new translation based on daily Korean language,[54] while the traditional translation was based on Chinese characters. The pronunciation of the first Korean translation is also the pronunciation of the Chinese characters in Korean.

The word "οὐσία" is the feminine present participle of εἰμί (I am), whose present infinitive is εἶναι (to be). In ancient Greek, one can see the clear connection between the word 'substance' and the 'to be' verb. From the traditional translation of 'substance' as *silche* [sheel-chae][55] in Korean though, one can almost never assume the connection between the 'to be' verb and *silche*. The new translation in Korean, therefore, utilized the matching word of 'to be' verb in Korean to reveal the connection. The categories are conceptualized for understanding the εἶναι (to be/being) of existing things, yet the word 'εἶναι' is commonly translated as *jonjae* [john-jae] in Korean.[56] The matching words for the 'to be' verb that also function as copula in ordinary Korean are *itda* [eet-da][57] and *ida* [ee-da].[58] *Jonjae* does not function as a copula in Korean. The most closely matching terminology for *jonjae* in English is 'existence' rather than 'to be.' As the standard translation for εἶναι, *jonjae* is utilized in a philosophical context supposedly with the signification and the implication that the word 'εἶναι' carries as philosophical terminology. Furthermore, the Korean word *jonjae*, as a word based on Chinese characters, has its own significations. It is one word that is composed of two characters which are ideograms.

**Table 1.1 Categories**

| Greek | Latin | German | English | Chinese | Korean (1) | Korean (2) |
|---|---|---|---|---|---|---|
| οὐσία | substantia | Substanz | substance | 實體 | 실체 silche [sheel-chae] | 있는것 inneungeot [een-nen-gut] 무엇임 mueosim [moo-aw-sheem] |
| πόσον | quantitas | Quantität | quantity | 量 | 양 yang [yang] | 얼마만큼 eolmamankeum [awl-ma-man-kem] |
| ποῖον | qualitas | Qualität | quality | 質 | 질 jil [jeel] | 어떠함 eotteoham [aw-taw-ham] |
| πρός τι | relation | Relation | relation | 關係 | 관계 gwangye [kwan-kyae] | 어떤 것에 걸림 eotteon geose geollim [aw-tawn-gaw-sae-gaw-leem] |
| ποῦ | ubi | wo | where | 場所 | 장소 jangso [jang-so] | 어디에 eodie [aw-dee-ae] |
| ποτέ | quando | wann | when | 時間 | 시간 sigan [shee-gan] | 언제 eonje [awn-jae] |
| κεῖσθαι | situs | Lage | situation | 姿勢 | 자세 jase [ja-sae] | 어떻게 있음 eotteoke isseum [aw-taw-kae-ee-sem] |
| ἔχειν | habitus | haben | possession | 所有 | 소유 soyu [so-you] | 가짐 gajim [ka-jeem] |
| ποιεῖν | action | tun, wirken | act | 能動 | 능동 neungdong [neng-dong] | 입힘 ipim [ee-peem] |
| πάσχειν | passio | erleiden | being acted upon | 受動 | 수동 sudong [soo-dong] | 입음 ibeum [ee-bem] |

Therefore, each character signifies a number of meanings, which are not simply evaporated when they are used to form a translated terminology.

Both characters that form the one word *jonjae* have their roots in the meaning of 'asking after a person, if the person is well.' The meaning of 'to be' is derived from this original meaning. The character *jon* [jon] (存)⁵⁹ is composed with two parts: the one part *jae* [jae] (才)⁶⁰ represents a sprout, and the other part *ja* [ja] (子)⁶¹ represents a child (son); therefore the character created by these two characters combined meant originally 'asking if the child is well (living)' and later it started to mean 'to be.' Still now this character signifies not only 'to be' but also 'to live,' 'to look after,' 'to console,' 'to think about someone,' 'to miss someone,' 'to feel sorry for,' 'to sympathize,' and so on. The second character *jae* also means 'to ask if someone is well,' 'to take care of.' In philosophical texts, when the terminology *jonjae* is used, readers do not usually read these meanings in the context, especially in a translated context. I would not insist that there is always some meaningful interpretation that is inferred from the etymological background of a word. The point is that it is still worth to note here that when εἶναι is translated in Korean—and the same for Chinese and Japanese in this case—it comes with an extended spectrum of meanings that reflect the different tradition of understanding existence, especially related to human existence.

One of the significant representations of the word *jonjae* (not as a mere translated word of 'εἶναι' but as a philosophical terminology) lies in its fundamental connection between existence (being) and relation. The readers whose mother tongue is Korean would think with the word *jonjae*, and their understanding of this word would associate it with this meaning—whether noticing it or not—rather than with εἶναι, because even if they are not aware of the etymology of these characters, this way of understanding being is rooted in their culture and daily life that differs from the culture of εἶναι. Although the terminology "Dasein" in the context of fundamental ontology is given a whole new definition, the meaning and the common usage of this ordinary German word "Dasein" linger on in the analysis of the human Dasein. It is probably not a coincidence that a trace of this fundamental connection between existence and relation is found in the investigation of the 'we' in Korean, precisely in the analysis of the pre-subjective 'we.'

So what difference does the language make for philosophizing? I would not be able to explain exactly how the difference of language affects the way of thinking in a philosophical context in general. The effect should differ case by case according to the topics, terminologies, the history of the discourse, and so on. I would not argue that language difference implies an impossibility of discussion or an inevitable misunderstanding that acts in contrast to universal human—philosophical—understanding. Despite differences in cultural and linguistic background, we all know from direct and indirect experiences that we can communicate, understand, and discuss with each other on the same (shared) philosophical topics. However, as in the case of *jonjae*, there are concepts, ideas, or simply words that reveal other colors of the spectrum of our understanding of certain matters: the colors that may have been hidden, forgotten, faded away, or that simply do not exist on this side.

As I initiated my research on intersubjectivity and questioned what—and who—the 'we' means, I became aware of this ordinary expression in Korean, 'ouri [oo-ree][62] husband,' which literally means 'our husband.' As I felt estranged from this ordinary—but odd in English—expression of the 'we' in Korean, the distance from the familiarity of daily life made room for philosophical queries. Does this particular linguistic practice have any significance for our understanding of the we-ness? This might give us some clue, maybe a small and subtle hint, for approaching the study of intersubjectivity from a perspective that has not been caught in our sight yet, I thought.

There are a few things that I would like to make absolutely clear, which are the things that I would neither want to nor be able to argue or prove through this investigation. First of all, the purpose of this investigation is not to surprise philosophers without a Korean language and cultural background by introducing some unknown and mysterious (linguistic) practices of this foreign language and culture. Nor is it to assert superiority or inferiority of any language or culture. There is no intention to insist on how special any particular language is compared to any other language. Furthermore, it is not only to simply show the difference and the similarity between different languages.

How am I going to deal with the problem of the 'we' philosophically in the Korean context? The following questions will guide our investigation:

(1) What do we understand by the 'we' and the 'I'?
(2) What is the significance of our way of saying 'I' and 'we' in relation to the understanding of self?
(3) Is there a possibility to understand intersubjectivity and subjectivity from a different perspective? If so, how?

In the following chapter 2, I will illustrate the use of *ouri* in Korean in detail with examples. Then, in chapter 3, I will introduce the use of the Korean word *jagi* [ja-kee], which means 'self,' but which is also utilized as a second- and the third-person singular pronoun, followed by a discussion on two other pronouns *neo* [naw] and *dangsin* [dang-sheen], both used as a second-person singular pronoun. In chapter 4, I will deal with self as subject in three different voices: passive, active, and medio-active. A discussion of self in terms of 'self-in-relation' follows, and I will introduce the notion of 'pre-subjective we' in chapter 5, which I represent mathematically in chapter 6. In chapter 7, the structure of 'we' will be analyzed in diagrams and knots. In chapter 8, I will introduce multiple theories on intersubjective self and explain the difference and significance of pre-subjective 'we' in comparison to them. Then in chapter 9, I highlight the notion of relation as the core of presubjectivity. In chapter 10, the discussion continues with the aspects of feelings and corporeality of the we-ness. Then in chapter 11, I talk about collective and cultural memory with the history of the Koryo Saram along with an analysis of border and home, whose story reveals the possibility of telling us a persuasive story of the 'we' as humanity.

## NOTES

1. David Carr, "Cogitamus Ergo Sumus: The Intentionality of the First-Person Plural," *The Monist* 69, no. 4 (1986): 524.
2. Mattia Gallotti and Chris D. Frith, "Social Cognition in the We-Mode," *Trends in Cognitive Sciences* 17, no. 4 (2013): 160.
3. See John J. Gumperz, "The Speech Community," in *Language and Social Context : Selected Readings*, ed. Pier Paolo Giglioli (Harmondsworth, Middlesex, Eng.: Penguin Books, 1990), 219.
4. Gallotti and Frith, "Social Cognition in the We-Mode," 2.
5. Gallotti and Frith, "Social Cognition in the We-Mode," 5.
6. Gallotti and Frith introduce the following sentence that illustrates two possible ways of reading it, one in the irreducible we-mode and the other not: "Renzo Piano and Richard Rogers designed the Pompidou Centre" expresses the idea that each architect made his own contribution to the final creation. Or, it also allows a collective reading: they did it jointly. The first reading means that "Piano, like Rogers, designed parts of the Pompidou Centre" which suggests that action predicates are distributed over the individuals (Gallotti and Frith, "Social Cognition in the We-Mode," 2).
7. Gallotti and Frith, "Social Cognition in the We-Mode," 2.
8. Gallotti and Frith, "Social Cognition in the We-Mode," 2.
9. Gallotti and Frith, "Social Cognition in the We-Mode," 5.
10. Elisa Pellencin et al., "Social Perception of Others Shapes One's Own Multisensory Peripersonal Space," *Cortex* 104 (2018): 163–79.
11. Gallotti and Frith, "Social Cognition in the We-Mode," 5.
12. Asif Agha, *Language and Social Relations*, vol. 24 (Cambridge: Cambridge University Press, 2006).
13. Richard J. Parmentier, *Signs in Society: Studies in Semiotic Anthropology* (Bloomington: Indiana University Press, 1994).
14. Raffaella Zanuttini et al., "A Syntactic Analysis of Interpretive Restrictions on Imperative, Promissive, and Exhortative Subjects," *Natural Language & Linguistic Theory* 30, no. 4 (November 1, 2012): 1231–74; Lan Kim, "A Note on Imposter Expressions in Korean," *Linguistics*, no. 71 (2015): 139–60; Jaehoon Choi, "Jussive Subjects as Imposters," *Linguistics*, no. 74 (2016): 3–24.
15. Tejaswini Niranjana, "Alternative Frames? Questions for Comparative Research in the Third World," *Inter-Asia Cultural Studies* 1, no. 1 (2000): 108.
16. Niranjana, "Alternative Frames?," 108.

17. Niranjana, "Alternative Frames?," 109.

18. Talal Asad, "The Concept of Cultural Translation in British Social Anthropology," *Writing Culture: The Poetics and Politics of Ethnography*, ed. James Clifford and George E. Marcus (Berkeley: University of California Press, 1986), quoted in Niranjana, "Alternative Frames?" 109.

19. Niranjana, "Alternative Frames?" 109.

20. Niranjana, "Alternative Frames?" 109.

21. Niranjana, "Alternative Frames?" 109.

22. Niranjana, "Alternative Frames?" 109.

23. Niranjana, "Alternative Frames?" 110.

24. Kwame Anthony Appiah, "Ethnophilosophy and Its Critics," in *Philosophy from Africa: A Text with Readings*, ed. P. H. Coetzee and A. J. P. Roux (London/New York: Routledge, 1998), 148, emphasis in original, quoted in Niranjana, "Alternative Frames?" 110.

25. Niranjana, "Alternative Frames?" 110.

26. Meenakshi Mukherjee, "A Phrase in a Talk on 'The Caribbean and Us,'" in *IACLALS Annual Conference* (Mysore, 1995), quoted in Niranjana, "Alternative Frames?" 110.

27. Niranjana, "Alternative Frames?" 110.

28. Franz Fanon, *Black Skin, White Masks*, trans. Charles Lam Markmann (New York: Grove Press, 1968).

29. Walter Rodney, *The Groundings with My Brothers* (London: Verso Books, 2019), 33–34, quoted in Niranjana, "Alternative Frames?" 112.

30. Niranjana, "Alternative Frames?," 110

31. Mark Sandiford, *Qallunaat!: Why White People Are Funny* (ONF/NFB, 2006), http://www.nfb.ca/film/qallunaat_why_white_people_are_funny/?fbclid=IwAR3x_a0M8taD1RStt59Z-weMTmWMUB2syQQpRU7prHLfDGkhgJo_-1xpSck.

32. Sandiford, *Qallunaat!*.

33. Sandiford, *Qallunaat!*.

34. Niranjana, "Alternative Frames?" 111.

35. Niranjana, "Alternative Frames?" 111.

36. Niranjana, "Alternative Frames?," 111.

37. Paul Ricoeur, *Soi-même comme un autre* (Paris: Éditions du Seuil, 1990).

38. Robert Bernasconi, "Must We Avoid Speaking of Religion? The Truths of Religions," *Research in Phenomenology* 39, no. 2 (2009): 204.

39. Bernasconi, "Must We Avoid Speaking of Religion?" 205.

40. Bernasconi, "Must We Avoid Speaking of Religion?" 205.

41. 저희.

42. Hamid Dabashi, "Can Non-Europeans Think? What Happens with Thinkers Who Operate Outside the European Philosophical 'Pedigree'?," *Al-Jazeera*, accessed November 20, 2017, http://www.aljazeera.com/indepth/opinion/2013/01/2013114142638797542.html.

43. Gumperz, "The Speech Community," 219.

44. Joshua A. Fishman, "The Sociology of Language," in *Language and Social Context : Selected Readings*, ed. Pier Paolo Giglioli (Harmondsworth, Middlesex, Eng.: Penguin Books, 1990): 45.

45. Gumperz, "The Speech Community," 220.

46. Teun A. van Dijk, "Introduction: Dialogue as Discourse and Interaction," in *Handbook of Discourse Analysis*, ed. Teun A. van Dijk, Volume 3 (Cambridge, MA: Academic Press, 1985): 5.

47. Dell H. Hymes, "The Ethnography of Speaking," in *Anthropology and Human Behavior*, ed. T. Gladwin and W.C. Sturtevant (Washington, DC: Anthropological Society of Washington, 1962), quoted in van Dijk, "Introduction: Dialogue," 7.

48. Van Dijk, "Introduction: Dialogue," 8.

49. Hannah Arendt, *Essays in Understanding 1930–1954: Formation, Exile and Totalitarianism* (New York: Schocken, 1994), 442.

50. Part of this discussion appears in Hye Young Kim, "A Phenomenological Approach to the Korean 'We': A Study in Social Intentionality," *Frontiers of Philosophy in China 12*, no. 4 (2017): 612–632.

51. Martin Heidegger, *Sein und Zeit* (Tübingen: Max Niemeyer Verlag, 2006), 6.

52. Hermann Bonitz, *Über die Kategorien des Aristoteles*, vol. 10 (Vienna: Braumüller in Komm, 1853); Otto Apelt, "Die Kategorien des Aristoteles," in *Beiträge zur Geschichte der Griechischen Philosophie*, ed. Otto Apelt (Leipzig: Meiner, 1891), 101–216, 120; Allan Bäck, *Aristotle's Theory of Predication*, vol. 84 (Leiden: Brill, 2000); John P. Anton, "On the Meaning of Kategoria in Aristotle's Categories," in *Essays in Ancient Greek Philosophy V: Aristotle's Ontology* (New York: SUNY Press, 1992).

53. This section is written based on my presentation "Kategorien Aristoteles: Koreanisch?" at the Free University of Berlin in 2017 and the discussion with Professor Wilhelm Schmidt-Biggemann (Free University of Berlin).

54. Aristotle, *Categories, De Interpretatione*, trans. Jinseong Kim (Seoul: E J Books, 2005).

55. 실체.
56. 존재.
57. 있다.
58. 이다.
59. 존.
60. 재.
61. 자.
62. 우리.

*Chapter 2*

# We in Korean

## 1. *OURI* IN KOREAN

As Brinck, Reddy, and Zahavi also claim, "The importance of verbal language and symbolization for developing the forms of we must not be neglected,"[1] when it comes to investigating the 'we.' Another important aspect that must not be neglected is the variety of verbal languages and symbolizations for developing the forms of the 'we.' But what are 'we' and 'I'? Are they words? If they are words, then this means that we can define them as such and such. 'I' is a pronoun that refers to the first-person singular, and 'we' is the first-person plural. One uses 'I' to refer to him/herself and 'we' to refer to a group of people including themselves. Or are they concepts (*Begriff*), the core set of common features of certain objects after abstracting, that is, removing unnecessary and irrelevant elements?[2] Or do they express a concept? When 'I' is used to refer to oneself, what does this oneself refer to? This oneself refers to a person who is an autonomous individual with subjective experiences of which he/she is aware of. From this, we could probably say that 'I' expresses the I-ness, the subject, the ego. Then what about 'we'? Is 'we' a collection of two or more 'I's'? Or could 'we' express more than that? What we would like to understand is *was das Wort von ihm will*,[3] what the word wants from itself, by investigating words as they are perceived as such.

From this point of view, I attempt to investigate the way the 'we' is verbalized in ordinary Korean language. First of all, for our investigation into the 'we,' it would make more sense to introduce the 'we' in Korean and explain how it is used. As I briefly mentioned in the introduction, in Korean, there is an expression 'our husband' or 'our wife.' The Korean word *ouri* means 'we,' 'our,' and 'us.'

The *Dictionary of the National Institute of Korean Language*[4] defines *ouri* as follows:

(a) First-person pronoun that indicates the speaker herself and the listener or multiple people including herself and the listener.
   The way that we (*ouri*) will go forward.
   What is there that we (*ouri*) cannot do if we do it together?
   Mother, should we (*ouri*) go to Mt. Dobong today?[5]
(b) First-person pronoun that indicates multiple people, including the speaker herself, while talking to someone who is not older or whose social status is not higher.
   We (*ouri*) go now, cheer up.
   One day you invited us (*ouri*) [couple].
   What did we (*ouri*) do that you are doing this?[6]
(c) (In front of certain nouns) a word that a speaker uses to express close relations with a certain person while talking to a person who is either not older or whose social status is not higher than the speaker herself.
   Our (*ouri*) mom.
   Our (*ouri*) wife.
   Our (*ouri*) husband.[7]

The third definition of *ouri* that means 'our' in English is not an unusual usage for English speakers. For example, one says 'our mom' and 'our brother' in English. However, expressions such as '*ouri* wife' or '*ouri* husband' sound strange to those who do not speak Korean. This explanation of 'our' in Korean could give us the impression that this usage of 'our' in Korean is almost always used as the exclusive 'we,' which does not include the listener. However, I find it problematic to say that the 'we' in Korean in the form of 'our someone' always indicates the exclusive 'we.'

Another problem is that the 'we' as a genitive (possessive) pronoun in the form of 'our' in Korean is not exactly the same as 'our' in English. For convenience, one says that *ouri* is both nominative and genitive pronouns in Korean, but it is probably more accurate to say that there is no genitive form of the 'we' in Korean. It is possible to make the genitive form of the 'we' by adding the suffix *ui* [eui][8] to *ouri* as *ouriui*. The suffix *ui* functions as 'of' in English. So, the literal translation of *ouriui* would be 'of *ouri*,' that is, 'of us' or 'of ours.' *Ouriui* is not an uncommon expression, but it is more usual to say *ouri* for 'our someone' or 'our something.' Not always, but often, *ouriui* sounds superfluous in daily conversation, or more serious and formal in some cases. Grammatically, one can say that *ouri* in '*ouri* husband' is therefore used as an adjective in this sense, but this is only a grammatical explication. In a daily conversation in Korean, *ouri* as a nominative pronoun and *ouri* as '*ouri* someone' are used as the same word with the same significance but not as homonyms.

Now I will show some more detailed cases of the use of 'we' and 'our' in Korean in oral and written contexts. The collection of the examples and the data analysis are based on the article "The Use of the First Person Plural Possessive Pronoun *Woorie* in Korean Language" (2005)[9] published in the *Journal of Korean Language Education*. The source of the oral texts was the Korean drama script *Love on a Jujube Tree*,[10] and the written data were gathered from J. K. Rowling's *Harry Potter and the Sorcerer's Stone* and its Korean translation,[11] and a Korean short story *A Guest in the Reception Room*[12] written by Yoseop Ju and its English translation.[13]

Following the data analysis, the article suggests a sociolinguistic interpretation of the use of the *ouri*, which claims that *ouri* reflects the character of Korean society as a traditionally collective society and that this collectivism in Korea is based on Confucianism, as in other Asian countries as well, due to its agricultural lifestyle that requires cooperation for farming labor, which led them to put more emphasis on the value of community.[14] Family especially is the most important community that one belongs to in this society. This could explain the fact that the most common situation where *ouri* is used is when Koreans talk about their family, referring to their parents as 'our mother' or 'our parents.' However, what speakers mean to convey is merely 'my mother' and 'my parents.'[15] In this situation, *ouri* is not meant to be plural and inclusive of the other speaker.[16] *Ouri* has developed a special use beyond marking a simple plural.[17] It is not at all an unreasonable way of explaining the use of *ouri* in Korean to one who learns Korean as a foreign language to say that *ouri* is used in the sense as if everyone were "just one big, happy family."[18]

In fact, a very common way of interpreting the use of *ouri* in relation to Korean culture is that *ouri* is proof of the group mentality that dominates over individuals in Korea.[19] Many would agree with this sentiment. Classic examples for this are that Koreans refer to their language not as 'Korean' but as 'our language' and their country not as 'Korea' but as 'our country.'[20] It is not only usually so, but some Korean language instructors for Koreans insist that it is not correct for a Korean to say or write 'Korea' instead of 'our country' or 'Korean' instead of 'our language.'

I do not oppose this interpretation of the relationship between the use of *ouri* and the history and the character of the Korean society, but what underlies this particular way of saying *ouri* in Korean is not unique only to Korean culture and the traditional way of being in Korea. Rather, this could say something about our way of understanding self and other, something that exists in other cultures and languages but has faded away, like a fraction of our self-portrait that has been washed off and blurred. This is what I want to explore.

The following sentences are examples of oral uses of *ouri* derived from the drama *Love on a Jujube Tree*. Jeong classifies the different uses of *ouri* within these examples under the three categories: (a) general, (b) inclusive, and (c) exclusive.[21]

(1) Maybe the reason we can sell a lot is that the tofu made of our (*ouri*) genuine beans is rare.[22]

Here, *ouri* beans refer to the beans produced in Korea. Jeong sees this *ouri* as the general *ouri*, because this *ouri* refers to "the entire population" of Korea, including everyone in Korea who is not present in the conversation, as well as the speaker and the listener.

(2) You'll see. You will hear she is leaving our (*ouri*) town sooner or later.[23]

The scope of *ouri* in this sentence includes both speaker and listener, and this *ouri* refers to the town where they both live. Therefore, it is an inclusive 'we.'

(3) However, our (*ouri*) father is really angry about it.[24]
(4) Our (*ouri*) husband gave it to me as a wedding anniversary present two years ago.[25]
(5) If our (*ouri*) wife knows this, I'll be in trouble.[26]

Jeong argues that the *ouri* in our father, our husband, and our wife is limited in the scope of reference to the speaker only. In these cases, *ouri* has nothing to do with the interlocutor or the third persons outside these speech acts. Therefore, it is an exclusive 'we.'[27] The *ouri* in these cases means 'my,' but one can say 'our father' in English as well if the speaker has siblings, and in the case of 'our father' in English, it would still be an exclusive 'we.' However, Koreans will surely say '*ouri* father' instead of 'my father' whether they have siblings or not. Jeong takes these expressions as proof for the fact that the relationship that is associated with family members, friends, or related group members is highly valued in Korea, and it is assumed that Koreans intend to have their interlocutors recognize that they belong to certain types of relationships and to emphasize that they are not isolated individuals, but members of a family or a group with whom they can share connectedness and a sense of belonging.[28]

(6) People say that *Mr. Seunghoon* (you) is pretending to like me because of *my* money.[29]
(7) Can you imagine how I felt when this gossip fell into *my* ear?[30]
(8) Even though I know how *my* younger brother feels.[31]

When the speaker talks about their private belongings, personal possession, or their own body, they say 'my' in Korean as well, as shown in examples (6) and (7). The difference between the uses of 'my' and 'our' lies in the distinction of whether they are associated with interpersonal relationships or not. For example, 'my money' in (6) or 'my ear' in (7) are 'my' instead of 'our' because they have nothing to do with the relationship with other people.[32]

Note that in (6) the listener is Mr. Seunghoon, and the speaker is talking directly to him while referring to him as 'Mr. Seunghoon' instead of calling him 'you.' This is because calling the other person 'you' in Korean is very unusual. I will discuss this in chapter 3, section 2 "You in Korean: *Neo* and *Dangsin*."

What is interesting about 'our family member' in Korean is that, for younger siblings, Koreans exceptionally usually say 'my' as well as 'our' as seen in the example of (8). However, this is restricted to only refer to those who are younger. On the other hand, when they refer to someone older or in a higher hierarchic position, 'my' is rarely used. As Jeong also points out, *nae hyeong*, [nae hyung][33] which means 'my older brother' in Korean, sounds awkward to the ears of Korean speakers. It is also a fair point that Koreans take it not only as awkward but even impolite to use the first-person singular, because they feel like it emphasizes and focuses 'too much' on the individuality of the person that they refer to. In Korean, therefore, 'our father' is regarded as a humble and modest expression.[34]

However, *ouri* is more frequently used in oral and informal discourse than in written or formal discourse.[35] The following example is taken from an essay written in Korean. Here one can notice the uses of 'my' which more than likely would be replaced with 'our' in oral discourse.

(9) The magpies that live in *my* neighborhood are lucky. . . . The nest of magpies in *my* neighborhood is old, but the nest on the poplar tree in *my* hometown is older than that.[36]

However, in the literary style in Korean, the possessive pronouns 'my' or 'our' are omitted because of the emotional distance between the author and the readers. Jeong insists that persistent use of 'my' or 'our' could give an impression that the writer is being self-indulgent.[37] Often the first-person possessive pronouns for family members such as grandparents, parents, and siblings are dropped in order to provide a more neutral and objective tone to the text.

(10) After ($\Phi$) father, who had his business, passed away after a long disease, *our* family abruptly became bankrupt. ($\Phi$) Brother left to make money, but there was no news for more than a year from him. ($\Phi$) Mother and I were suffering from the demanding debtor.[38]

The data collected from the literature translation highlights the different uses of the first-person possessive pronouns between English and Korean. The following examples are from the Korean translation of *Harry Potter and the Sorcerer's Stone*.[39] I marked the first-person pronouns that are changed in the Korean translation in bold and added the pronouns that were used in the Korean translated version next to each changed pronoun in brackets. The pronouns that were directly translated are marked in italic. For example, in (11), the original text in English uses the pronoun 'my,' but in Korean it is translated as 'our.'

(11) **My** (*ouri*) aunt and uncle and cousin are, though. Wish I'd had three wizard brothers.[40]
(12) Nobody in *my* (*ouri*) family's magic at all, it was ever such a surprise when I got *my* ($\Phi$) letter, but I was so pleased, of course.[41]
(13) **My** (*ouri*) dad says it must've been a powerful Dark wizard to get round Gringotts.[42]
(14) Think *my* name's funny, do you? No need to ask who you are. **My** (*ouri*) father told me all the Weasleys have red hair, freckles, and more children than they can afford.[43]

In the examples (11) through (14), one can notice that most of the cases of the first-person singular possessive pronoun 'my' are translated into *ouri*. All the cases of 'my' that refer to relational deictics such as 'my aunt and uncle,' 'my family,' and 'our father' are translated into 'our,' which reflects the predominant use of *ouri* in Korean. However, 'my name' in (14) is translated as 'my name' in Korean because this case is associated with a personal concern instead of a personal relationship.[44]

The following example shows a case when a Korean text is translated into English. This text is from the Korean short story *The Guest in My Mom's House*. Here as well, I marked the pronouns that were changed in bold and added the pronoun that was used in the original Korean text. For example, 'my father' in the English translation was 'our father' in the original Korean.

(15) Grandmother says that *my* (*ouri*) father died one month before I was born, and he and $\Phi$ (*ouri*) mom had only been married for one year. **My** (*ouri*) father's home was far away from here, but he was a teacher at the school in *our* town so even after he married $\Phi$ (*ouri*) mom, they never went to live in *his* parent's house (*the house of the in-laws*) like other people do.[45]

As in the case of the Korean translation from English, in this reversed case, one can see the same pattern of translation where 'our' in Korean is translated as 'my' in English or without a possessive determiner. However, there is another interesting point in this text, which is the appearance of the third-person pronoun in the English translation. In Korean, one would never refer to their father or their mother as 'he' or 'she,' neither in the nominative nor possessive form. Therefore, expressions such as 'his parents' house' would never be used in the Korean context to refer to the home of one's grandparents on the father's side. The literal translation of the original Korean text for this expression is 'the house of the in-laws.'

Jeong concludes that the use of *ouri* in Korean implies that Koreans intend to show their connectedness to a certain group and their sense of belonging, as language is a socially accepted convention that can be used to identify oneself as a member of a social network.[46] This case study and data analysis present some different perspectives of another culture based on different linguistic patterns. However, we need more than that. In a philosophical context, I pose the question: What does it really mean when the 'we' and the 'our' are said in such a way? What does it say about our understanding of self, other, subjectivity, and intersubjectivity?

## 2. OUR HUSBAND

To help the readers to have a better sense of how *ouri* is used in Korean, I would like to examine the following conversation that I have set up for our investigation with a consistent context. This is a conversation in Korean that takes place at a restaurant among four speakers: (*A*) daughter, (*B*) father, (*C*) *A*'s friend, and (*D*) waiter. The waiter in this conversation seems to be around the same age as the father. Stephen (*E*) is *A*'s husband but is not present at the restaurant.

(16)  *A*: Dad, did you like the card that our husband made for you?
(17)  *B*: Yes! I still have it here. Our Stephen is so funny. I love the joke on the card!
      (*C* arrives at the restaurant and *A* shows the card to *C*.)
(18)  *A*: Look, this is the card that our husband made for our dad.
(19)  *C*: Oh, our Stephen did a good job! This is pretty funny.
(20)  *A*: Yes, our family was very amused.
      (As *C* is looking at the card, *D* approaches the table and sees the card.)
      *D*: Is this a handmade card? It looks nice!
(21)  *B*: Thanks. Our son-in-law made it for me. Here, he came up with this joke.
(22)  *D*: Ha, hilarious! Stephen is the name of (father's) son-in-law?
      *B*: Yes.
(23)  *D*: Very nice. I guess our Stephen must be a funny guy!

There are seven different cases of 'our' in this conversation.

(16) our husband
    Speaker: daughter
    Listener: father

In this case, the daughter, her husband, and the father are related, which means 'our' is said among related people. By 'our husband,' the speaker, who is talking about her husband, means 'my husband,' but it is not 'my husband' for the father. Therefore, it is, in fact, not 'our husband' for the father. The daughter can say 'our husband' to the father, but the father cannot say 'our husband' for the daughter's husband. Or the daughter, in this case, can also say 'husband' without 'our,' and the meaning of the sentence is unchanged. Therefore, A can say either 'our husband,' 'husband,' or 'my husband' in this case without changing the meaning, but each case comes with a different nuance. For example, 'my husband' is not the most natural expression in Korean, even if it is grammatically correct, while 'husband' sounds natural and is also grammatically correct.

According to the definition by the National Institute of Korean Language, *ouri* is used when speaking to a person who is either not older or whose social status is not higher than the speaker. However, as in the case of (1), it is neither unnatural nor uncommon that children, either young or grown, use *ouri* with their close family members. When the relationship of the speaker with the listener is more vertical or not intimate enough, one is supposed to use the honorific form of the word *ouri*, which is *jeohi* [jaw-hee].[47] Therefore, here, the daughter can also say '*jeohi* husband' instead of '*ouri* husband.' I will deal with this form in the following chapter.

(17) our Stephen
    Speaker: father
    Listener: daughter

The father, the daughter, and Stephen, the husband, are related. It may not be said very frequently, but 'our someone' can be said among related people in other languages, especially when the speaker wants to express their intimate relationship or their affection for the person who is spoken of. In this case, however, the speaker (the father) is older than the daughter, so the father would not say '*jeohi* Stephen.'

(18) our husband
    Speaker: daughter
    Listener: daughter's friend

our dad
    Speaker: daughter
    Listener: daughter's friend

Here, the daughter and her friend are related, but not in a familial relation. In this case, the friend cannot say 'our husband' either. However, the friend can say 'our father' or 'father' without a possessive pronoun, as explained in the earlier section.

(19)  our Stephen
    Speaker: daughter's friend
    Listener: daughter/father

As shown here, the friend can say 'our Stephen.' But can the friend say *'jeohi* Stephen' in this case? The father is older than the friend, and the relationship between them is not as intimate as the one between the father and the daughter. But the friend would not say *'jeohi* Stephen,' because *jeohi* could more strongly imply the meaning of the exclusive 'we,' such that Stephen belongs to the group of the friend rather than the group of the father or the daughter.

(20)  our family
    Speaker: daughter
    Listener: daughter's friend/father

The 'we' in 'our family' said by the daughter could be interpreted as the exclusive 'we' to the friend and the inclusive 'we' to the father. In this case, among the father, the daughter, and the friend, not only the two familially related speakers, the father and the daughter, but also the friend can say 'our family.' However, 'our family' as said by the friend does not refer to the same family of the daughter and father. Therefore, the friend can say both 'our family' and 'my family.' The father and the daughter can also say both, but they would say 'my family' only when they are talking to the friend, not when they are talking to each other.

(21)  our son-in-law
    Speaker: father
    Listener: waiter/daughter/daughter's friend

As the father says 'our son-in-law,' the targeted listener is the waiter, because the father is responding to the waiter. One could assume that the father uses the 'our' as the exclusive 'we,' meaning his wife and himself by 'our.' This can be replaced by 'my son-in-law.'

(22) (father's) son-in-law
   Speaker: waiter
   Listener: father

Here, the waiter refers to *A*'s father as 'father' as he is talking to *A*'s father. These two people are not related, and clearly *A*'s father is not the waiter's father. However, still the waiter uses 'father' without a possessive pronoun. In English, in this kind of situation, one would say 'your son-in-law,' which would never be said in Korean. Addressing the father, the listener, as 'you' is basically forbidden in Korean. Instead, in this situation, one could also say 'teacher's son-in-law' or 'son-in-law' without any possessive pronoun. If the listener is a man who is supposedly older, whether that person has children or not, one could address the person as 'father,' and if it's a woman, one could say 'mother' instead of 'you.' I will examine this phenomenon whereby a speaker uses a title of relationship such as 'father,' even if the listener is neither their father nor related at all, in more detail in later chapters.

(23) our Stephen
   Speaker: waiter
   Listener: father/daughter/daughter's friend

This 'our Stephen' is said by a person who is related neither to Stephen nor any of the other speakers of the conversation. Neither does this person know Stephen nor does the person really know if Stephen actually exists. Obviously, this is not what everyone would say about someone they do not know to someone they do not know. While the expression 'our husband' is a common expression, this expression of 'our someone' said by an unrelated person is more situation-specific than 'our husband,' which means it depends on the speaker's personality, such as whether the speaker is extroverted or socially awkward, or on the atmosphere of the conversation. However, it is not an extraordinary situation for an unrelated person to say 'our someone,' who is unrelated to the speaker, the listener, or the person who is spoken of, if that someone is a third person who is not present, as is 'our Stephen' in this conversation.

One could argue that it depends on the situation and that the 'we' is also said in English among unrelated people. Let's say there are two sisters with a dog, and a visitor who is visiting the sisters is also present, and the dog is very friendly to the visitor. One of the sisters could say the following to the visitor in English:

(24) One of the sisters: Our dog recognizes us, dog people. We all love dogs.

Here, we have three different types of the 'we':

   (a) our dog

When one of the sisters is referring to their dog as 'our dog' to the visitor, it is used in the sense of the exclusive 'we,' which means that the dog belongs to the 'we' group of owners of the dog, in which the visitor is not included. Therefore, the visitor would not refer to the dog as 'our dog' to the sisters, as long as the visitor does not share ownership over the dog, no matter how close the visitor is to the dog or the sisters.

However, if this conversation takes place in Korean, it is not hard to envision the situation where the visitor says 'our dog' to refer to this dog that belongs to the sisters. In fact, the visitor would say 'our dog' to express her affectionate feelings toward the dog and also intimate feelings for the sisters, even if the visitor is not necessarily closely related to the sisters or the dog. Of course, it is possible to imagine the case where this 'our' is used as a fraudulent 'we,' meant to exaggerate intimacy to disguise one's true feelings or to manipulate, but regardless it is neither uncommon nor unnatural for the visitor to say 'our dog' referring to the sisters' dog in this situation.[48]

(b) us, dog people

The 'we' in 'us, dog people' is obviously said as the inclusive 'we.' This 'we' refers to the group of the people who like dogs. As they say 'us, dog people,' the sisters imply that the visitor must like dogs and therefore belongs to this group to which the sisters also belong because liking dogs unites this certain group of people. The sisters and the visitor, all of them, are included in this 'we.' But the sisters could also mean 'us, dog people,' excluding the visitor but including the third others who are not present in the conversation. In this case, this would be an exclusive 'we.'

(c) we all love dogs

The 'we' in this case could be both the inclusive 'we' and the nosistic 'we.' The nosistic 'we' is the 'we' that is used to refer to oneself to express a personal opinion, such as the royal 'we' or the editorial 'we.' When it is thought to be the inclusive 'we,' this 'we' refers to the two sisters, the visitors, and the dog people group. But this 'we' could also be read as a nosistic 'we' that expresses the sister's personal opinion with her belief that everyone loves dogs. The nosistic 'we' is used quite frequently in everyday life, for example, as when one says, 'We need to reduce the use of plastic.' I will talk more about nosism in chapter 2, section 6.

Then what is the significance of the 'our someone' in Korean? Does the 'we' in 'our someone' in Korean refer to the exclusive or the inclusive 'we'? Or is it rather a nosistic 'we'? Or is there another side of the we-ness in it?

## 3. INCLUSIVE AND EXCLUSIVE WE

Is 'our husband' an exclusive 'we'? Or could it be inclusive? Or both? Or neither?

The use of inclusive and exclusive 'we' is common in many languages. If a brother and a sister talk about their mom to someone else who is not their sibling, they would refer to their mom as 'our mom,' excluding the listener from the 'we' group of 'our mom.'

The exclusive form of the 'we' is used frequently in expressions such as 'our nation,' 'our team,' or 'our class,' and the exclusiveness of this 'we' group opposed to the ones who do not belong to this group is the main point of the we-expression in this case. A certain nation, team, or class is an already-formed group with a certain social or political membership that has a shared purpose, activity, or history. The idea of identity is deeply related to the exclusive 'we.' At the same time, on the other side of the token, the sense of the 'we' as the inclusive 'we' is strongly present within the group talking to the other members of the group. This is more significant in the 'we who' form such as we the people, we the Koreans, we the Green Bay Packers, we the class of 2020.

Let us see more closely how the exclusive 'we' and inclusive 'we' work. Here is another short conversation between Annie, Basti, and a dog. Annie is holding a dog in her arms. She was on the way to see the mother dog.

> *Annie:* Do you want to come with us? We are going for a walk and going to see his mother.
> *Basti:* Sure, we can go together to see his mom.
> *Annie:* We will have fun going for a walk together.

I will mark the 'we' in this conversation and distinguish the inclusive and exclusive relations among the two people, the two dogs, and the ones who are present and not present at the time of the conversation.

(a) We are going to see his mom.
(b) Do you want to come with us?
(c) We are going for a walk.
(d) We can go together to see his mom.
(e) We will have fun going for a walk together.

The inclusive and exclusive relations among Annie, Basti, the dog, and the mother dog are as follows:

(a) exclusive we: Annie, the dog
(b) exclusive we: Annie, the dog

(c) inclusive we: Annie, the dog, the mother dog
(d) inclusive we: Annie, the dog, Basti
(e) inclusive we: Annie, the dog, Basti, the mother dog

This is the map of the different ranges of the inclusive and exclusive we.

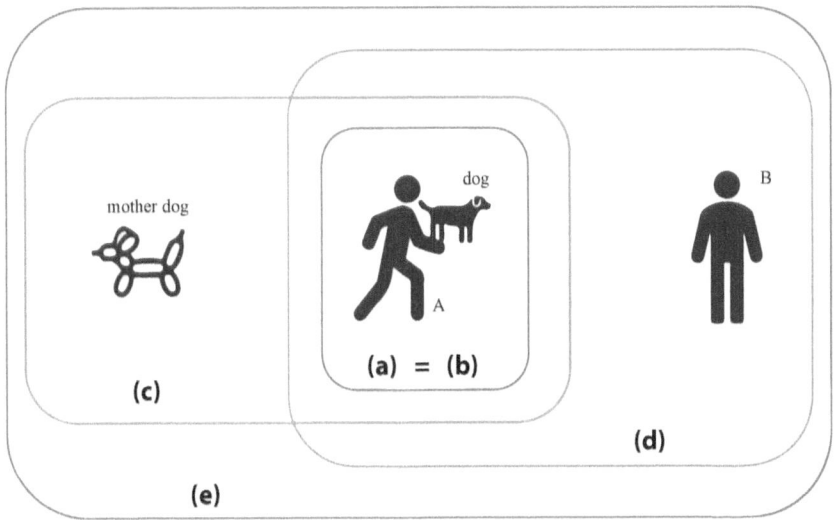

The exclusive 'we' is not necessarily used to emphasize the relationship, the membership, or the belongingness of the speaker and the object of the utterance, as shown in the above examples. When Annie says 'we' as an exclusive we in which Basti and the mother dog are not included, she does not intend to emphasize her intimate relationship with the dog in contrast to Basti or the mother dog. It is the 'we' that defines and expresses the border of the subject. In this context, when Annie decided to go with the dog to see the mother dog, the mother dog does not belong to this 'we' because the mother dog cannot participate in the joint action (going together) of Annie and the dog. And Basti was not informed about this joint action before Annie told him, therefore Basti could not belong to this 'we' either. The 'we,' in the case of (a) and (b), uttered by Annie, is the exclusive we that is conditioned to be the exclusive we. I will call this exclusive we the 'neutral exclusive' we. The neutral we is more frequent in the form of the nominative pronoun than in the possessive pronoun. The 'neutral' we does not necessarily entail a strong sense of identification or a clear intention of excluding the listeners. The exclusiveness in the case of the neutral exclusive we is given rather than intended, and the exclusiveness merely provides clarification in the sentence.

However, there are cases of the exclusive we that are not used for grammatical and contextual clarity, but to point at the exclusiveness of the group that is spoken about. I will call this we the 'strong exclusive' we.

In order to understand the sense of the 'we' utterance, it depends on the type of the 'we,' whether it is intended to simply make the context of the conversation clear, that is, to clarify the object of the utterance, or it is intended to emphasize the 'we' group with which the speaker identifies, excluding the listener. The 'we' in the form of the 'our' that relates to the aspect of identity is often used with more of a sense of exclusiveness: in the form of 'ours but not yours.' When social or political membership and identification is involved, the stronger exclusive we is expressed in the possessive form such as 'our nation,' 'our people,' 'our culture,' and so on.

Then now, let's examine the different cases of the 'we' in Korean from the above conversation at the restaurant (see chapter 2 section 2).

(16)  our husband
         Speaker: daughter
         Listener: father

On the one hand, this 'we' is the exclusive we, because it is technically 'my husband,' which means that the speaker (I) and the husband of the speaker (my husband) are included in the 'we' of 'our husband,' while the father, the listener, is excluded in this 'we' group. There are studies that argue that the 'our' in the case of 'our husband' or 'our wife' is used only in the exclusive scope, where the speaker intends to emphasize the intimate relationship to the object of the utterance while excluding the listener. Hence, the strong exclusive we.

On the other hand, however, the intention of creating a distinction between the inner and the outer circle within the conversation is neither always recognized nor justified. Especially in this case, the listener is the father of the speaker, another intimate family member, so the speaker does not have to clarify the intimate relationship or prove her membership to the family.

If she says 'my husband,' which is not impossible—it is grammatically correct and often preferred in the written context in Korean—in this context to her father, this expression clearly presents the case that she wants to clarify her relationship with her husband and her membership to the family for which only she and her husband are the members, excluding the listener, the father, from this family group.

Also, the husband who is ours but not yours (listener) is different than the family that is 'ours' but not yours (listener), because the husband is a single person, not a group to which more than one person can belong or identify with. If it is a thing, for example, 'our table' that more than one person has ownership over, the exclusive scope of the 'we' is more clearly displayed.

The husband that is ours is not exactly a group in which the listener is not included or a thing that the listener does not share.

Definitely, 'our husband' is often used with the connotation of the exclusive we, excluding the listener from the speaker's relationship with the husband, and this is a logical and convenient way of comprehending this unusual expression in Korean, especially for Korean language learners. This view is already very well-known and widespread in the research in sociocultural linguistics, anthropology, ethnography, and so on. However, this we-expression has a wider scope than the one of the strong exclusive we. This explanation does not unveil the whole picture of this linguistic phenomenon with its cognitive, epistemological, metaphysical, and existential respects.

(17)  our Stephen
        Speaker: father
        Listener: daughter

In this case, it is even more bizarre to assume that the father is saying 'our Stephen' about the husband of the listener, who is his own daughter, to show his intimate relationship to Stephen while excluding the daughter from this group. What the speaker intends to say is definitely not 'it is only about me and Stephen, not you.' Obviously, the speaker says 'our someone' to express affectionate feelings and a close relationship to this someone, but this 'our someone' is not said to exclude the listener.

The expression 'our Stephen' is not always completely interchangeable with 'my Stephen,' which makes it hard to define this 'we' as the exclusive we. The framework of the exclusive and inclusive we is not sufficient for analyzing the we-ness of this case.

(18)  our husband
        Speaker: daughter
        Listener: daughter's friend
      our dad
        Speaker: daughter
        Listener: daughter's friend

Since this is said to a friend who does not belong to the family, the 'our' in this case could be interpreted with a stronger connotation of the exclusive we than the first 'our husband' that is said to the father. The same could be applied for 'our dad.' Therefore, this 'we' could be thought of as both neutral and strong exclusive we. However, it is not satisfying to declare that it is necessary for the speaker to clarify the membership relationship to the person that is spoken about against the listener who does not share the membership in this situation. One says 'our husband' mostly in this kind of situation, but not because the speaker wants to emphasize that the husband is the speaker's husband and not the listener's. In English as well, when one says 'my husband' in this situation, it is to clarify the object of the utterance is the speaker's husband, not anyone else's husband, including the listener, but it is not to emphasize that it is not the listener's husband, to exclude the listener. However, the exclusive we as in the case of exclusive 'our country' is often said to emphasize the distinction of 'my country' from the listener's country.

(19) our Stephen
     Speaker: daughter's friend
     Listener: daughter/father

In this case, it definitely is not a strong exclusive we. However, the speaker says this to express their sympathetic and favorable feelings toward the person that they are talking about. In this sense, it would be possible to argue that it is rather an inclusive we 'in spirit,' because the speaker creates this we group by relating oneself to Stephen, and therefore includes oneself to this we group where the speaker, the listener, and Stephen are all included.

(20) our family
     Speaker: daughter
     Listener: daughter's friend/father

It is not specific to Korean to say 'our family' in a similar way as 'our mom.' In English, for example, one says 'our family' referring to the family to which the speaker belongs together with other family members. Especially, in this case, the father is present with the daughter as she says 'our family,' so she could mean simply 'my and my father's family' opposed to the listener who does not belong to this family, hence the neutral exclusive we. Of course, there is a chance that it is said as a strong exclusive we, although it is quite unlikely in this given situation.

However, 'our family' in Korean in this situation is yet different from the one in English, in the sense that one would say 'my family' in English, if the father is not present, but in Korean, one would still more than likely say 'our family' rather than 'my family,' even if the father is not there.

(21) our son-in-law
     Speaker: father
     Listener: waiter/daughter/daughter's friend

There are situations where the speaker can say 'our son-in-law,' for example, when it is said with the spouse in thought, even if the spouse is not present at the site of the conversation. The speaker could mean that the son-in-law is not only his son-in-law but his and his wife's son-in-law. One could say that the father in this conversation meant his son-in-law is also his wife's son-in-law and he and his wife are the 'we.' From this point of view, it is not odd to say this in other languages as well. However, I would say that normally it is said in a similar way as 'our husband' is said, rather than taking the not-present spouse into account in referring to their children in common. Thus, neither exclusive nor inclusive necessarily.

(22) our Stephen
       Speaker: waiter
       Listener: father/daughter/daughter's friend

This expression among unrelated people is not impossible in other languages either, even if it is not frequently said. In Korean, and in other languages as well, the situation in which 'our someone' is uttered is mostly either when the speaker wants to emphasize positive feelings toward the person who is spoken about or when the speaker wants to express deep sympathetic feelings for that someone.

However, another interesting feature of the 'we' in Korean in the form of 'our someone' or 'our something' is that it is sometimes said almost habitually to soften the atmosphere and what is going to be talked about by adding 'our' before the rest of the speech. The utterance of 'our,' which sounds the same as 'we' in Korean, prepares the listeners, giving them an impression of welcoming and embracing. In this case, the contents of the speech or the object of 'our' are not that important for the saying of 'our.' However, there are still things that would never be said with 'our' in Korean; for example, 'our Japan' or 'our USA' would never be said in Korean by a Korean person. It is possible to say 'our neighbor Japan' or 'our partner USA,' but not alone with the name of the other countries, because they cannot be replaced with 'my,' which implies belongingness, unless the speaker has multiple nationalities including Korean, American, and Japanese.

But 'our Stephen' can be said by the waiter, even if Stephen is not his. The waiter, who neither has met Stephen, nor knows Stephen, nor knows if Stephen even really exists, can say 'our Stephen.' It is similar to 'our Stephen' said by the friend. The difference is that the waiter is not related to Stephen at all, unlike the friend whose friend is Stephen's wife. It is not exclusive, neither neutral nor strong, but it may be inclusive, in a way, according to the same reason above in the case of 'our Stephen' uttered by the friend.

In effect, 'our husband' can also be said by a stranger. In this conversation situation, the waiter could possibly say 'our husband' to the wife. But strangely enough, the related people would not say 'our husband' to the wife, and when it is said by the stranger, it can be said only to the wife. In this case, the stranger who says 'our husband' or 'our wife' to the spouse of the person who is talked about will always add the honorific suffix *bun* [boon][49] as 'our husband-*bun*.'[50] Although this sort of phrase is often used by a person who provides service when they want to express kindness, politeness, and their positive feelings toward the person who they talk to, 'our someone' in the form of 'our *title of the relationship*' with an honorific suffix such as *nim* [neem][51] and *bun* [boon] is a commonly used expression in Korean, such as 'our brother-*bun*,' 'our father-*nim*,' or 'our aunt-*nim*.' The title of the relationship matches the relationship of the listener to the person who is talked about. For example, if I am trying to buy a shirt for my husband and one of the staff of the shop is helping me, the staff could ask, 'What color does *our husband-bun* like?' The same sentence could be said without any possessive pronoun, too, as in 'What color does *husband-bun* like?'

Another thing that I would like to pay attention to is the way this *ouri* in 'our husband' is stated by an unrelated person. There are two ways with a subtle difference.

(a) *ouri* husband
(b) *ouri,* husband

In the second case, there is a very short pause between *ouri* and 'husband.' With this (almost unnoticeable) pause, this *ouri* sounds like 'we' instead of 'our' to the ear of native Korean speakers. Maybe 'ear' is not even the right expression, because both 'we' and 'our' in Korean is *ouri*.[52] So, they sound the same, either as 'we' or 'our' in any case, but the first *ouri* without a comma *sounds* like an adjective that is attached to 'husband' meaning 'our,' but 'our' said for the wife, the listener. However, the second *ouri* with a comma sounds like 'we' immediately, then even when 'husband' is said after this tiny pause, the strong impression of the *ouri* as 'we' lingers. It sounds ambiguous, in fact, if this person wishes to mean 'we, husband' or 'our husband.'[53]

It is also because *ouri* is almost habitually said in Korean. Therefore, even if they didn't want to neither necessarily express their extra kindness or feelings of closeness, nor have the feeling of belongingness at all before saying what they really want to say, sometimes they say *ouri* at the beginning of a sentence. This habitual use of 'we' seems to point at the "one big happy family"[54] *ouri*, which is neither inclusive nor exclusive between the speaker, listener, and the one who is spoken about.

What is the significance of this 'one big happy family?' Whether it really is a happy family or not is another problem, but it is one big family, even if we all could have our black sheep in the family. About the feeling of being in or out of this family, I will say more in the last chapter. And in any case, this one big family could be regarded as *the* representative example of traditionally agricultural, Confucian society, but I see this as the exposition and the acknowledgment of the *web* of relation. What I mean by this *web* will be discussed in detail in chapters 5–9.

Yet, there is another case of 'our husband' that was not included in the above conversation.

(25) "Our husband is Stephen."

Let's say that (25) is true, and, thus, the phrase 'our husband' refers to Stephen. The question is what this 'our' refers to here. One could say that it depends on the context of the exchange. Suppose that a group of people, including the speaker, Stephen, and so on are doing research on husbands. We ask men who are married to put a piece of paper with their names in a bowl from which one person will be selected. The speaker draws a paper on which is written the name 'Stephen.' The speaker utters (25), which is perfectly intelligible in the context.[55] This indicates that the rule for the use of 'our' in English is that it refers to one or more individuals relevant in the context. These can be people, but they need not be. In the example above, there is no reason to treat the group of researchers as an extended self. Moreover, Stephen himself might well be in the group of researchers.

In this example, however, the husband in "Our husband is Stephen" is different from 'our husband' uttered by the person whose husband is actually Stephen. In the first case, where researchers who work on husbands say 'our husband,' this 'husband' refers to the subject of their research, which neither expresses nor indicates the relationship of the speaker to the person named Stephen. 'Our' here indicates the group who research on husbands together—a specific group who are gathered to form a particular group. One can transform "our husband is Stephen" to "The topic (husband) of our research is Stephen." Meanwhile, when the person whose husband is actually Stephen says, "Our husband is Stephen," 'husband' here indicates my relationship to Stephen. So this person cannot say "Our husband is Stephen" formulated in a different way than this. And in this case, 'our' doesn't necessarily indicate any relevant group(s) of the 'we,' where *I* (whose husband is Stephen), Stephen, and the person(s) who *I* am talking to belong together with a certain membership or relationship.

## 4. TWO LEVELS OF WE-NESS IN CONVERSATION

When we say 'we' or 'our' in a conversation, there are two levels of we-ness.

First, there is we-ness in the event of conversation. This denotes the relation between the participants of the conversation.

*I* (speaker) talk to *you* (listener).
*I* (speaker/listener) see *you* (listener/speaker).

*I* (listener) hear *you* (speaker).
*I* (listener/speaker) respond to *you* (speaker/listener).

The speaker and the listener form a 'we.' The 'we' that refers to their copresence in the interaction does not always have to be uttered. Even if the 'we' between the speaker and the listener is not uttered, the participants in the I-Thou structure form a latent we-group. This is the condition of mutual knowledge and joint action.

Second, there is we-ness that is uttered.

(26) (a) *We* (speaker and speaker's husband) want to invite *you* (listener).
(27) (b) *Our* husband said hi to *you* (listener).
(28) (c) *Our* husband gave (d) *us* (speaker and listener) these concert tickets.

The speaker says (a) 'we' in which the listener is not included. This exclusive 'we' is uttered. The uttered 'we' is the we group with which the speaker proactively identifies. Within the I-Thou framework, we could say that there are three I-Thou situations here: (1) I-Thou between the speaker and the listener; (2) I-Thou of the speaker and the speaker's husband; (3) I-Thou between the uttered 'we' as an extended 'I' (speaker and the husband) and 'you' (the listener).

In sentence (26), the (a) 'we' that belongs to the second I-Thou was uttered. But the 'we' of the first I-Thou between the conversation participants is not uttered in (26), even though present, therefore this 'we' is a latent 'we' in this context. It could be said that there is another latent 'we' in this sentence, which is the third I-Thou between 'we' (extended I) and 'you.' In sentence (28), the we as (d) 'us' referring to the speaker and the listener is not latent, because the speaker identifies herself with the 'we' together with the listener, and this 'we' is uttered.

(26)
(a) we (uttered): speaker + the husband of the speaker
we (latent): speaker + listener
we (latent): (speaker + the husband) + listener
(28)
(d) us (uttered): speaker + listener

How about the 'we' in sentences (27) and (28) uttered as (b)/(c) 'our husband'? According to the three I-Thou models I suggested above, the 'we' in 'our husband' seems to fit the third I-Thou (extended I + Thou). But this 'we' is not latent, unlike in (26). Who belongs to the 'we' as extended 'I' is not fully clear. The listener could be considered as the Thou of the third I-Thou, but the listener is also not excluded from this we-ness in 'our husband.' Rather the listener could be considered to be included in this extended I.

(27)
(b) / (c) our husband (uttered): speaker + husband + ( )

I have shown above that 'our husband' can be exclusive, but neither always, nor necessarily. Within the parenthesis above, the listener, or a third person, or both the listener and a third person, that is, anyone can be included.

## 5. JEOHI

There are two different words for the first-person singular: *na* [na][56] and *jeo* [jaw].[57] *Jeo* [jaw] is an honorific expression to humble oneself toward the interlocutor, but they both mean 'I' with no semantic difference between the two other than the honorific distinction. For the first-person plural, there are two words as well: *ouri* and *jeohi* [jaw-hee].[58] *Jeohi* is regarded as the plural form of *jeo*, but the use and meaning of this word is more complicated than that of a simply plural form of *jeo* or an honorific form of *ouri*.

The use of *ouri* and *jeohi* can be distinguished in their relation to *neo* [naw],[59] the second-person singular.[60] *Jeohi* is used by the speaker who refers to herself as *jeo* and who is referred to by the interlocutor as *neo*. The interlocutor who can call the other *neo* refers to herself as *na*. On the other hand, *ouri* can be used by both interlocutors; the person who refers to herself as *na* and the person who refers to herself as *jeo*.

Let's say there are two people *A* and *B*. *A* is older than *B*, therefore, *A* refers to herself as *na*, while *B* refers to herself as *jeo* in conversation with *A*. This means that *A* can call *B neo*. However, *B* cannot call *A neo*. *B* will try to avoid mentioning *A* at all or find another way to refer to *A*, which I will discuss in detail in chapter 3, section 2. So, we have the following (arrow signifies "to refer to"):

$A > B$ ($B$ uses honorific language)

a. $A \rightarrow A$ : *na*
b. $B \rightarrow B$ : *jeo*
c. $A \rightarrow B$ : *neo*
d. $B \rightarrow A$ : Φ (or the name of the title, relationship, etc.)

When one refers to a group in which one, the other, or both belong to, we have the following cases ($C$ is a third person):

e. $A \rightarrow AB$ : *ouri*
f. $A \rightarrow AC$ : *ouri*
g. $B \rightarrow BC$ : *jeohi*
h. $B \rightarrow BA$ : *ouri* (or *jeohi*)
i. $A \rightarrow BC$ : *neohi* [naw-hee][61]
j. $B \rightarrow AC$ : Φ (or the names of the title, relationship, etc., of A and C)
k. $A \rightarrow ABC$ : *ouri*
l. $B \rightarrow BAC$ : *ouri* (or *jeohi*)

*Neohi* is the second-person plural. The group referred to as *neohi* refers to themselves as *jeohi* but not *ouri*. The group that refers to the other group as *neohi* refers to themselves as *ouri*. But the group that refers to everyone, including the speaker, the listener, and a third party, refers to themselves as *ouri*. *Ouri* is used to refer to everyone. The question is (1) whether *jeohi* can replace *ouri* in the case of *ouri* everyone, as seen in *h* and *l*; (2) whether this can be explained in the framework of exclusive and inclusive we.

The distinction between the inclusive and exclusive forms is almost universally found among the Austronesian languages and the languages of northern Australia.[62] However, it is rather questionable whether the framework of exclusiveness and inclusiveness is the right frame of reference for analyzing the use of *ouri* and *jeohi*. According to the clusivity rule, *ouri* functions as both the inclusive and exclusive we, although we have seen above that this framework does not fully cover the dimensions of the use of *ouri*. Furthermore, *ouri* as the exclusive we is also conditional, able to be said only in cases when the listener is of equal age or younger than the speaker, or when the speaker and the listener are very close in age.

Compared to the use of *ouri*, *jeohi* seems to have more of an exclusive meaning, but, even so, whether *jeohi* should be considered as the exclusive we is controversial. If *jeohi* is considered only as the plural of *jeo*, grammatically it is more logical to regard *jeohi* as exclusive, because *jeohi* is an honorific word that is used to lower the speaking self, thus, logically—under the condition that *jeohi* is the plural of *jeo*—it is not sound to include the interlocutor(s) toward whom the speaker has lowered herself in the 'we' group of *jeohi*.

A child can ask her grandmother, "Did *jeohi* family come from the north?," referring to "their," the grandmother and the grandchild's family, as *jeohi* family. In this case, the grandmother also belongs to the *jeohi*. One can notice that *jeohi* is used very frequently in such contexts, but I see this as an honorific error. The right way to refer to their "shared" family both by the grandmother and the grandchild is not *jeohi* but *ouri*, because the members of *jeohi* are supposed to be lower in status before the listener. The grandmother is lowered when she is referred to as *jeohi* along with the speaker, causing the error.

Colloquially, however, *jeohi* is used frequently to include the interlocutor(s) who is older, hierarchically higher, or a stranger. For example, in the situation where someone seems very familiar but I cannot recall who that is, I could ask, "Have *jeohi* met before?" In this case, 'technically' one should say *ouri*, because everyone who belongs to the group of *jeohi* including *myself* and the interlocutor are humbled. But conventionally, many would say *jeohi* instead of *ouri* in this case, because (1) *ouri* could sound/feel too intimate, (2) *ouri* could sound/feel rude, even if it is grammatically correct and therefore would technically be neither impolite nor inappropriate to refer to oneself and the stranger as *ouri*. There is no complete consent over the use and the meaning of *jeohi*. For example, not all agree with my view that a granddaughter referring to her family as *jeohi* family while talking to her grandmother is an honorific error.[63]

*Jeohi* is used not necessarily to exclude the listener but rather to express respect for the listener. The distance the speaker creates in her conversation room by saying *jeohi* is an expression of respect in most cases rather than an instance of separating herself deliberately from the listener. Therefore, it is insufficient to define *jeohi* as an exclusive we per se. Of course, *jeohi* could also draw a clear line between the speaker and the listener, when it is necessary to distinguish the other from 'me' or 'us.' *Jeohi*, however, does not sound as aggressive and exclusive as the first-person singular form 'my.' For example, it is not intended to exclude the listener when one says "*Jeohi* [our] husband is from this town." *Jeohi* in this statement gives information about the listener, perhaps that this listener is older, or someone with a higher social status than the speaker, or not close to the speaker. *Jeohi* is a modest way of saying 'we,' or 'my.' Sometimes, *jeohi* is considered as not distinguished from *jeo-ui* (of mine), when it is used to mean 'my.'

However, in the case of 'our Stephen' as in sentence (23), "Our Stephen must be a funny guy," as spoken by the waiter, a stranger, *jeohi* cannot replace *ouri*, because the waiter and Stephen do not belong to a group to which the father does not belong. The 'we' in 'our Stephen' spoken by a person who does not share any social identification or group membership with Stephen includes everyone; the speaker, the listener, and the third person, either related or unrelated, present or absent.

What is significant about the patterns of using the 'we' in Korean is that the speaker uses the we even if she refers to herself in the first-person singular. For example, in Korean, 'our home' is a common expression, said in the form of '*ouri/jeohi* home,' which refers to 'my home,' with 'my' referring to the speaker. The speaker, of course, could have meant 'our home,' which belongs not only to herself but to her other family members as well. But even if the speaker who says '*ouri/jeohi* home' is a single person who lives alone or has never had a family in her entire life and has always lived alone, she would still say '*ouri/jeohi* home' when she wants to talk about her home to others. In this case, one can see that the 'we' (our, us) is more commonly used in Korean than 'I' (my, me) to mean the actual 'I' (the first-person singular). This use of the 'we' as an extended self is more clearly represented in possessive expressions such as '*ouri/jeohi* home' or '*ouri/jeohi* husband.'

There are some languages that have a pronoun expressing 'we' which is used for expressing 'I.' For example, in Qawasqar, a language from Chile, *cecaw qjeq'ja qjenaq afxat* could mean "I ran yesterday" or "We ran yesterday," and there is no way to decide from the sentence alone if it refers to 'I' or 'we' who ran yesterday. This usage is rather uncommon, but there are languages with no specialized plural pronouns, as with Maricopa, a Native American language.[64] In Korean, there is a distinction between 'I' and 'we,' and they are used in different contexts unlike in Qawasqar. However, *ouri* is a more commonly used expression for representing oneself, while 'I' is used intentionally to refer to the 'own-ness' of the self in special cases.

## 6. NOSISM

In European languages, there are cases where the 'we' acts as an extended self, such as *pluralis excellentiae*, which refers to plural words that take singular forms, and *pluralis majestatis*, also known as the royal we, the phenomenon in which a single person holding a high office, such as a sovereign or religious leader, refers to herself as 'we.' *Pluralis majestatis* is a representative example of *nosism*, which refers to the phenomenon of using 'we' instead of the first-person singular to refer to oneself when expressing one's personal opinions. Another example is the editorial 'we,' which is used by editorial columnists in newspapers or in other media when they, as an individual, refer to themselves as 'we,' thereby casting themselves in the role of a spokesperson. The author's 'we,' or *pluralis modestiae*, is a similar case and is the common practice in the mathematical or scientific literature of referring to a generic third person as 'we.' An example of this occurs in the following quote: "We see that our extension of the principle of relativity implies the necessity of the law of the equality of inertial and gravitational mass."[65] In the sentence "We may not think the scientists are lying, but are we able truly to believe what they tell us?"[66] from *The Guardian*, the 'we' here refers to the reader and the author, as the author assumes that the reader agrees with the ideas that the author is presenting. This is a common practice in philosophical works, as well as in comments in computer code.[67]

The 'we' of *pluralis majestatis* and *pluralis modestiae* refers to one person who represents the other. I wrote in my paper "A Phenomenological Approach to the Korean 'We'"[68] that this 'we' can be considered as a collection of selves as well as an extended self. But I think that it is in fact more plausible to consider *pluralis majestatis* only as an extended self, because the 'we' implies God and the king, in the sense that God is the king and the king is God, so the self-identity of the king (A) is extended in the form of the 'we' as 'the king (A) = God (B)' or sometimes 'the king (A) = the people (C).' The royal 'we' with God in three persons and the people is plural but is not collective, as in the sense of a gathering of individuals.

The 'we' in *pluralis modestiae* comes about in the process of transforming oneself into the 'we,' which assumes the agreement of the other, in this case, the reader. I once considered this as a collection of individuals based on a presumption of mutual agreement. The author 'envisages' and 'imagines' a community of readers.[69] However, it is an exaggeration, I think, to regard this community that is imagined in the head of the author as a we group created by a gathering of individuals.

In the use of the 'we' in Korean, when one says 'our home,' referring to one's own home which is not shared with anyone else, this 'we' is not necessarily a result of (A + B), but seems to refer to an extension of the self. However, the structure of *pluralis majestatis* and *pluralis modestiae* seems to be different from that of 'our husband': The 'central self' as the subject that is extended in nosism is 'I,' the king, the queen, the pope, or the author, while the 'central self' that is extended in 'our husband' is not only 'I,' the speaker, but could also be the other(s).

(1) Nosism
Extended I = (A) + (C)
   (A): I (The king/The queen/The pope/writer)
   (C): other(s)
The self that is extended is the 'I.'
→ extended (A)

The king, the queen, the pope, or the writer as the subjective speaking 'I' is extended.
→ (C) is anonymous, imaginary, or ontically vacant.

(2) Our husband
Extended Self (husband or I) = (A+B) + (B) (+ (C))
   (A+B): Our (I + My husband + maybe others)
   (B): husband
The self that is extended is both the speaking 'I' (my) and the husband.
→ extended (A+B), extended (A), extended (B), (extended (C))
Husband is another self in 'our husband.'
→ (B) is neither anonymous, nor imaginary, nor ontically vacant.

I have already mentioned that *ouri* contains all the meanings of 'we,' 'us,' and 'our.' '*Ouri* husband' seems to function more as 'we, husband' or 'us, husband' than 'our husband' as 'the husband of you and I,' unless one says '*ouriui* husband' (the husband of ours) with the suffix *ui*. In that case, it sounds like 'our husband' meaning 'our husband in common.' Here, the 'we' in '*ouri* husband' is not the combination of the speaking 'I' with other individuals, including the husband, but an extended self of the speaker, the husband, or/and possibly others.

Both nosism and the *ouri* express an extended self in the plural form. However, what do we understand by this 'self'? We need to investigate 'self' in this regard. To spill the beans, *ouri* has another dimension beyond that of the nosistic self: *ouri* represents a pre-subjective selfhood that is fundamental-ontologically 'in-relation.' This points at the self that is necessarily in relation with others without a specific status as a particular subject such as a royal or a writer. Before we go into the discussion on pre-subjective self-in-relation, in the following two chapters (chapters 3 and 4), we will briefly see how the self has been understood in philosophy from different perspectives.

## NOTES

1. Ingar Brinck et al., "The Primacy of the 'We'?," in *Embodiment, Enaction, and Culture: Investigating the Constitution of the Shared World*, ed. Christoph Durt, Thomas Fuchs, Christian Tewes (Cambridge, MA: MIT Press, 2017), 141.

2. Ernst Mach, *Beiträge zur Analyse der Empfindungen* (Jena: Verlag von Gustav Fischer, 1886), 149, quoted in Filip Mattens, "Introducing Terms. Philosophical Vocabulary, Neologism and the Temporal Aspect of Meaning," in *Meaning and Language: Phenomenological Perspectives*, ed. Filip Mattens (Dordrecht: Springer, 2008), 283.

3. Ernst Mach, *Die Prinzipien der Wärmelehre* (Leipzig: Johann Ambrosius Barth, 1900), 404, quoted in Mattens, "Introducing Terms," 323.

4. In *The Dictionary of the National Institute of Korean Language*, n.d., https://stdict.korean.go.kr/search/searchView.do.

5. 우리가 나아갈 길/ 우리 둘이 힘을 합치면 못할 일이 뭐가 있겠니? / 어머니, 우리 오늘 도봉산에 갈까요? (my translation).

6. 우리 먼저 나간다. 수고해라/ 언젠가 자네가 우리 부부를 초대한 적이 있었지./ 우리가 당신한테 무슨 잘못을 했다고 이러시오? (my translation).

7. 우리 엄마/ 우리 마누라/ 우리 신랑.

8. 의.

9. Kyeong-Ouk Jeong, "The Use of the First Person Plural Possessive Pronoun Woorie in Korean Language," *Journal of Korean Language Education* 16, no. 3 (2005). The author of this article Romanizes the Korean word 우리 (*ouri*) as *woorie* presumably to suggest to the readers a pronunciation that is closer to the actual pronunciation of the word in Korean, 405–422.

10. *Love on a Jujube Tree* (대추나무 사랑 걸렸네) was a weekly drama broadcasted between September 9, 1990, and October 10, 2007, by KBS. The English translation of the title is different in the article by Jeong (2005).

11. J. K. Rowling, *Harry Potter and the Sorcerer's Stone (Korean Edition)*, trans. Hyewon Kim (Seoul: Munhak-Sucheop, 2016), quoted in Jeong, "The Use of the First Person Plural."

12. Yoseop Ju, *The Guest in My Mom's House* (Seoul: Cheongmoksa, 1935), quoted in Jeong, "The Use of the First Person Plural."

13. Yoseop Ju, "The Guest in My Mom's House," trans. Joseph Ruesing, *Korea Journal* 25, no. 11 (November 1985), quoted in Jeong, "The Use of the First Person Plural."

14. Jeong, "The Use of the First Person Plural," 407.

15. Richard Harris, *Roadmap to Korean: Everything You Ever Wanted to Know about the Language*. 2nd Edition (Seoul: Hollym, 2005), 121.

16. Harris, *Roadmap to Korean*, 121.

17. Iksop Lee and S. Robert Ramsey, *The Korean Language* (Albany, NY: SUNY Press, 2000), quoted in Jeong, "The Use of the First Person Plural," 407.

18. Harris, *Roadmap to Korean*, 121.

19. Harris, *Roadmap to Korean*, 121.

20. Harris, *Roadmap to Korean*, 121.

21. (a) The general scope that can be applied to anyone associated; (2) the inclusive scope that can be applied to both speaker and listener; (c) the exclusive scope that can be applied to the speaker only (Marianne, Celce-Murcia and Diane Larsen-Freeman, *The Grammar Book : An ESL/EFL Teacher's Course* [Boston: Heinle & Heinle, 1999], 304, quoted in Jeong, "The Use of the First Person Plural," 409–410). The collected data are taken from Jeong, "The Use of the First Person Plural." The article presents the original sentences in Korean in the text, but I will present the sentence only in English in the text and move the sentences in Korean to footnotes. I made minor changes to the translated sentences in English (Jeong, "The Use of the First Person Plural," 411–412).

22. 순수 우리 콩으로 만든 두부들이 별로 없으니까 어쩌면 잘 팔릴 거예요.

23. 두고 봐요. 우리 동네서 얼마 살지 못하고 떠난다는 소리 나올테니까!

24. 하지만 우리 아버지가 지금 보통으로 화가 나신게 아니라구요.
25. 우리 남편이 재작년에 결혼기념일이라고 선물해 준 거야.
26. 우리 마누라가 알면 난 즉시 징계감이유.
27. Jeong, "The Use of the First Person Plural," 410–411.
28. Jeong, "The Use of the First Person Plural," 411.
29. 승훈 씨가 나를 좋아하는 것은 순전히 내 재산을 노린 거라구.
30. 내 귀에 그런 얘기가 들려올 때 기분 어땠겠어?
31. 내 동생 맘을 모르는 바는 아니지만.
32. Jeong, "The Use of the First Person Plural," 412.
33. 내 형.
34. Jeong, "The Use of the First Person Plural," 412.
35. Jeong, "The Use of the First Person Plural," 413.
36. 나의 이웃에 사는 까치들은 복이 많다 . . . 내 이웃에 있는 까치 둥지도 오래되었지만, 내 고향 마을의 미루나무 위에 지어진 둥지는 더 오래 되었다 (Jeong, "The Use of the First Person Plural," 413).
37. Jeong, "The Use of the First Person Plural," 414–415.
38. 사업을 하시던 아버지께서 오랜 투병 끝에 돌아가시고, 우리 집안은 급격하게 몰락했다. 형은 돈 벌러 간다고 나가 일 년이 넘도록 소식이 없고 어머니와 나는 매일 빚쟁이에게 시달리면서 지겨운 생활을 하고 있었다 (Jeong, "The Use of the First Person Plural," 414).
39. Jeong, "The Use of the First Person Plural," 418–419.
40. 우리 이모와 이모부와 사촌은 그래. 내게도 마법사 형제가 세 명 쯤 있으면 좋겠어 (Jeong, "The Use of the First Person Plural," 418).
41. 우리 가족 중에는 아무도 마술을 해본 적이 없어서, 내가 Φ 편지를 받았을 때 정말 놀랐었어. 물론 나는 굉장히 기뻤지만 (Jeong, "The Use of the First Person Plural," 418).
42. 우리 아빠는 그린고트까지 손을 뻗은 건 틀림없이 강력한 어둠의 마법사짓 일거라고 하시지만 (Jeong, "The Use of the First Person Plural," 418).
43. 내 이름이 웃긴다 이거니? 네가 누군지는 물어보지 않아도 알겠구나. 위즐리 가족은 모두 빨간 머리에, 주근깨투성이에다 형편에 맞지 않게 아이들을 턱없이 많이 낳았다고 우리 아버지가 그러셨거든 (Jeong, "The Use of the First Person Plural," 418–419).
44. Jeong, "The Use of the First Person Plural," 419.
45. 외할머니 말씀을 들으면 우리 아버지는 내가 이 세상에 나오기 한 달 전에 돌아가셨대요. 우리 어머니하고 결혼한 지는 일 년만이고요. 우리 아버지의 본집은 어디 멀리 있는데, 마침 이 동리 학교에 교사로 오게 되기 때문에 결혼 후에도 우리 어머니는 시집으로 가지 않고 여기 이 집을 사고 (바로 이 집은 우리 외할머니댁 옆집이지요) 여기서 살다가 일 년이 못 되어 갑자기 돌아가셨대요 (Jeong, "The Use of the First Person Plural," 419).
46. James Paul Gee, "What Is Literacy," in *Negotiating Academic Literacies: Teaching and Learning across Languages and Cultures*, ed. Vivian Zamel and Ruth Spack (Mahwah, NJ: Lawrence Erlbaum, 1998), quoted in Jeong, "The Use of the First Person Plural," 421.
47. 저희.
48. See also Kim "A Phenomenological Approach to the Korean 'We.'"

49. 분.
50. 우리 남편분.
51. 님.
52. 'Us' is *ouri* as well.
53. It is indeed very subtle, and it could be very sensitive according to the situation, for example, politically in relation to Japan for Koreans. Korea was colonized by Japan for nearly forty years, and the end of colonization was hastily performed without much of an autonomous and independent action of the Korean people. Many of the pro-Japanese officials in Korea, who are sometimes compared to the officials who served the Nazi German regime in other European countries, stayed in power, and, in fact, still do up until this point. The episode of a Korean politician who—presumably—accidentally said "*ouri* Japan" in public and was very much in trouble provides a good example that shows the habitual way of Koreans of saying *ouri* and the political sensitivity of this issue in relation to the recent history of Korea. She claimed that it was a mistake due to her habitual way of speaking. Namely, I assume that she probably meant saying *ouri* before any sentence, to give herself time to think and make room for others to get ready for her speech. Unfortunately, though, there already had been a strong suspicion that she and her family have been pro-Japan, therefore, her apology was not very well accepted. The truth of matter is that it is hard to think of a Korean politician or even a nonpolitician saying "*ouri* Japan" on purpose, especially in public, even if they actually are pro-Japan and are conscious about it. Not to defend her at any rate, but it probably was more than likely a mistake, the second case of saying '*ouri* something or someone' with a comma as '*ouri*, Japan.' I guess, you never know, but even the dumbest politician would not dare to say that in Korea, considering which, one can see through this episode how deeply it is habituated to say the word *ouri* in Korean.
54. Harris, *Roadmap to Korean*.
55. Example from Steven Davis (Professor Emeritus of Philosophy at Simon Fraser University and Carleton University).
56. 나.
57. 저.
58. 저희. Part of the discussion on *jeohi* appears also in Kim, "A Phenomenological Approach to the Korean 'We.'"
59. 너.
60. Comment from So Jeong Park (Associate Professor, Korean Philosophy Department Chair, College of Confucian Studies & Eastern Philosophy, Sungkyunkwan University).
61. 너희.
62. See Michael Cysouw, "Inclusive/Exclusive Distinction in Independent Pronouns," *The World Atlas of Language Structures Online* (Munich: Max Planck Digital Library), 2008.
63. Comment from Jae Hoon Yeon (Professor of Korean Language and Linguistics, SOAS University of London).
64. Cysouw, "Inclusive/Exclusive Distinction in Independent Pronouns."
65. Albert Einstein, *Relativity: The Special and General Theory*, trans. Robert W. Lawson (London: Methuen & Co., 1920).

66. Jonathan Safran Foer, "Why We Must Cut out Meat and Dairy before Dinner to Save the Planet," *The Guardian*, September 28, 2019, https://www.theguardian.com/books/2019/sep/28/meat-of-the-matter-the-inconvenient-truth-about-what-we-eat.

67. These forms of the 'we' can be substituted with 'one' from time to time. It is *man* in German and *on* in French. It is interesting to note that *on* in French is also used in the place of *nous*, the 'we.' The 'you' can function similarly to the 'we,' not only in scientific literature, but also in spoken language, in such sentences as "You have to eat more vegetables," where 'you' is used not necessarily to refer to the addressee as the specific 'you,' but rather the 'we' in the general sense.

68. Kim, "A Phenomenological Approach to the Korean 'We.'"

69. David Carr describes how the author's 'we' is formed and used in his discussion of the narrative self and the communal *Besinnung* of history-writing: "The author bravely and hopefully envisages a community of readers, each as clear-minded and discerning as the author himself, jointly addressing themselves to the task of investigating some problem, say, the connection between time, narrative, and history. The author leads the way, occasionally (for example, at the beginning of each chapter) reminding his readers what 'we' have accomplished and what remains to be done. He imagines them vigorously nodding their heads at each turn in the argument" (David Carr, *Time, Narrative, and History* [Bloomington: Indiana University Press, 1991], 157).

*Chapter 3*

# Self in Korean

## 1. SELF IN KOREAN: *JAGI*

The use of the word *jagi* [ja-kee],[1] which means 'self' in Korean, is peculiar. *Jagi* consists of two Chinese characters 自 [ja] and 己 [kee]. The etymology of this word relates to the act of 'pointing to oneself.' The first character 自 originates from the shape of the nose of a person. Alone, it means 'self,' because one has to point at her nose to point at, or rather, call oneself 'self.' This word in Korean is used to address the second-person singular 'you,' the third-person singular 'he/she,' or 'one' as everyone. For example:

(29) "*Jagi* busy today?"[2]
(30) "*Jagi* didn't want to go there."[3]
(31) "Our *jagi*, did you have dinner yet?"[4]
(32) "*Jagi* should take care of *jagi*'s own belongings."[5]
(33) "I had to trust *jagi jasin*."[6]

In (29), 'self' refers to the second-person singular 'you,' in (30) the third-person singular she/he, in (31) 'self' is used as a term of endearment, and in (32) 'self' functions as 'one' in English referring to 'everyone.' And in (33), 'self' refers to the speaker herself. However, for *jagi* to be used to refer to the speaker herself, usually it is said together with the word *jasin* [ja-sheen] which also means 'self.' *Jasin* is composed of two Chinese characters *ja* (自) and *sin* (身); *ja* meaning 'self' and *sin* meaning 'body.' *Jasin*, therefore, literally means 'self-body.'

They can be translated as follows:

(29) Are *you* busy today?
(30) *He/she* didn't want to go there.

(31) *My sweetheart*, did you have dinner yet?
(32) *One* should take care of *one*'s own belongings.
(33) I had to trust *myself*.

Since this word *jagi* is used to refer to the first, the second, and the third person, I would like to apply it to the meta-name framework that utilizes the logic of 'shift' invented by the mathematician Louis Kauffman. This is how it works:

> Naming objects occurs, and when it does, a pointer is notated in memory from A (the name) to B (the object) as A → B. When there is a naming A → B, it is shifted to ♯A(name) → BA(object-name). That is, the name is appended to the object and sets up a new or meta-name ♯A for this composite object made of thing and name. This shifting process is noticed and given a name M. Thus M(name) → ♯(object). M is the name of the meta-naming process. This naming is shifted to form ♯M(name) → ♯M(object-name) and abbreviated to I = ♯M. I am the meta-name of my meta-naming process.[7]

Here let us apply the word *jagi* to this shift rule. When we say *jagi* in Korean, it means either you, he, she, they, or one. Therefore, *jagi* is the name for the objects 'you, he, she, they, or one.' So we have 'Self → you/he/she/they/one' and you can shift it to '#self → you-self (yourself)/he-self (himself)/she-self (herself)/they-self (themselves)/one-self.' Here 'self' is a name. But let us do the same with the word 'I,' the meta-name of my meta-naming process. 'I' means self, therefore, I → Self.

This can be further shifted to #I → I-self (myself). Here 'self' is not a name, but an object of the name, because 'I' is the meta-name of calling my-self. Each person—you, she, he, they, one—uses this meta-name 'I' to call oneself. Each person says 'I.' 'You,' 'she,' 'he,' and 'they' are 'you,' 'she,' 'he,' and 'they' based on each person's relation to the other. These who-word-names are used relatively. This shows how the word *jagi* can be used as an indexical, like the word 'I.' However, *jagi* is not dependent on a relation, unlike the pronouns 'you,' 'she,' 'he,' 'they,' or 'one.' *Jagi* is used in a way that is free from or outside of the relative I-you, I-she, I-he frame. This may be related to the fact that the Korean language did not natively develop third-person pronouns. In fact, the Korean words that match 'he' or 'she' in English are imported words from European languages to Japanese and then to Korean.[8] But even to address the person in front of you as *neo* [naw],[9] which means 'you,' is barely used or used reluctantly, because it comes with a strong feeling of disconnection. In this context, the 'I' does not seem to be the necessary center of the relationship, or more precisely, the starting point for understanding/framing relationships.

Self, *jagi* in Korean, is the name of each person's self, not as 'you,' 'he,' or 'she' in contrast to the 'I,' but each person's own person, or self, set as their own center. Thus, there are multiple centers in a conversation/interaction. Each person uses the meta-name 'I,' and each person is not relativized, or 'othered,' by the other 'I.' In this context, 'I' is the meta-name that each self uses in contrast to the other. The other is 'I' for oneself but not for *me*. *I* am 'I' for *myself*, and only *I* can call *myself* 'I.' Others cannot call *me* 'I,' while they can call each one of themselves 'I.' Each self is each one's own person which is addressed by the identical name 'self.' The self is therefore everyone. *I* can call *myself* and others 'self,' and others can call themselves and *me* 'self.' *Jagi* (self) is not used relatively. Therefore, I argue that 'self' is not only a meta-name that everyone can use to refer to oneself but a *pan-meta-name*, meaning one name that can be used to refer to everyone including oneself and every other person at the same time. Self is, therefore, self and other at the same time: paradox. I will show how this paradox could be resolved in the following chapter. The word 'self' in Korean seems to represent this 'resolved' paradox.

In linguistics, there are several studies on *jagi*, especially concerning its binding-theoretic status.[10] Simply, the goal is to study to whom *jagi* refers in the sentence. In the context of these studies, *jagi* has been considered as a long-distance anaphor, that is, a word that refers back to an earlier word at a distance. The antecedent of *jagi* is found both locally and at a distance. One of the core defining features of long-distance anaphors is that they are monomorphemic, which means that they consist of only one morpheme, an individual basic unit of language. This is demonstrable both in Germanic *zich* (Dutch) and *seg* (Norwegian) as well as in the East Asian *ziji* (Chinese) and *zibun* (Japanese).[11] However, while *jagi* fits the character of the other anaphors, linguists argue that there are also some fundamental differences[12] which challenge the core notion of what it means to be an anaphor. In Korean, *jagi* can take extrasentential antecedents, or not have antecedents at all, for instance, when it is used to refer to the listener in the conversation (you) or the third person (he/she) as seen in the above examples.[13] Some linguists argue that empathy may play a role in the interpretation of *jagi*.[14] Empathy refers to the speaker's variable degree of identification with a person (potential antecedent) participating in the event or state described by the sentence.[15]

Although *jagi* can be regarded as an indexical, *jagi* is used to refer to self and other at the same time, while 'I' cannot be said to refer to another person, even if the other can say 'I' for themselves. One can call only oneself 'I' and call others other names such as 'you,' 'she,' or 'he,' whereas *jagi* expresses the simultaneous multipolarity of self.

52                    Chapter 3

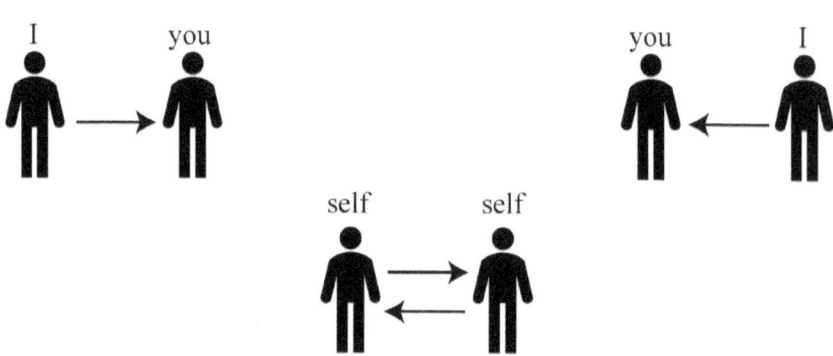

In self as *jagi* (I, you, she, he, they), the structure of subject-object seems to wither. *Jagi* blurs the linguistic articulation of distinction between self and other. Self as *jagi* does not lose its subjective attributes, but the speaking self calls the other literally 'self' instead of 'you,' 'she,' 'he,' or 'they,' in contrast to 'I.' The other is not expressively other in the word 'self.' The opposition of the other as something else, that is, 'object,' in contrast to 'I' disappears when one says *jagi*.

## 2. YOU IN KOREAN: *NEO* AND *DANGSIN*

While the word 'self' is used to refer to 'you,' the actual second-person singular pronoun, *neo*, is hardly used in Korean. It is said only to a person who is the same age or younger, but pretty much only when they are closely related. However, even between close friends and siblings, it is used rather reluctantly when they are aged, and it is regarded to be rude or even low when an aged person calls another person *neo* in certain cases. Especially between people who are not close or who do not know each other very well, it is strictly forbidden to use the word *neo*. This is because calling somebody 'you' in Korean gives the impression that the speaker draws a very clear line of distinction opposed to the listener and thereby creates distance. If it is said to another person whom the speaker does not know very well, it gives an impression that the speaker puts no respect on the listener, and perhaps even looks down on the person. Saying 'you' in Korean, therefore, has a tacit implication: 'I am I, and you are you, and I am aware of this.'

This is also because *neo* is not the honorific form of the word 'you.' There are several honorific forms of the word. Koreans would try to avoid saying 'you' as much as possible, and when it is necessary to address another person, they would use different forms of 'you.' To call a younger person, one could use the words *jane* [jah-nae][16] or *geudae* [gue-dae].[17] If it is 'you' for an older person or a stranger, one says *seonsaengnim* [sun-saeng-neem],[18] which literally means 'teacher' or sometimes, to an older person, one says 'father' (*abeonim* [ah-baw-neem])[19] or 'mother' (*eomeonim* [aw-maw-neem][20]), in the way that the waiter address the father as 'father' in the sentence (22) from chapter 2, section 2. It is an interesting phenomenon that one calls an unrelated person 'teacher,' 'father,' and 'mother.' From a sociocultural perspective, this can be interpreted as demonstrating that the understanding of self and other in Korean society and culture is fundamentally rooted in relationship. This is interesting, however, not only from a sociocultural point of view but also from a philosophical perspective.

*Dangsin* [dahng-sheen][21] is another word that means 'you' in Korean. However, the use of this 'you' is quite confusing. First of all, the literal meaning of *dangsin* is you, and this word can be used to call the listener. However, the uses of this word are not consistent with other words that refer to 'you.' I will explain with examples.

(34) I will try to be a good husband to *dangsin*.[22]

Here, *dangsin* is said to refer to 'you' who is the partner of the speaker. This word is used often between a married couple to refer to each other. When it is said to the spouse in a married relationship, it subtly expresses respect and care for the spouse.

(35) (Φ) won't forget the sacrifice of *dangsin*.[23]

*Dangsin* is often used in literature. When it is used in the written context, it is used as an honorific form of 'you.' Also, this sentence (35) lacks a subject, but from the context, one could presume that it is either 'we' or 'I,' though probably more than likely 'we.' But most of the time, this sort of sentence would be expressed without a subject. In fact, when it is said with 'I' or 'we,' it sounds almost superfluous.

(36) What? *Dangsin*? How dare you call me *dangsin*?[24]

Nevertheless, at the same time, as shown in (36), the exact same word *dangsin* can be as inappropriate and aggressive as 'you' in a hostile situation. Calling the other person *dangsin* could be considered to be very rude. One can say and hear this in an intense situation when people fight or argue fiercely. In this case, *dangsin* functions as *neo*, but still not as strong as calling another *neo* in an argument. It can be used when someone wants to create distance from the opponent by calling the other person *neo*. But calling someone who one does not know *neo* is completely inappropriate. Therefore, one uses this softened form of 'you,' but perhaps sarcastically, because the speaker has no respect for the listener in this situation. This is, in a way, a disguised *neo*, to keep one's last dignity, not so much for the listener, but, in effect, for the speaker themselves. But of course, when the fight goes out of control, one could say *neo*, but this expresses absolute disrespect and insult toward the other person. If it is said between total strangers, this plain second-person singular pronoun functions basically as a pejorative. But as mentioned repeatedly, this word literally only points at 'you,' as simple as that, yet its use is not so simple at all.

(37)  Father cannot stand it when a strong person looks down on the weak, even if that person has nothing to do with *dangsin*.[25]

This is not any less confusing compared to the former use. In this context, *dangsin* is used as an honorific form of *jagi*[26] to refer to a third-person singular with respect. This is not only honorific but highly honorific. It sounds rather formal, even if it is said often in daily conversation. One would use *dangsin* to refer to a third-person singular pronoun in place of she, he, or *jagi*, when one wants to express their respect on the person referred to, even when that person is absent.

There is some truth to the trivial comparison of cultures, in which one says that the idea of individuality is not as significant in East Asian cultures as compared to the West. The word *gaein* [kae-een][27] in Korean means 'individual,' but this word is a newly formulated one to translate 'individual' from Western literature to Chinese, Japanese, and Korean.[28] It is, however, a logical leap to use this as proof for the umbrella argument that the concept of individuality is absent in the past and present of Asian society. First, political, social, ontological, and metaphysical concepts of individuality should be distinguished from each other. Second, it is necessary to investigate whether a translation of a concept is an initiation of a completely different way of understanding, or the discovery of a word for an already existing way of understanding.

The word 'subject' is translated as *juche* [joo-chae][29] in Korean and similarly in other East Asian languages. Even if this word is used to refer to 'subject' and 'subjectivity' as a philosophical concept, the ordinary use of this word in daily context, namely, not as a translated word in Western philosophical literature, is to refer to 'the major part' of a group, a body, or a thing, or the major actor of a certain action or an event. This word has a strong connotation of 'owner' or 'head,' because of the character *ju* [joo][30] which means 'main' or 'primary.' The literal meaning of the other character *che* [chae][31] is 'body.' So, it rather points at the 'head of the body.' The connotation of the differentiation of each individual subject from an object or another subject in contrast to the subject is not so significant in the everyday understanding of the word 'subject' in Korean. In this context, the second-person singular pronoun 'you' is a word that disconnects a person from the 'body' where the person belongs to as a part. Although this way of understanding is more visible in current East Asian cultures, it is not only a culture-specific phenomenon, as in the analogy of Jesus as the vine with his followers as the branches or the church as the body of Christ. This represents a variety of the way of understanding self, other, and relation. The way of understanding self and life has been diverse and variable throughout history.

## 3. TO BE AND TO HAVE: *ITDA* IN KOREAN

We surely are bodily beings. It is my fingers that are now typing these words, my eyes are seeing them, and I am breathing through my nose and my lungs. I am a body, but I am also more than just a body. I am a body and I have a body. Self as bodily being reveals these two sides: 'being' as 'to be' and 'to have' (the body). In *Être et Avoir*, Gabriel Marcel distinguishes *être* (to be) from *avoir* (to have).[32] The way he deals with *être* stands close to that of *Sein* by Heidegger, in which, however, Marcel brings up the body to the discussion of *être*. He writes that "incarnation is the situation of a being who appears to be himself, as it were, *bound* to a body [emphasis in original]." Incarnation is the central 'given' of the metaphysics which stands in opposition to the *cogito*. About the body, one can neither say that it is *I*, nor that it is not *I*, nor that it is *for me*. Here, the opposition of subject and object is transcended from the start.[33] Properly speaking, one cannot say that one has a body, but "the mysterious relation uniting me to the body is at the foundation of all my powers of having."[34] However, he also writes that "in order to have effectively, it is necessary to be in some degree, that is to say, in this case, to be immediately for one's-self, to feel one's-self, as it were, affected or modified."[35] He refers to this as a mutual interdependence of having and being.

Merleau-Ponty approaches 'to be' and 'to have' in a differently yet not completely incompatible way with that of Marcel in *Phénoménologie de la Perception*. He lends 'to be' a weak sense of existence or predication while considering 'to have' as something in relation to the subject that projects itself in the sense of having an idea, a desire, fear, and so on.[36] For Merleau-Ponty, the difference between 'I am my body' and 'I have my body' designates the relation between my bodily being and my subjectivity:[37] my body is an expressive being that expresses my subjectivity.[38] Thomas Fuchs differentiates *Körper* from *Leib* based on the distinction between *haben* (to have) and *sein* (to be). They both mean 'body' in German, but *Leib* refers to the vital body in which we are incarnated, while we have and use the *Körper*.[39] Thus, *Leib* is what we *are*, while *Körper* is what we *have*.

The core concept for understanding the τί ἐστι (being) of τόδε τι (this one) by Aristotle[40] was εἶναι (to be). This verb is translated into Korean as *itda* [eet-da] or *ida* [ee-da]. The latter one, *ida*, is used when the verb functions as a copula, in the same way that 'is' is used in the sentence 'The tree *is* green.' The former one, *itda*, focuses on the existence of the thing that is talked about, like ἔστι(ν) with the accent on the first syllable to emphasize the being of the subject over the predicates that signify the properties of the subject. The meaning of the word *itda* is very similar to those of the 'to be' verb in English or *sein* in German, but this word *itda* also means 'to have.' It is expressed as 'a thing or a person *is* to the subject.' In Korean, therefore, one would say 'a brother is to me' instead of 'I have a brother.' The expression 'to have someone' is rarely used in Korean. The only exception is when someone is pregnant, then one can say 'I have a baby.' Other than that, 'to have someone' with the verb *gajida* [ka-jee-da][41] (to have) is almost never said for a person that, in other languages, would take the person as the object of the verb, 'to have.'

One can say something similar in German as well: *mir ist ein Bruder* for 'I have a brother.' But at the same time, the expression 'there is' in German is made with the 'to have' verb as *es gibt* (it gives [it is given (that) . . .]). In French as well, one uses *avoir* (to have) in the expression *il-y-a*, to say 'there is.' It is not an extraordinarily odd linguistic phenomenon that the 'to be' and the 'to have' verbs have cross-usage, not only in Korean but cross-culturally. Yet the 'to have' verb in Korean is never used in the way it is in German and French. In *es gibt*, and *il-y-a*, the impersonal pronoun 'it' is used as a dummy subject or placeholder, while in Korean, the subject—and especially a pronoun in the place of the subject—is usually omitted in sentences.

In Korean, it is possible to say 'a brother is to me' without 'to me.' One often says 'a brother is' meaning 'I have a brother.' The verb *itda* functions as a 'to have' verb that does not require an object. When one says 'I have a brother' in the form of 'to me, is a brother,' or 'a brother is,' it implies that 'I and my brother are there (together)' rather than 'I have a brother,' where 'a brother' stands as an object to the subject 'I.' In fact, in Korean, the majority of native speakers do not say 'a brother is to me' but rather 'I, a brother is.' Some insist that this expression in Korean should be considered grammatically wrong, and therefore it ought to be said as 'to me, a brother is.' However, in everyday conversation and in literature, this expression 'I, a brother is' is ordinarily said and written. Martin Luther King Jr.'s speech "I have a dream" is translated into Korean as both 'to me, a dream is' and 'I, a dream is.' After the publication of the autobiography of Martin Luther King Jr. in Korean under the title of 'to me, a dream is,' the other translation became less popular and is often taken as an incorrect expression. However, this expression is valid, and especially when it comes to other people in relation to me, such as brother, parents, or friends, this double-subject sentence structure is ordinarily and frequently used. In fact, the expression 'to me, a brother is' sounds unnatural in an informal situation. Usually one would say 'a brother is' or 'I, a brother is' as an answer to the question of whether one has siblings, but also mostly without 'I.'

As I mentioned, in the structure of the sentence 'I, a brother is,' the brother is not an object to the 'I.' It is different than 'I have a brother,' where 'I' as the subject has an object of the verb, the brother. I think that this sentence structure of 'a brother is' for 'I have a brother' reflects the difference between 'to be' and 'to have.' Marcel talks about *avoir* in the sense of possession as 'I have something' while he takes *être* in the sense of existential 'belongingness' as 'I am my body' or 'I am my life.' But for Merleau-Ponty, *avoir* reveals the status of the subject that is reflective and conscious, while *être* is taken as in the sense of 'a tree is there' or 'it is green.' The verb 'to have' in 'I have a brother' refers to the possession of something. When it is not a thing but a person who is related to me, though, 'to have' is not a very plausible way of expressing the interpersonal relation, because a relationship with other human beings is not the same as a proprietary relationship with things. When the subject 'I' is not uttered, what is placed at the forefront of the utterance is the relatedness of myself with my brother, which is revealed by the verb 'to be.' It is the same in the case of 'I, a brother is.' The 'I' in 'I, a brother is,' cannot be considered the same as the I in 'I have a brother.' Marcel explains that 'to have' comes with the notion of 'to contain': "The haver is the subject in so far as it carries with it a container."[42] But in 'being,' a 'non-autonomy' which he calls "very freedom" is rooted, which transcends all possible possessions, "at a point either short of self or beyond self."[43]

In principle, in order to have a brother, one has to be there first and to be able to say that 'a brother is' one has to 'know' the relationship between myself and the brother, which necessarily comes with 'knowing' that I myself am there first. This subjectivity of the 'I' as the subject of 'knowing' is clearly expressed in 'I have a brother.' This 'I,' the subject, is the subject of knowing, understanding, and speaking. 'A brother is' means 'the brother is my brother' which points at the relationship between my brother and I, which also implies the 'being' of myself and the brother and our relatedness. Unlike in 'I have a brother,' in 'a brother is,' the subject 'I' is not expressed as a precondition for expressing the selfness, otherness, and the relation between the two, both grammatically and phenomenologically. Marcel wrote in his journal of metaphysics, "It is impossible to exaggerate how much better the formula *es denkt in mir* is than *cogito ergo sum*, which lets us in for pure subjectivism. The 'I think' is not the spring of inspiration. Far from it, it actually dams the flow."[44] It is not my intention to deny subjectivity, but it should be critically reflected upon that the concept of subject is taken for granted, both linguistically and philosophically, and its status and necessity are almost never again questioned. It has become dogmatic in our way of thinking. What do we understand by subject? It is one of the core ideas of understanding and investigating the self. But what is self at all? Can we understand selfhood outside of the boundary of subjectivity of the 'I'?

## NOTES

1. 자기.
2. 자기 오늘 바빠?
3. 자기는 가기 싫대.
4. 우리 자기, 저녁 먹었어?
5. 자기 물건은 자기가 챙겨야지.
6. 자기 자신을 믿어야 했어.
7. Louis H. Kauffman, "Categorical Pairs and the Indicative Shift," *Applied Mathematics and Computation* 218, no. 16 (2012): 7989–8004.
8. Akira Yanabu, *History of the Birth of Translated Words in Modern Japan (Honyakugo Seiritsu Jijyo)*, trans. Ok-Hee Kim (Seoul: Maeumsanchaek, 2001).
9. 너.
10. Nikki Adams and Thomas J. Conners. "Imposters and their implications for third-person feature specification," *Linguistics*, forthcoming.
11. Leonard M. Faltz, *Reflexivization: A Study in Universal Syntax* (London/New York: Routledge, 2016); Pierre Pica, "On the Nature of the Reflexivization Cycle," *Proceedings of the North East Linguistic Society* 17, no. 2 (1987): 483–500, quoted in Chung-Hye Han and Dennis Ryan Storoshenko, "Semantic Binding of Long-Distance Anaphor Caki in Korean," *Language* 88, no. 4 (2012): 764.
12. Han and Storoshenko, "Semantic Binding," 764.
13. Especially, even if Chinese *ziji* and Korean *jagi* use the same Chinese characters, 自己, Chinese *ziji* does not have inherent Φ-features (third person) while Korean *jagi* has them. (Han and Storschenko, "Semantic Binding," 769).
14. Susumu Kuno, *Functional Syntax: Anaphora, Discourse and Empathy* (Chicago: University of Chicago Press, 1987); Peter Sells, "Aspects of Logophoricity," *Linguistic Inquiry* 18, no. 3 (1987), quoted in Han and Storschenko, "Semantic Binding," 785.
15. Kuno, *Functional Syntax*, quoted in Han and Storschenko, "Semantic Binding," 785.
16. 자네.
17. 그대.
18. 선생님.
19. 아버님.
20. 어머님.
21. 당신 當身.
22. 당신에게 좋은 남편이 되도록 노력하겠소. (In *The Dictionary of the National Institute of Korean Language*, n.d., https://stdict.korean.go.kr/search/searchView.do.) (My translation).

23. 당신의 희생을 잊지 않겠습니다.(In *The Dictionary of the National Institute of Korean Language*, n.d., https://stdict.korean.go.kr/search/searchView.do.) (My translation).

24. 뭐? 당신? 누구한테 당신이야. (In *The Dictionary of the National Institute of Korean Language*, n.d., https://stdict.korean.go.kr/search/searchView.do.) (My translation).

25. 아버지는 당신과는 아무 상관없는 사람이라도 강자가 약자를 능멸하는 것을 보면 참지 못하신다. (In *The Dictionary of the National Institute of Korean Language*, n.d., https://stdict.korean.go.kr/search/searchView.do.) (My translation).

26. As in the example of (b) She/He didn't want to go there.

27. 개인 個人.

28. Yanabu, *History of the Birth of Translated Words*, 193–205.

29. 주체 主體.

30. 주 主.

31. 체 體.

32. Gabriel Marcel, *Être et Avoir* (Paris: Fernand Aubier, 1935).

33. Gabriel Marcel, *Being and Having*, translated by Katharine Farrer (Westminster: Dacre Press, 1949), 11–12.

34. Marcel, *Being and Having*, 84.

35. Marcel, *Being and Having*, 134.

36. Maurice Merleau-Ponty, *Phénoménologie de la Perception* (Paris: Gallimard, 1945), 203.

37. Evan Thompson, *Mind in Life. Biology, Phenomenology, and the Sciences of Mind* (Cambridge, MA: The Belknap Press of Harvard University Press, 2007), 247; Merleau-Ponty, *Phénoménologie de la Perception*, 203–232.

38. Thompson, *Mind in Life*, 246; Merleau-Ponty, *Phénoménologie de la Perception*, 203–232.

39. Thomas Fuchs, "Zwischen Leib und Körper," in *Leib und Leben. Perspektiven für eine neue Kultur der Körperlichkeit*, ed. Martin Hähnel and Marcus Knaup, Darmstadt: WBG, 2013, 82.

40. Aristotle, *Categories*.

41. 가지다.

42. Marcel, *Being and Having*, 84.

43. Marcel, *Being and Having*, 174.

44. Marcel, *Being and Having*, 27.

*Chapter 4*

# Self as Subject

## 1. SUBJECT

### 1.1. Subject and Object

A subject is conscious and relates to an object with the first-person perspective as self in contrast to other. A subject also has predicates. A subject as consciousness reflects on something, including itself. In other words, when a subject is conscious, it is always conscious of something, and this something is an object. An object that a subject reflects on is in relation to that subject but is always outside of the subject; therefore, this object is other, rather than self.

Zahavi calls for attention on the distinction between having a first-person perspective and being able to articulate it linguistically, labeling the former as a weak first-person perspective and the latter as a strong first-person perspective.[1] According to Baker, a weak first-person phenomenon refers to merely having a subjective point of view, which is not yet enough for having self-awareness. One can have self-awareness only when one is able to think of oneself as oneself.[2] In other words, the ability to take oneself as oneself, that is, an objectified self, is crucial for the possession of self-awareness.

When self-awareness is taken as a per se social phenomenon, becoming an object to oneself in virtue of one's social relations to others is the core of being conscious of oneself. According to Mead, self-consciousness is constituted by adopting the perspectives of the other toward oneself.[3] However, at the same time, he claims that consciousness and self-consciousness are not on the same level. "A man alone has, fortunately or unfortunately, access to his own toothache, but that is not what we mean by self-consciousness."[4] Another way of approaching consciousness, as Carruthers claims, is to study the mental states of being conscious in contrast to being nonconscious.[5]

## 1.2. Intentionality

A conscious being has an intentionality toward an object. Intentionality is characterized by an epistemic difference between the subject and the object of experience.[6] Intentionality is a process of objectification that allows us to encounter the other as an object. In other words, intentionality relates self to other, but in the way that the object that is perceived by the subject loses its alterity in relation to the subject. Zahavi quotes Lévinas for explaining this relation between an acting subject and an object, which I find quite sympathetic:

> Although intentionality does relate me to that which is foreign, it is, in Lévinas's words, a nonreciprocal relationship. It never makes me leave home. On the contrary, the knowing subject acts like the famous stone of the alchemists that transmutes everything it touches; it absorbs the foreign and different, annuls its *alterity*, and transforms it into the familiar and same [emphasis in original].[7]

There is a language that reveals precisely this relation in the speakers' daily practice of language. The Malagasy language does not operate on the system of subject and object based on the difference and identity of the two. Therefore, when one wants to say 'I see a rose' in Malagasy, something like 'a rose is seen by me' can be said, even if a word-to-word direct translation to English is not possible. According to native Malagasy speakers,[8] it is not natural for them to understand 'I' as a subject that stands face to face opposed to the object that *I* perceive or act on. Rather, once the object, in this case, 'a rose,' is perceived by *me*, *I* relate to this rose, so therefore it becomes a part of *myself*. This is uttered and explained without subject and object in Malagasy, but one can mirror the fundamental relationship between subject and object onto this Malagasy way of thinking.[9]

## 1.3. Reflection

Reflection as an intentional activity is possible through the relation between subject and object. The process of distancing oneself from the experiences of daily life and taking them as an object is crucial for reflection.[10] One needs to have the objects stand opposite to themselves for one to be able to observe them with distance. In reflection, one is "confronted with a relation"[11] between the reflecting and the reflected. In the pre-reflective state, there is only one experience: an experience without the difference between subject and object and their relation.

Here, one encounters a problem of these closely related yet not clearly distinguished terms: self-awareness, self-reflection, and self-consciousness.

They are used in multiple texts with similar, yet different meanings. In this section, I would like to briefly discuss the similarities and differences between these terms.

First, Hans Bernhard Schmid distinguishes self-awareness from self-reflection. He says that self-awareness is more basic than self-reflection. He says that we do not have to think about ourselves to have a sense of our perception, beliefs, and attitudes. Therefore, the basic self-awareness is pre-reflective.[12] In this sense, Schmid argues that self-awareness is not a proper intentional act that is directed at the subject, but it is rather a feature or component of an intentional act.[13] In self-reflection, however, a subject makes itself the object of its intentional act. Schmid writes that self-reflection involves a thematic awareness of the subject itself, which means that self-reflection involves a distinction between the subject as the subject of an act and self as the object of the act.

Sartre speaks of pre-reflective self-awareness as "an immediate and non-cognitive 'relation' of the self to itself,"[14] hence not yet with a difference between the observer and the observed within the self. According to Sartre, pre-reflective self-awareness is one of the two different modes of existence that consciousness has.[15] Zahavi explains that we are acquainted with our own subjectivity in a different way than when we are acquainted with objects because first-person self-reference involves a non-objectifying self-acquaintance.[16]

Self-consciousness, explains Zahavi, is about being conscious of something. In this regard, Uriah Kriegel makes a distinction between the "qualitative character" (the "what it is like") and the "subjective character" (the "for me") of consciousness.[17] Simply stated, it is related to know that both the consciousness of an object and the consciousness of the self (who is conscious of an object) are both mine. The tentative distinction between them can be summarized as follows:

*self-awareness*   pre-reflective
*self-reflection*   self as the subject of an intentional act
              self as the object of an intentional act
*self-consciousness* consciousness of consciousness
              difference and identity of self and other

A distinctive feature of reflection, according to Zahavi, is that the first-person singular effectuates an inner pluralization. 'I,' the reflecting subject can have 'I' the reflected subject, through which it can distance itself from itself. In this sense, he refers to reflection as a kind of self-awareness that is essentially characterized by an internal differentiation and alterity.[18] However, he also argues that reflection does not split me into two different egos, because "by saying 'I,' I am affirming the identity between the reflecting and the reflected subject."[19] The unity of the reflecting and the reflected subject is the very condition of reflection along with alterity. This identity of the two is inherited from the pre-reflective state. Identity and difference of the 'I' is the core of the idea of subjectivity, as Fichte already deciphered in the framework of 'I = I.'

What I would like to pay extra attention to here is that the unity of the self-differentiating 'I' is affirmed by 'saying I.' Calling requires an object: calling someone or something. The act of calling unfolds the division and the unity of the calling and the called. As we saw in the logic of 'shift' (see chapter 3, section 1) concerning the meta-name 'I,' by calling myself (object) 'I' (name), self is objectified—not that self is an object—and the identity of the objectified self and the calling self is obtained through the act of calling. The act of saying 'I' is not just saying a word that is determined to signify an object. Calling self 'I,' 'we,' 'self,' or something else reveals the way of the self-understanding. But 'how' I call self 'what' is not absolute. The other ways that 'I' is said in different cultures and times reflect the way that self and other are perceived and comprehended *there* at *that moment*. This simple, ordinary word 'I' comes with the full scope of understanding of self and other, and this scope has diverse spectra.

## 1.4. I, the Subject

What is the significance of the ordinary word 'I'? Wittgenstein refers to it as one of the most misleading representational techniques in our language. He describes, "The word 'I' in the mouth of a man refers to the man who says it."[20] This word is uttered to point to herself as the character 自 [ja] in *jagi* (self) originated from the figure of a person who is pointing to one's own nose. Very often, as Wittgenstein writes as well, a person who says it actually points to herself with her finger.[21] But, he also says, it is "quite superfluous"[22] to point to herself, because it is *she* who points. The referred of the first-person pronoun 'I,' when used as subject, cannot be mistaken by the referrer, which Sydney Shoemaker called "absolute immunity to error through misidentification."[23] This act of pointing might be only to attract attention to what is pointed at. The distinction between the pointer and the pointed displays the different uses of the word 'I,' as Wittgenstein differentiated the use of the word 'I' between "the use as object" and "the use as subject."[24] The way of conceiving the self could be found in its profound relation to our perception which is, in principle, bodily. The immediate examples for the uses of the 'I' for both subject and object are bodily perceptual expressions such as "*I* see so-and-so," "*I* am trying to lift my arm," "*I* have a toothache," "*My* arm is broken," "*I* have a bump on *my* forehead," or "The wind is blowing *my* hair about."[25]

On the other hand, however, in introspection, it has been commonly assumed that the self in the awareness of self would be something nonbodily. Strawson reduces the self-body relation into a "straightforward part-whole relation."[26] Shoemaker views bodily entities as individuated in part by their bodily properties and their spatial relation to other things, and perception of them is meant to provide information about such properties and relationships, but introspection does not provide such information; therefore introspection is not perception at all, or it is the perception of something nonbodily.[27] Wittgenstein as well points out that in the case in which 'I' is used as subject, "we don't use it because we recognize a person by his bodily characteristics; and this creates the illusion that we use this word to refer to something bodiless."[28] As long as we dwell in the system of subject rooted in *cogito ergo sum*, this conclusion seems inescapable no matter which direction the argument stems from and leans toward. We are, though, inevitably bodily entities.

Another way of grasping the sense of 'I' is to regard 'I' as synonymous with 'this self,'[29] in which 'I' means something like 'the subject of this,' where 'this' names some object of immediate experience.[30] The pointing to 'this' distinguishes the subject of the experience from the ones that are distinct from 'I,' 'this' subject. Strawson argues that 'I' is not univocal. He distinguishes the use of 'I' between the use of 'I' as the human being considered as a whole and 'I' as "some sort of inner subject," which he refers to as a "thin subject."[31] According to him, the reference of 'I' is fluid, and we move naturally between these two conceptions of 'I,' sometimes meaning one, or the other, or both. Shoemaker also explains that when 'I' is used as the first-person pronoun, its reference is determined by "the causal role of the beliefs it is used to express."[32] But what exactly is this 'I' for the human being as a whole? Does it mean the entirety of human species? Or the collective group of individual human entities? Or the representative and necessary qualities of being human? I think that the distinction between "the human being as a whole" and a "thin subject" brings us back to the framework of understanding τί ἐστι (being) of τόδε τι (this one):[33] 'I' as a thin subject refers to 'this self' that represents the οὐσία of the human being. 'I,' either as 'this self' or the human being as a whole, all this sums up, again, to the frame of 'I,' the subject.

Self as subject has itself as an objectified self. The primary relation in this context is the relation between self and the objectified self. Self as subject is grounded in this self-referential relation. But it doesn't have to be in relation with the other yet. The self-referential relation of the self in/with itself is an ideational relation, not yet representing the 'actual' relation between self and other. The problem of self-referential relation is that it falls into an infinite regress of self-objectification within oneself for self-representing (self-reference).

The subject 'I' has to have an objectified 'I.'

I = I

The objectified 'I' is identical with the subjective 'I.' Therefore, the second 'I' also requires an objectified 'I' to be 'I' that is identical with the first 'I.'

I = I
   I = I

And this 'I' requires another 'I,' and another, and another, and another . . . ad infinitum.

I = I
   I = I
      I = I
         I = I

Or, in the form of the second 'I' goes back to the first 'I' and the first goes to the second again and so on and so forth. In this everlasting pendulum between the two that are only within oneself, the system of 'I' is self-enclosed.

I ↔ I

Wittgenstein points out the problem of using the word 'I' that represents immediate experience. He suggests replacing the way of speaking by another, through which immediate experience would be represented without using the person pronoun, and this would reveal what was logically essential in the representation. The first-person pronoun 'I' is used to represent the first-person experiences that are supposed to express the privileged status of 'me' as the center of this expression of language. However, we soon find out that the privileged status of 'my' language that has 'me' as its center cannot be expressed with the language with 'me' as its center, because, as Wittgenstein explains,

> If I do it in the language with 'me' as its center, the exceptional status of the description of this language in its own terms becomes nothing remarkable, and in terms of another language my language occupies no privileged status whatever.—The privileged status lies in the application, but if I describe this application, the privileged status does not find expression, because the description depends on the language in which it is couched.[34]

The first-person pronoun 'I' as subject is inevitably self-referential with 'I' itself as its center, which falls into the infinite regress of self-representation. The differentiation of languages that yields the privileged status of 'my' language is possible only through "their application":[35] the description of the application by others with themselves as their centers. This, ironically, requires a multicentered, therefore, centerless relation of the self with the others. The phenomena of the multicentered usage of the word *jagi* (self) and the usual way of speaking without personal pronoun in the subject place in Korean seem to reflect this situation in our ordinary language. I think this positioning of the self and the other in a multicentered, therefore, centerless, relative relation can be grasped with an understanding of the spatial difference between inside and outside, which I present in chapter 6.

## 2. PASSIVE SUBJECT

The two major ways of dealing with the self as subject each have their own distinct approaches to the temporality of the self. First, the view that regards self as a minimal subject focuses on atemporal subjectivity, which is not derived from a constructed identity throughout the changes of time. Second, for the view that takes self in a narrative structure, temporality lies in the core of their understanding of the self. In the following sections, we will briefly go through these two discourses.

### 2.1. Subject of Experience

Strawson regards subjectivity as a synonym for 'experientiality.'[36] He distinguishes 'I' as a thin subject from the 'I' as the human being, which is considered as a whole. He argues that all thin subjects are minimal subjects and all minimal subjects are thin subjects.[37] For him, a thin subject is a thin subject of experience, and a thin subject of experience exists if there is an experience for which it is the subject.[38] The subject is identical with experience.[39] He explains that a minimal subject experiences the phenomenon of experiential-qualitative character, 'what-it's-likeness,' in which no real distinction between the subject of experience and that which is the object of experience exists. It is "internalistically understood."[40] He insists that understanding subjectivity as involving experience within the subject-object structure is the "venerable tradition of subjectivity."[41]

Dealing with subjectivity as a subject of experience appears to be a commonly accepted stance which precludes a discussion of subject-object structure. However, Strawson does not fully reject this venerable tradition either: he admits that there is a sense in which all subjectivity necessarily has subject-object structure. As Strawson himself says, to say that all experience has subject-object structure is not to say that all experience necessarily has subject-object structure 'phenomenologically speaking,' meaning that it is not to say that the subject-object structure of experience is always experienced by the experiencer. He continues,

> Nor is it to say that all experience has subject-object structure in any metaphysical sense that involves the idea that the subject of experience is irreducibly ontologically distinct from the content of experience.[42]

Exactly. Although his theory of minimal subject as subject of experience takes a different path than mine, the fact that subject-object structure is not the absolute core of selfhood is the point that I am trying to make as well.

### 2.2. Atemporality of Self: Minimal Subject

Self as subject must have not only the phenomenon of experiential qualitative character of "what it is like" but also "subjective character," which is "what it is like for me" as Kriegel describes.[43] Zahavi claims that this "for-me-ness" of experience is an essential constitutive aspect of experience that is at the very core of the first-person perspective.[44] The consciousness of my 'self' is non-observational, that is, it does not involve a perceptual or reflective act of consciousness. The first-person experience is immediate.[45] In this regard, self is regarded as subjectivity of experience itself.[46] Even if the experiential life of the self is world-related[47] and the self is immersed in conscious life,[48] the identity of self is defined in terms of givenness rather than in terms of temporal continuity.[49] This pre-reflective sense of mineness with a minimal, core, sense of self is referred to as minimal self. This subjective experience of self is "unextended in time."[50] The absolute immunity to error that applies to the use of 'I' as subject is grounded in this immediate, nonreflective access of mine to my own self.

### 2.3. Nonconceptual Self-Consciousness

Ulric Neisser distinguishes five kinds of self: ecological self, interpersonal self, extended self, private self, and conceptual self.[51] The self that is capable of using the first-person pronoun is, according to the distinctions of the selves by Neisser, the conceptual self. However, Bermúdez argues that self-consciousness emerges from a "nonconceptual first-person thought" which does not presuppose any linguistic or conceptual mastery.[52] According to

Bermúdez, nonconceptual self-consciousness is logically and ontogenetically more primitive than the higher forms of self-consciousness.[53] Nonconceptual first-person content is attained in perceptual experience: when perceiving objects, the perceiver gains prelinguistic and nonconceptual information about their own self. David Hume also wrote that "I never can catch *myself* at any time without a perception [emphasis in original]."[54] The self, according to Hume, is nothing but a bundle of momentary impressions that are strung together by the imagination.[55] The human infant is already equipped with a primitive self-consciousness that is embodied, enactive, and ecologically tuned within an environment. Then a phenomenological reflective approach follows that characterizes the self as a subject of experience.[56]

## 2.4. Nonreflective Self-consciousness

We have seen that the self as subject has its inevitable paradox of self-representation. To avoid this paradox, consciousness needs to have a nonreflective mode of self-awareness within its self-representing structure. Sartre argues self-consciousness is a pre-reflective and non-objectifying form of consciousness.[57] He writes,

> The I is the ego as unity of actions and the me is the ego as unity of states and the qualities. The distinction that one sets up between these two aspects of one reality appears to be simply functional, if not grammatical.[58]

The nonreflective consciousness renders the reflection possible; pre-reflective cogito is the condition of the Cartesian cogito.[59] According to Sartre, nonreflective consciousness must be considered as autonomous,[60] which says that the reflective cogito is not prior to nonreflective consciousness. Zahavi's notion of the pre-reflective sense of mine-ness with a minimal sense of self is situated in this frame.[61] Kriegel talks about this nonreflective mode of self-awareness in the structure of consciousness in the sense of intransitive self-consciousness.[62] According to Kriegel, intransitive self-consciousness is a nonreflective mode of self-awareness. The awareness of our conscious states is something we experience,[63] but there are such things as nonconscious, that is, nonreflective occurrent mental states.[64] Intransitive self-consciousness is a necessary condition for phenomenal consciousness; a mental state is phenomenally conscious only if it is intransitively self-conscious.[65] Setting up the premise of the ontological priority of nonreflective or pre-reflective self-consciousness over reflective consciousness is one way of avoiding the paradox of self-representation of the self as subject, yet the mysteriousness of the self-representation of self-consciousness lingers on.

## 3. ACTIVE SUBJECT

### 3.1. Temporality of Self: Narrative Self

I believe that such a nonconscious state exists and do not deny a consistent, non-changing minimal sense of self that transcends the spatiotemporal experiences of the world in which I am immersed in. However, the inevitable condition, the very core of human existence, is temporality in the sense that our existence is finite and is in a constant flow of change. Narrative plays a crucial role in the discussion on time and time-consciousness in relation to understanding the self. I *believe* that my 'I' when I was five years old and my 'I' now right at this moment share an unbreakable, common trace, or the core of being the same 'I.' As Shaun Gallagher describes, the minimal self is present in the flow of the narrative.[66] There is, though, not a single moment where we stop changing while we exist. Ontologically speaking, there is no true atemporal 'bracketed moment,' even when it is theoretically or phenomenologically bracketed in the middle of the ceaseless course of our existence.[67]

Not everyone, though, agrees that temporality constitutes the core of narrative. For example, Louis Mink, Wilhelm Schapp, and Hayden White claim that time is not essential to narrative.[68] In this view, human reality is nothing "in itself" but "mere sequence without beginning or end," and the narrative coherence is something imposed by the literary or historical imagination.[69] Roland Barthes and Claude Levi-Strauss speak of the illusional chronology of narrative (*l'illusion chronologique*), claiming that the order of chronological succession disappears in an atemporal matrix structure.[70] There are others, including Algirdas Julien Greimas, Claude Bremond, and many other structuralists,[71] who take the temporal features of narrative as a mere surface aspect and "anything beyond pure sequentiality as atemporal, quasi-logical structures and relations."[72] However, as David Carr explains, the events whose structures and relations are portrayed "unfold in time" and "their order of unfolding is important to their significance."[73] When I experience something such as a melody that is happening, my experience is itself something that happens, which means that it is an event.[74] The idea of an event is already that of something that *takes* time, that has "temporal thickness" with a beginning and an end.[75] The significance of having a beginning and an end lies in the finiteness.

The fundamental-ontological reason that temporality matters for human beings is due to the unavoidable finiteness of our existence—there is a beginning and an end of every single one of us. Temporality itself is our being, therefore, no discourse on our being, understanding, and self can be exempted from the discourse on temporality. Our experiences are temporally extended, whereby future, present, and past mutually determine one another as parts of a whole.[76] Carr claims that these experiences are not events that we encounter, but something that we live through.[77] He maintains that an individual's lifetime itself is a temporal configuration based on his interpretation of Dilthey's coherence of life. Human time is configured time in virtue of the structure of the events, experiences, and actions of human existence. The events, experiences, and actions are constituted by their beginnings, middles, and ends,[78] which shape a temporal sequence.[79]

The temporal thickness of an event that is experienced by a subject is *understood* as configured time through the reflection of the subject. Dilthey saw life itself as something akin to a melody, whose parts, that is, experiences, are related to each other, as individual notes are.[80] This melodic character of life is neither pre-given nor given naturally by simply living through it. The coherence of life (*Zusammenhang des Lebens*) has to be constituted by *Besinnung* (reflection)[81] which he relates to *Sinn* (sense) in the way that it suggests "making sense" of our actions and experiences. For Dilthey, the basic units of conscious life are "lived experiences" (*Erlebnisse*) which he views as "temporal wholes or configurations unified from within."[82] The configuration as 'making sense' refers to the aim, the end. It is narrative, according to Carr, that makes such configurations possible. Narrative is the way we obtain the coherence of life and understand our time, and thus grasp the sense of self.

## 3.2. Subject of Action

In his analysis of narrative self, Carr includes another important aspect to the discussion on self as subject: subject is not only a subject of experiences but also a subject of actions. This reveals another dimension of temporality of the subject. The focus on the experientiality of a subject is directed to the past, and thus the passive temporal experience, but an action of a subject has a purposive and means-end (*Besinnug*) character.[83] To perform an action is to achieve its end, therefore, activity is future-centered.[84] The "why" of this action refers to its "making sense" as a means-end.[85] Through narrative, Carr says, individuals make sense of their actions and experiences and constitute them temporally.[86] The structure of everyday life is, therefore, characterized by narrative.[87] Human existence and action "consist not in overcoming time, not in escaping it or arresting its flow, but in shaping and forming it," and "the narrative grasp of the story-teller is not a leap beyond time but a way of being in time."[88]

It is tantamount to how I interpreted the *Geschichtlichkeit* (historicity) by Heidegger in the light of Augustine's *Sinn* as *omne agens agit proper finem* (everything that acts, acts toward the end), in order to say that the quintessence of understanding of human existence lies in understanding the *Selbstvollzug* (self-fulfillment or self-action) of its temporality by fore-grasping the end as a possibility. The *Geschichte* (story or history) of each individual's *Geschehen* (occurrence) can be understood by the act of 'telling it' (*erzählen*) which presents and represents the very temporality of human existence, its sequential order (*zählen*) and its meaning or coherence (*Sinn*), through which we understand our own existence and our time.[89] It is not far from this context that Carr argues that narrative is our primary way of organizing and giving coherence to our experience by which he calls narrative a primary act of mind, quoting Barbara Hardy.[90] Paul Ricoeur is one of the representative narrative theorists who takes narrative as a universal, transcultural necessity for human existence. He says,

> Between the activity of narrating a story and the temporal character of human existence there exists a correlation that is not merely accidental but . . . presents a transcultural form of necessity. . . . Time becomes human to the extent that it is articulated through a narrative mode.[91]

### 3.3. Coherence of Life

For the coherence of narrative, the mineness of the experiences and the actions, that is, the unity of self, is required. Alasdair MacIntyre says that the unity of self resides in the unity of narrative that links birth to life to death as narrative from beginning to middle to end.[92] Marya Schechtman's hermeneutical interpretation of a narrative self shares similar ideas. She insists that selves are constituted by narratives. Selves, as fundamentally self-interpreting beings, lead their lives by understanding one's life as a narrative rather than merely having a history.[93] Michael Gazzinga writes that an interpreter constantly establishes a running narrative of our actions, emotions, thoughts, and dreams, and this is the glue that unifies the story and creates the sense of being a whole, rational agent. The narratives of our past pervade our awareness.[94]

Daniel Dennett regards the self as a dense constellation of interwoven narratives. He argues that our fundamental tactic of self-protection, self-control, and self-definition is telling stories. Human consciousness and narrative selfhood are the product of our tales.[95] The way we tell our stories is, however, different than that of professional storytellers. Dennett explains that we do not consciously and deliberately figure out what narratives to tell and how to tell them. Rather, he writes, "Our tales are spun, but for the most part we don't spin them; they spin us."[96] Dunnett calls this self a "nonminimal selfy" self, which Neisser referred to as the extended self.[97]

As Ricoeur said, the identity of the narrative self contains modification and transformation throughout one's lifetime.[98] In this context, Carr points out that the unity of self, not as an underlying identity, but as a life that hangs together and makes up a coherent life story, is not a pre-given condition but an achievement.[99] Gallagher sums up that the mineness of episodic memory depends on a minimal but consistently remodeled and reiterated sense of self.[100] The interrelation between the minimal-core self and the autobiographical-narrative self is complex. Dealing with these complexities, Antonio Damasio, Peter Goldie, and others add another dimension by discussing feelings and emotions.[101]

### 3.4. Intersubjectivity

Another crucial aspect of narrative self lies in intersubjectivity. As one of the five kinds of self-knowledge, Neisser presents the interpersonal self as "the self as engaged in immediate unreflective social interaction with another person."[102] He insists that, in principle, the ecological self is not separated from the interpersonal self. Taking studies of infancy as his validation, Neisser claims that intersubjectivity is based on direct perception rather than inference.[103] For example, Colwyn Trevarthen speaks of "primary intersubjectivity,"[104] and Daniel Stern speaks of "affect attunement"[105] between the mother and the baby. The mother and the baby mutually respond to each other's actions and feelings immediately and coherently. These experiments show that a complex form of mutual understanding, both naturally accepted and strongly regulated by the infant, develops already at the age of two to three months.[106] When we perceive the self, we do not perceive only the self. Neisser points out that all perceiving, as J. J. Gibson described, involves co-perception of self and environment, including both the social environment and the interpersonal self that is established in these interactions.[107]

One is self only among other selves, as Charles Taylor puts it.[108] He insists that one cannot be a self on one's own. I am a self only in relation to certain interlocutors.[109] The primary intersubjectivity or the affect attunement during exchanges of emotions and feelings has a 'protoconversational' character. But Taylor takes language as proof that the self is necessarily interpersonal. He argues that a language only exists and is maintained within a language community, which indicates one of the crucial features of the self: that a self can never be described without reference to those who surround it.[110] Taylor explains that the self-definition that is understood as an answer to the question of who I am finds its original sense in the interchange of speakers "in the family tree, in social space, in the geography of social statues and functions, in my intimate relations to the ones I love, and also crucially in the space of moral and spiritual orientation within which my most important defining relations are lived out."[111] Therefore, *my* self-understanding necessarily has temporal depth and incorporates narrative.[112]

MacIntyre illustrates that the concept of self without social embodiments and any rational history of its own, lacking a necessary social identity, has only an abstract and ghostly character.[113] According to MacIntyre, the unity of self is in the unity of a narrative.[114] Furthermore, the story of one's life is always embedded in the story of those communities from which one derives their identity. To have this identity as a social person is to find oneself placed at a certain point of a journey with set goals, making progress or failing to make progress toward the given ends.[115] An individual is born with a past, as one of the bearers of a tradition—whether desired or not, possessing a historical identity which coincides with a social identity.[116] In this sense, he says that "we are never more (or sometimes less) than the co-authors of our own narratives."[117] Schechtman also writes that narrative comes from the community with which an individual interacts. She points out that a narrative requires a moral framework, which again requires us to place ourselves in a historical tradition.[118] A crucial fact about history and tradition is that they are something that is shared with others, both from the past as well as the present.[119]

In *Soi-même comme un autre*, Ricoeur discusses the significance of the expression *soi-même*. In English and German, 'same' cannot be confused with 'self,' but in French the *soi* (self) is used in the form of *soi-même*, combined with *même* that signifies 'same,' the synonym of 'identical.' The equivocity of the term 'identical' is at the center of his reflections on personal and narrative identity and related to the temporality of the self.[120] According to Ricoeur, in the circle of the sameness-identity of the *idem*-identity, the otherness of the other offers nothing original under the shadow of the hierarchy of signification. The *ipse*-identity, on the other hand, involves a dialectic complementary to that of self and the other. The alterity is constitutive of identity (*ipséité*). Oneself as another (*soi-même en tant que . . . autre*)[121] suggests that oneself implies otherness to the degree that oneself cannot be thought of without the other, hence oneself in as much as being other, Ricoeur says, in Hegelian terms.[122] Hegel's notion of self as "the I that is We, the We that is I"[123] includes the otherness in self as a social and collective subject. Carr interprets Hegel's plural subject within his analysis of narrative in relation to time and history.[124] Historical temporality is social temporality in the sense that the past that is shared with others is within the experience of an individual and therefore affects the configuration of time of an individual. Carr quotes Dilthey's assertion that "we are historical beings first, before we are observers (*Betrachter*) of history,"[125] insisting that we as an individual and a historical being not only observe the historical world but are intertwined with it, through which *we* not only understand *ourselves* but constitute *ourselves*.

# 4. MEDIO-PASSIVE SUBJECT

## 4.1. Self, Other, and We

The kind of attribute that allows a subject to have subjectivity is related to the ability of being conscious. A subject is conscious, either of oneself or others, including other subjects and objects, or of oneself being conscious. Vogeley and Gallagher say that

> selves are experiential, ecological, and agentive; they are often engaged in reflective evaluations and judgments; they are capable of various forms of self-recognition, self-related cognition, self-narrative, and self-specific perception and movement. In many of these activities, selves are more "in-the-world" than "in-the-brain," and they are in-the-world as-subject more so than as-object.[126]

Under the auspices of consciousness, the discourse of subjectivity seems to be necessarily bound to the differentiation of self from other. Self is not other. In other words, self is distinguished by not-self, the other. What distinguishes self from the other? I am born once upon a time somewhere on the planet, I have memories, I sense and acknowledge things and phenomena, I relate with and interact with (other) people, I am this tall, I weigh this much, my hair is this color, my mother tongue is this language. I have a small scar on my knee from when I fell down on the ground running in the rain when I was seven years old. I think about the book that I read last week. I play piano and I run. I feel grateful and calm today. I am here and I understand that I am here. This 'I,' the self, the subject of senses, thoughts, feelings, understanding, and actions, is differentiated from the others who are not 'I.'

It is not a mystery that *I* as a minimal self and a person with history am here with this body that is not yours or any other's, but *mine*. If *I* neither express nor communicate, either verbally or physically, the other who is not *myself* would neither know what *I* think about right at this moment or last night, nor how *I* feel. No one else perceives this subtle itch on *my* arm or the weight of *my* hair on *my* scalp when *my* hair is down. *I* may be watching a film, but rather than focusing on the story of the film or the main character, *I* might be thinking about the wallpaper that appeared in the film that reminds *me* of the pattern and the tone of the wallpaper in the house where *I* grew up. Before *I* describe these feelings or thoughts externally, only *I* would have access to these thoughts and feelings. Only *I*, as a person, an individual, a subject, can be aware of these phenomena. Meanwhile, another person who was watching the same film together with me would have their own feelings and thoughts to which *I* have no access unless *I* communicate with that person or observe the external appearances of the person, such as physical reactions, and guess. Otherwise *I cannot know*. Whether the information of *my* perception and understanding is internal or external, the frontier—the irreducible distinction—between the inside and the outside plays the crucial role for differentiating self and other.[127]

The irreducible distinction between self and other is the starting point of an investigation of intersubjectivity, which is, as Sartre points out, an attempt to bridge the gap between self and other.[128] There has long been a concern about any account where the investigation proceeds from the 'I.' Habermas, for example, criticizes that any account of intersubjectivity in the concrete form of self-other relation will always have a persisting asymmetry between self and other which does not guarantee full reciprocity between the subjects.[129] In this context, Zahavi mentions the paradigm shift in twentieth-century philosophy from a philosophy of subjectivity to a philosophy of language and the confrontation between them, as he contrasts linguistic intersubjectivity to phenomenology. As a phenomenologist, Zahavi defends phenomenology as a philosophy of subjectivity while opposing the criticism of Habermas on phenomenology being blind to linguistic intersubjectivity, such as in a theory of communication, which assumes intersubjectivity is already provided by language.[130] However, this opposition between subjectivity and language seems to mislead us. Habermas's criticism on the everlasting gap between subjects as self and other is not totally unfair. Whether the philosophy of language is the most plausible alternative is another question. Instead, why not respond to the problem of subjectivity from a different perspective?

There have already been multiple accounts that try to handle this issue from different perspectives. One of them is an attempt to overcome the solipsistic state of subjectivity by conferring primacy on intersubjectivity. For example, Searle considers collective intentionality as primitive, by conceiving collective intention or action as sui generis instead of as construction or as collection of individual intentions.[131] Or, Scheler claims that our immediate perceptions of others neither relate to their bodies, nor their selves, nor souls, but to their integral wholes.[132]

Sartre, on the other hand, disagrees with the a priori feature of intersubjectivity in our understanding of self and other.[133] Zahavi also questions the primacy of the 'we' and talks about the danger of a radical anonymity prior to any distinction between self and other.[134] Zahavi's stance in this matter is quite clear and consistent. The distinction between self and other is the necessary condition for understanding intersubjectivity as well as subjectivity. In his joint paper with Brinck and Reddy, they conclude that the dyadic structure of I-Thou, that is, the 'I' and the 'you,' is conceptually and developmentally prior to the we,[135] after investigating the origins of self-other differentiation and consciousness of self, infant behavior with other persons immediately after birth, and the evidence of infant ability to act in acknowledgment of a jointness of experience or activity with others.[136]

In this context, they discuss the variety of the 'we' and suggest that

> we-ness is a changing developmental achievement gradually emerging in repeated episodes of engagement between infant and adult, with emotional expressivity playing an essential role in the communication and creation of meaning.[137]

There is a difference between identifying and being united with a certain group and knowing this reflectively, and they admit that a we-perspective is most often simply lived pre-reflectively, rather than being reflectively affirmed.[138] They point out that *I* can be aware of *myself* without being reflectively or pre-reflectively aware of *myself* as part of a 'we,' and *I* can be aware of another without that awareness necessarily giving rise to a shared we-perspective.[139]

Sociocultural and institutional forms of we-ness also presuppose the 'I' and the 'you,' and without reference to the differentiation of the 'I' and the 'you,' the 'we' cannot be fully explained.[140] However, the understanding of the 'I' and the 'you' has varied throughout the world and has been ever-changing through time, even within the same culture and tradition. For example, the subject was not always considered only within the scope of passivity or activity. There was a set of voice forms in ancient Greek that English does not have. Middle voice is a diathesis that faded away in Indo-European languages; it reflects a different way of understanding self and other than that of the modern era.

## 4.2. Middle Voice

In reading *Sein und Zeit*, many including Carr, Taylor, and myself, focused on the 'action' of *Dasein* who tells a story, through which its very existence obtains and maintains its *Sinn* (coherence, meaning, or end) in itself. In *Sorge und Geschichte*, I cannot say for others, but personally I did not take the medio-passive character of human *Dasein* that is neither fully active nor fully passive seriously into the account of my interpretation of *Dasein* as *Erzähler* (storyteller). Back then, I did not (consciously) reckon about the fact that there is a tie between the possibility of overcoming the subject-object structure of subjectivity and the medio-passive character of human existence. However, I laid one of the crucial points of my interpretation in the *Übereinstimmung* (accordance, in the sense of 'becoming one or complete' by 'overlapping') of the beginning and the end of this *story* that *we tell*, in which the story begins with its end. The fore-grasping of the end of the story is the beginning of the action of telling this story. What I failed to investigate more elaborately and clearly in this analysis was the fact that the paradoxical relation of the activity of existential understanding to the passivity of human existence, namely the end that had to be fore-grasped as the pre-given, unavoidable, necessary condition, yields room for a middle ground somewhere between the passive and the active, instead of rejecting both or taking only one fragile side, but having both: the middle voice.

Middle voice is an old Indo-European diathesis (*Genus verbi*, voice), which is neither active nor passive, but in between. The subject in middle voice is syntactically active but semantically passive, that is, the subject of verb is performing an action, but it can't actually perform itself. Stories from ancient times often begin with a prophecy that tells the end. The protagonists of the stories act according to their own will, following their own desires, with their full self-determination and autonomy, yet they find themselves in the fetters of their fate in the end. Acknowledging the limitation of human free will and the vulnerability of human existence was once a more common way of understanding human subjectivity. The ancient manner of storytelling that begins with the end represents the perspective of middle voice, namely that we are a subject in between activity and passivity. *I* create and understand the coherence of *my* own life with *my* own autonomy (*Selbstbestimmung*) and *my* free will, but *my* autonomous power over *my* life is always within the boundary of *my* being human that is in the hand of the other, whoever that might be, but clearly not *mine*. The presence of middle voice in the ancient Greek language projects and reflects the way of self-understanding of their time.

Defining self as subject in terms of experientiality and action also mirrors and expresses our current time of understanding where our language functions based on two voices, passive and active. The loss or absence of the middle voice brings forth a different way of understanding the self ontologically, metaphysically, and existentially. This points at the fact that the picture of self in the system of cogito is a reflection of a certain linguistic, cultural, social, historical, and temporal scope, rather than an absolute reference that bears an ahistorical, universal truth of understanding the self. I understand middle voice as an attempt to *resolve* the paradox of the understanding of the human subject that invariably clashes with the other subjects, and whose existence and subjectivity are beyond *my* realm of subjectivity, yet to whom *I* am fundamentally bound. The Greek gods or the Absolute exemplified this other that *I* am tied to, but the core of this helpless side of *my* subjectivity is profoundly attached to the otherness of the other. The linguistic forms of middle voice have disappeared, but the fundamental bond of *my* being to other beings and the inevitable limitedness of *my* being did not disappear, whether noticed or not in our current language. It is within this framework that I present pre-subjective self-in-relation, whose trace is more clearly found in another sphere of culture, as one of the possible ways that might *resolve* the paradox of self and other in the self as 'we.'

# NOTES

1. Dan Zahavi, *Subjectivity and Selfhood: Investigating the First-Person Perspective* (Cambridge, MA: MIT Press, 2008).
2. Lynne Rudder Baker, *Persons and Bodies: A Constitution View* (Cambridge: Cambridge University Press, 2000), 60, 67, quoted in Zahavi, *Subjectivity and Selfhood*, 13.
3. George Herbert Mead, *Mind, Self, and Society: From the Standpoint of a Social Behaviorist* (Chicago: University of Chicago Press, 1962), 164, 172, quoted in Zahavi, *Subjectivity and Selfhood*, 14.
4. Mead, *Mind, Self, and Society*, 163; 171–172, quoted in Zahavi, *Subjectivity and Selfhood*, 2005, 14.
5. Peter Carruthers, *Language, Thought and Consciousness: An Essay in Philosophical Psychology* (Cambridge: Cambridge University Press, 1998), 148, quoted in Zahavi, *Subjectivity and Selfhood*, 18.
6. In this sense, Zahavi explains that self-consciousness implies some form of identity. "Every higher-order theory operates with a duality: one mental state takes another mental state as its object," in which the identity of the first-order and the second-order mental state should be guaranteed (Zahavi, *Subjectivity and Selfhood*, 28). But this comes with the defect that a nonconscious second-order mental state cannot identify a first-order mental state as belonging to the same mind (Zahavi, *Subjectivity and Selfhood*, 29). Hence, we encounter the self-representing paradox of consciousness (see Uriah Kriegel, *Subjective Consciousness: A Self-Representational Theory*, Oxford: OUP, 2009; Uriah Kriegel, "Consciousness, Permanent Self-Awareness, and Higher-Order Monitoring," *Dialogue* 41, no. 3 (2002): 517–40).
7. Emmanuel Lévinas, *Cahier de l'Herne*, ed. C. Chalier and M. Abensour (Paris: L'Herne, 1991), 52, quoted in Zahavi, *Subjectivity and Selfhood*, 172.
8. I heard this explanation during my public philosophy lecture in Antananarivo, Madagascar, in February 2017. The audience of the lecture was mostly college students and young people around the same age. My lecture was in English and translated to Malagasy. While I was explaining the notion of subjectivity as the core idea of German idealism, the translator needed a more detailed explanation to indirectly translate the objectification of the subject. It was extremely complicated to decipher this idea in Malagasy, especially for those who did not study philosophy. The Malagasy academics in the field of philosophy did not react the same way to this discussion, because they are bilingual, using French as their academic language, even if they use Malagasy for their daily conversation.
9. Not in written form, but in informal conversation I once faced an opposition to this explanation. The argument was that the so-called Malagasy way of 'thinking' without subject and object is a simple misunderstanding due to ignorance, and that they simply do not know the system of subject and object, but that does not mean that

they do not think in the subject-object structure. It is controversial. But back then, I could not agree with such a determined affirmation, and I still do not.

10. Zahavi, *Subjectivity and Selfhood*, 64.
11. Zahavi, *Subjectivity and Selfhood*, 64.
12. Hans Bernhard Schmid, "Plural Self-Awareness," *Phenomenology and the Cognitive Sciences* 13, no. 1 (March 1, 2014): 12.
13. Self-awareness is not always reflective, but there is a self-awareness that is present in self-reflection (see Schmid, "Plural Self-Awareness," 13).
14. Jean-Paul Sartre, *Being and Nothingness* (New York: Washington Square Press, 1992), 19, quoted in Zahavi, *Subjectivity and Selfhood*, 21.
15. Sartre, *Being and Nothingness*, 19, quoted in Zahavi, *Subjectivity and Selfhood*, 21.
16. Zahavi, *Subjectivity and Selfhood*, 27.
17. Kriegel, *Subjective Consciousness*.
18. Hermann Ulrich Asemissen, "Egologische Reflexion," *Kant-Studien* 50, no. 1–4 (1959): 262, quoted in Zahavi, *Subjectivity and Selfhood*, 91.
19. Zahavi, *Subjectivity and Selfhood*, 91.
20. Ludwig Wittgenstein, *Preliminary Studies for the "Philosophical Investigations." Generally known as The Blue and Brown Books* (Oxford: Blackwell Publishing, 2007), 67.
21. Wittgenstein, *Preliminary Studies*, 67.
22. Wittgenstein, *Preliminary Studies*, 67.
23. Sydney Shoemaker, *Identity, Cause, and Mind*. Oxford: Oxford University Press, 2003, 8; "Immunity principle" (Shaun Gallagher, "Philosophical Conceptions of the Self: Implications for Cognitive Science," *Trend in Cognitive Science* 2000, 15).
24. Wittgenstein, *Preliminary Studies*, 66.
25. Wittgenstein, *Preliminary Studies*, 66.
26. Galen Strawson, *Real Materialism and Other Essays* (Oxford: Oxford University Press, 2008), 131.
27. Sydney Shoemaker, *The First-person Perspective and Other Essays* (Cambridge: Cambridge University Press, 1996), 17–18.
28. Wittgenstein, *Preliminary Studies*, 69.
29. Shoemaker, *The First-person Perspective*, 14.
30. Shoemaker, *The First-person Perspective*, 14.
31. Strawson, *Real Materialism*, 158.
32. Shoemaker, *The First-person Perspective*, 17.
33. Aristotle, *Categories*.
34. Ludwig Wittgenstein, *Philosophical Remarks*, ed. Rush Rhees, trans. Raymond Hargreaves and Roger White (Oxford: Basil Blackwell, 1998), 89.
35. Wittgenstein, *Philosophical Remarks*, 89.
36. Galen Strawson, "The Minimal Subject," in *The Oxford Handbook of the Self*, ed. Shaun Gallagher (Oxford: Oxford University Press, 2011), 259.
37. Strawson, "The Minimal Subject," 262.
38. Strawson, "The Minimal Subject," 260–261.

39. Descartes, Kant, Willam James (Strawson, "The Minimal Subject," 260).
40. Strawson, "The Minimal Subject," 259–260.
41. Strawson, "The Minimal Subject," 259.
42. Strawson, "The Minimal Subject," 259.
43. Kriegel, *Subjective Consciousness*.
44. Dan Zahavi, "Unity of Consciousness," in *The Oxford Handbook of the Self*, ed. Shaun Gallagher (Oxford: Oxford University Press, 2011), 327.
45. Gallagher, "Philosophical Conceptions," 15.
46. Zahavi, "Unity of Consciousness," 328.
47. Zahavi, "Unity of Consciousness," 328.
48. Zahavi, *Subjectivity and Selfhood*, 125.
49. Zahavi, "Unity of Consciousness," 329. Zahavi compares this to the empirical subjectivity of the "pure I" (*reines Ich*) as "transcendence in the immanence (*Transzendenz in der Immanenz*)" by Husserl (Husserl, *Ideen zu einer reinen Phänomenologie und phänomenologischen Philosophie. Erstes Buch. Allgemeine Einführung in die reine Phänomenologie* [Den Haag: Martinus Nijhoff, 1973], 124).
50. Gallagher, "Philosophical Conceptions," 15.
51. Ulric Neisser, "Five Kinds of Self-Knowledge," *Philosophical Psychology*, 1:1 (1988): 35–59.
52. José Luis Bermúdez, *The Paradox of Self-Consciousness* (Cambridge, MA: The MIT Press, 1998), 269.
53. Bermúdez, *The Paradox of Self-Consciousness*, 294.
54. David Hume, *A Treatise of Human Nature* (Oxford: Clarendon Press, 1888), 252.
55. Hume, *A Treatise of Human Nature*, 252; Gallagher, "Philosophical Conceptions," 19.
56. Gallagher, "Philosophical Conceptions," 17–18.
57. Sartre, *Being and Nothingness*, 9–17.
58. Jean-Paul Sartre, *La Transcendance de l'Ego* (Paris: Librairie Philosophique J. Vrin, 2012), 44 (my translation).
59. Sartre, *Being and Nothingness*, 13.
60. Sartre, *La Transcendance*, 41.
61. Dan Zahavi, "The Experiential Self: Objections and Clarifications," in *Self, No Self? Perspectives from Analytic, Phenomenological, and Indian Traditions*, ed. Mark Siderits, Evan Thompson, and Dan Zahavi (Oxford: Oxford University Press, 2011).
62. Uriah Kriegel, "Consciousness as Intransitive Self-Consciousness: Two Views and an Argument," *Canadian Journal of Philosophy*, 33, no. 1 (March 2003): 103–132.
63. Kriegel, "Consciousness as Intransitive Self-Consciousness," 120.
64. Kriegel, "Consciousness as Intransitive Self-Consciousness," 116.
65. Kriegel, "Consciousness as Intransitive Self-Consciousness," 125.
66. Gallagher, "Philosophical Conceptions," 15.
67. Husserl also has nowhere recourse to a substantial, underlying, persisting ego that exists outside the multiplicity of temporal phrases (David Carr, *Time, Narrative,*

*and History*, 25); the problem of the transcendental ego (*transzendentales Ich*) is fundamentally related to the problem of time. For further detailed discussions on the problem of time and the transcendental ego in the Husserlian framework, see Klaus Held, *Lebendige Gegewart. Die Frage nach der Seinsweise des transzendentalen Ich bei Edmund Husserl. Entwickelt am Leitfaden der Zeitproblematik* (Den Haag: Martinus Nijhoff, 1966).

68. Louis O. Mink, "History and Fiction as Modes of Comprehension," *New Literary History* I (1970): 555; Wilhelm Schapp, *In Geschichten Verstrickt*, 2nd ed. (Wiesbaden: B. Heymann, 1976), 144, quoted in Carr, *Time*, 50.

69. Carr, *Time*, 88.

70. *l'Ordre de succession chronologique se resorbe dans une structure matricielle atemporelle* (Roland Barthes, "Introduction à l'analyse structure des récrits," *Communications 8* [1996]: 12, quoted in Carr, *Time*, 50).

71. Claude Bremond, *Logique du récit* (Paris: Seuil, 1973); A. J. Greimas, *Sémantique structurale* (Paris: Larousse, 1966), quoted in Carr, *Time*, 50.

72. Carr, *Time*, 50.

73. Carr, *Time*, 50.

74. Carr, *Time*, 26.

75. Carr, *Time*, 24.

76. Carr, *Time*, 31.

77. Carr, *Time*, 47.

78. Carr, *Time*, 53.

79. Carr, *Time*, 81.

80. Wilhelm Dilthey, *Gesammelte Schriften*, vol. VII, 5th edition, ed. B. Groethuysen (Stuttgart: B. Teubner, 1968), 234, quoted in Carr, *Time*, 57. I discuss the part-whole structure in the context of 'understanding' music and show the structure of (the epistemology of) music in a geometrical manner in: Hye Young Kim, "Music, Consciousness, and Knots: Visualization of Music," in *Ecrire comme composer: le rôle des diagrammes*, ed. Franck Jedrzejewski, Antonia Soulez, Carlos Lobo. Sampzon, France: Delatour, forthcoming and Hye Young Kim, "'Visualisation de la musique dans l'espace': pour une compréhension de la spatialité et de la temporalité de la musique," *Intentio*, forthcoming.

81. Dilthey, *Gesammelte Schriften*, 196–98, quoted in Carr, *Time*, 57.

82. Carr, *Time*, 56.

83. Carr, *Time*, 31.

84. Carr, *Time*, 39, 49.

85. Carr, *Time*, 87.

86. Carr, *Time*, 63.

87. Carr, *Time*, 64.

88. Carr, *Time*, 89.

89. Hye Young Kim, *Sorge und Geschichte: Phänomenologische Untersuchung im Anschluss an Heidegger* (Berlin: Duncker und Humblot, 2015); Hye Young Kim, "Care and History: Phenomenology of Dasein in the Framework of Martin Heidegger's Being and Time," *Existentia* XXIV FASC.1-2, 2014). See also, Wilhelm Schmidt-Biggemann, *Apokalypse und Philologie* (Göttingen: V&R Unipress, 2007).

90. Carr, *Time*, 65.
91. Paul Ricoeur, *Temps et récit*, tome I (Paris: Seuil, 1983), 85, quoted in Carr, *Time*, 182.
92. Alasdair MacIntyre, *After Virtue. A Study in Moral Theory* (Notre Dame, IN: University of Notre Dame Press, 2007), 205.
93. Marya Schechtman, "The Narrative Self," in *The Oxford Handbook of the Self*, ed. Shaun Gallagher (Oxford: Oxford University Press, 2011), 395.
94. Michael S. Gazzinga, *The Mind's Past* (Berkeley and Los Angeles: University of California Press, 1998), 174.
95. Daniel C. Dennett, *Consciousness Explained* (New York: Back Bay Books, 1991), 418.
96. Dennett, *Consciousness*, 418.
97. Gallagher, "Philosophical Conceptions," 15.
98. Ricoeur, *Temps et récit*.
99. Carr, *Time*, 97.
100. Gallagher, "Philosophical Conceptions," 20.
101. Antonio Damasio, *The Feelings of What Happens* (New York: Mariner Books, 2000), Peter Goldie, *The Mess Inside, Narrative, Emotion, and the Mind* (Oxford: Oxford University Press, 2012).
102. Neisser, "Five Kinds," 41.
103. Neisser, "Five Kinds," 42.
104. Colwyn Trevarthen, "Communication and Cooperation in Early Infancy. A Description of Primary Intersubjectivity," in *Before Speech: The Beginning of Human Communication*, ed. M. Bullowa (London: Cambridge University Press, 1979), 321–347.
105. Daniel Stern, *The Interpersonal World of the Infant. A View from Psychoanalysis and Development Psychology* (London: Karnac Books, 1998).
106. Trevarthen, "Communication," 346.
107. J. J. Gibson, *The Ecological Approach to Visual Perception* (Boston: Houghton Mifflin, 1979), quoted in *Neisser*, "Five Kinds," 43.
108. Charles Taylor, *Sources of the Self. The Making of the Modern Identity* (Cambridge, MA: Harvard University Press, 1989), 35.
109. Taylor, *Sources of the Self*, 36.
110. Taylor, *Sources of the Self*, 35.
111. Taylor, *Sources of the Self*, 35.
112. Taylor, *Sources of the Self*, 50.
113. MacIntyre, *After Virtue*, 33.
114. MacIntyre, *After Virtue*, 205.
115. MacIntyre, *After Virtue*, 34.
116. MacIntyre, *After Virtue*, 221.
117. MacIntyre, *After Virtue*, 213.
118. Schechtman, "The Narrative Self," 405.
119. This aspect of history and tradition is crucial for Carr's discussion on historicity. In this context, Carr mentions that the authenticity of Heidegger's *Dasein* as a bearer of tradition (or standing in the tradition already as *gewesensein*, that is,

'having been there') should not be read as a lone isolated entity that dies alone. David Hoy's interpretation of the historicity of *Dasein* holds the same stance (David C. Hoy, "History, Historicity, and Historiography in *Being and Time*," in *Heidegger and Modern Philosophy*, ed. Michael Murray [New Haven and London: Yale University Press, 1978], 329–354). This point of view lies in their focus on the historicity in the interpretation of *Dasein* that includes others from the past in the self-understanding of *Dasein*, but, as Carr himself admits as well, the contemporary others and the direct interactions with them are absent in the analysis of *Dasein* apart from its inauthentic being as *verfallen in das Man* (lost in the anonymous they). I am not convinced by the view that the involvement of others of the past (but not of the present) is enough to 'save' *Dasein* from its existential solitude. *Dasein*'s authenticity is grounded in its *Jemeinigkeit* (my-own-ness) that is fundamentally related to *Dasein*'s *Vorlaufen-zum-Tode* (fore-running toward death), that is, its own death as a possibility of its own being. Despite the fact that *Dasein* is an *In-der-Welt-sein* (Being-in-the-world) that takes over and stands in the tradition and the fact that its inauthentic being with others is an equally crucial aspect of its self-understanding, the core of Heidegger's analysis of *Dasein* as *Sein-zum-Tode* (Being-toward-death) lies in its solitary self-understanding, therefore, it does not have enough room for others in its system. *Dasein*, after all, is *dasjenige Seiende, dem es in seinem Sein um sein Sein selbst geht* (Heidegger, *Sein un Zeit*, Tübingen: Max Niemeyer Verlag, 2006, 12; Kim, *Sorge und Geschichte*, 27).

120. Ricoeur, *Soi-même*, 14; Paul Ricoeur, *Oneself as Another*, trans. Kathleen Blamey (Chicago and London: University of Chicago Press, 1992), 3.

121. Ricoeur, *Soi-même*, 14.

122. Ricoeur, *Oneself as Another*, 3.

123. G. W. F. Hegel, *Phenomenology of Spirit*, trans. A. V. Miller (Oxford: Clarendon Press, 1977), 110.

124. Carr, *Time*, 138–146.

125. Dilthey, *Gesammelte Schriften*, 277–78, quoted in Carr, *Time*, 3, 178.

126. Kai Vogeley and Shaun Gallagher, "Self in the Brain," in *The Oxford Handbook of the Self*, ed. Shaun Gallagher (Oxford: Oxford University Press, 2011), 129.

127. Besides these epistemological and ontological differences between self and other, one can think of the social and political significance of a person. I have the right to live as a citizen of a certain country and vote in political elections. Each person who is recognized as a certain nationality has the right to proclaim, to defend, and to practice their legal rights. One vote per person is a symbolic and practical representation of the sociopolitical status of a person as an individual.

128. Jean-Paul Sartre, *Being and Nothingness*, trans. Hazel E. Barnes, vol. 330 (New York: Philosophical Library, 1956), quoted in Zahavi, *Subjectivity and Selfhood*, 170.

129. Jürgen Habermas, *Theorie des kommunikativen Handelns - Band II: Zur Kritik der funktionalistischen Vernunft* (Frankfurt am Main: Suhrkamp, 1981); Jürgen Habermas, *Vorstudien und Ergänzungen zur Theorie des kommunikativen Handelns* (Frankfurt am Main: Suhrkamp, 1984); Jürgen Habermas, *Nachmetaphysisches Denken* (Frankfurt am Main: Suhrkamp, 1988), quoted in Zahavi, *Subjectivity and Selfhood*, 148.

130. Zahavi, *Subjectivity and Selfhood*, 147.

131. John Searle, *The Construction of Social Reality* (New York: Simon and Schuster, 1995).

132. Max Scheler, *The Nature of Sympathy*, trans. Peter Heath (New York: Routledge, 2017), 261.

133. Jean-Paul Sartre, *Being and Nothingness*, 293–295, 412, quoted in Zahavi, *Subjectivity and Selfhood*, 170.

134. Zahavi, *Subjectivity and Selfhood*, 170.

135. Brinck et al., "The Primacy of the 'We'?," 143.

136. Brinck et al., "The Primacy of the 'We'?," 133–134.

137. Brinck et al., "The Primacy of the 'We'?," 139.

138. Brinck et al., "The Primacy of the 'We'?," 141.

139. Brinck et al., "The Primacy of the 'We'?," 143.

140. Brinck et al., "The Primacy of the 'We'?," 142.

*Chapter 5*

# Self in Pre-subjective Relation

## 1. SELF-IN-RELATION: SELF AS WE

The linguistic practice of saying '*ouri* husband' represents pre-subjective self as 'we.' When the self is 'we,' the self-ness of the self is not dependent on the self-representation of the self because of the irreducible distinction between self and other within the 'we.' A self can be aware of a relation without reflection on its self-ness based on the self-objectifying or self-representing system of the 'I,' the subject. Pre-subjective self refers to the fundamental-ontological condition of the self that is necessarily in relation with others.

I suggest that we approach the 'we' neither from a self-centered nor from a selfless point of view in which the 'we' is only either a collection of individuals or an anonymous whole, but based on 'relation.' This relation is pre-subjective, by which I mean that the conscious, reflective, subjective self with intentionality is not the conceptual basis of the relation. Relation is there, even if one does not conceptually posit oneself as a subject and stand in contrast to another. The pre-subjective relation is prior to the consciousness of the distinction between self and other and is not formed by separate individual subjects coming together and consciously relating to each other.

In the sense that a pre-subjective self is not conscious of a differentiation between subject and object, it is comparable to pre-reflective consciousness. Pre-reflective experience refers to the experience without a differentiation between subject, object, and their relation. But presubjectivity is not a subject's state of experience. Rather, the pre-subjective state of self is what a pre-reflective subject can be aware of. In the experience of a pre-reflective subject, relation with the other does not play a crucial role, but relation is the core of the pre-subjective self as 'we.'

## 2. PRE-SUBJECTIVE SELF

A subject can be aware of the pre-subjective state of self that is fundamental-ontologically in relation, and the awareness of relation can be prior to the awareness of distinction between self and other, even though relation already presumes that there is a distinction. If the we-ness is pre-distinction, it falls right back into the we-ness as the undifferentiated anonymous whole. The distinction in the awareness of relation is not obliterated, but the distinction can be conceived posteriorly, meaning that the awareness of distinction is not the precondition of the awareness of relation. When a baby and the mother are aware of each other as 'one,' this oneness does not point at an undifferentiated oneness. Rather it is a recognition of the relation between the two. We can be in relation and be aware of it without being conscious of the difference between self and other as well as *my* self-ness as subject. Although the distinctness of self is present in relation, the consciousness of self-ness in contrast to not-self is neither the beginning nor the basis of the awareness of relation.

Epistemologically, the consciousness of a primary distinction between *this* and *that* is the starting point of any knowledge. An epistemological priority of distinction, however, does not refer to an irreducible metaphysical distinction between different entities that is pre-given. A primary distinction that initiates the very first differentiation in the void is the precondition of understanding (see chapter 6), and it is an epistemological/mathematical imagination. Our ontological/existential understanding of distinction between self and other, on the other hand, does not and cannot start from this primary distinction in an undifferentiated void, because we exist in the world, never alone in the void. Existing in any social form, in any culture, in any style of life, or in any existential ideology, we never experience our self in the midst of an undifferentiated anonymous whole. Even the fetus in a mother's womb is not an unseparated entity from the mother. They are connected as if they were one body, but they are not an undifferentiated whole. There is a *primary* relation. We are in relation in the 'we' that is not a collection of individuals who convey the concept of self as the 'I' as subject, but of the 'we' that we are born into: the world.

I call this world the *web* of relation. The awareness of an irreducible metaphysical distinction between self and other comes after or simultaneously with the awareness of the relation in which we are born, but not prior. The reason that I call it 'relation' and not 'world' is to have us notice the *web* in which I am placed in intermingled relation with the others which is there prior to *my* consciousness of it. In the following chapter, I will show how a spatial understanding of the difference and identity (self and other) of the self as *we* in this *web* is possible. In chapter 7, I will try to visualize the structure of the relation in we-ness, applying the principle of primary distinction and link as membership in knot set theory, the principle of which I will explain in further detail in chapter 6. Such a visualization would help us to have more of an intuitive picture of the spatial understanding of distinction and unity. It is important to remark here that pre-subjective does not mean a-subjective. Namely, the acknowledgment of pre-subjective relation is not to deny the subjective self and its intentional acts in its way of relating to the other within the subject-object structure. I will say more about this in chapter 8 as I compare pre-subjective we-ness with other accounts.

## 3. HISTORI-POLITICAL PROBLEM OF SUBJECTIVITY

Before moving over to chapter 6 for a mathematical representation of the pre-subjective self-in-relation, I would like to mention a historical, political, and philosophical background of the problem of subjectivity. In chapter 1, I started the discussion with addressing the problem of colonialism in philosophy, in which the discourse of subjectivity is deeply rooted. The core of subjectivity lies in the freedom (*Freiheit des Menschen*), the self-determination (*Selbstbestimmung*), and the autonomy (*Autonomie*) of a conscious human being, which is the firm—and dogmatic at this point—foundation of modern Western philosophy.[1] 'Who' could represent and understand this core is a fundamentally philosophical yet also very power-sensitive question: the status of the 'true' representative of this core philosophical notion of 'being human' matters. The foundation of German idealism is subjectivity that penetrates the core of the human being as an autonomous free entity. The following quote from Hegel shows this struggle for the status of the 'true' subject even within the West:

> The philosophy of Kant, Fichte, and Schelling. In these philosophies, the [French] revolution as in the form of idea is grounded and articulated.... In this grand epoch of world history ... only two nations have participated, the German and the French nation. . . . This principle is in Germany as idea (*Gedanke*), spirit (*Geist*), concept (*Begriff*), and it stepped out into actuality (*Wirklichkeit*) in France.[2]

This principle refers to the self-determination and the autonomy of a free human being.

According to this philosophy, as long as we are human, each one of us is a free, autonomous person, but the fact that the East is mundanely described as a so-called Confucianist society where genuine concept of freedom of an individual is neither understood nor realized shows how widely, profoundly, and distortedly this subjectivity philosophy-politics is rooted in our way of viewing 'us' and the other who doesn't belong to this 'us.' Challenging subjectivity falls necessarily within this scope of discussion, whether desired or not.

There are many pro-drop (pronoun dropping) languages in the world, and Korean is one of them, which means that one usually speaks without a subject in Korean. This phenomenon can well be interpreted as an ellipsis that intends to save saying predictable elements, which implies that the subject of the sentence is still there but simply not uttered. I do not oppose this view completely, but at the same time, when one says 'had a meal?' (Did you have a meal?) in Korean, even if the 'you' in the conversation is present, the you, the subject of the sentence 'had a meal,' is not automatically and necessarily presumed to be omitted as in non-pro-drop languages such as Indo-European languages. It is explained so because (1) this has to be explained in European languages for Western readers and (2) even if it is explained in Korean linguistically, the references for the linguistic theories that are used to analyze the Korean language stem from the West.

I was faced with this problem as I was trying to describe and understand the phenomenon of saying 'our husband' by utilizing preexisting philosophical theories which stem from the West and are written in European languages. I distinctly felt a shortage of words and lack of systematic methodology for explaining this 'foreign' phenomenon in the frame that originates from the culture where this phenomenon does not exist—at least at this time—without turning to molding and fitting it in the 'standard' frame. The Malagasy language, for example, does not have the subject-object structure, as I mentioned. It is explained and translated into English in the passive form, which is the closest example of explaining how their sentences are structured. But that does not mean that I understand their way of speaking and understanding things. This felt like an impossible mission, but the biggest challenge or obstacle that had to be overcome for this study was not this difficulty of ineffability between different cultures, languages, and worldviews, but the unquestioned authority of the unchallenged system of subjectivity, and the thoroughly habituated way of conceiving 'being' within this system, in which not only merely philosophical debates but also 'the world' operates.

However, I assert that the notion of pre-subjective self-in-relation is not idiosyncratic only to a certain culture. The core idea of pre-subjective self lies in the acknowledgment of a primary and necessary unity (with other selves) and distinction (from other selves) of a self. MacIntyre also points out that it is a common phenomenon that an individual identifies oneself and is identified by others through one's membership in a variety of social groups, that is, as a sister, cousin, grandchild, member of this family, that village, this tribe.

He says it is so in many premodern, traditional societies, yet it is still so in the present world. As MacIntyre writes, these are neither the characteristics that belong to human beings accidently nor superficial elements that are to be cast off to discover "the real me." Rather, they are pan of my substance.³ As a fundamentally social being, we inherit "a particular space within an interlocking set of social relationships." Without this space, one is "nobody, or at best a stranger or an outcast."⁴ We have already seen in our previous discussion on narrative self that not only MacIntyre, but many others, including Dilthey, Heidegger, and Carr, have regarded the individual as a historical being, bearing or standing in the tradition or "in the cultures that are historically predecessors"⁵ of their own. The ways we think and act can never be separated from the cultures or the traditions in which we are placed.

I see that my idea of pre-subjective self-in-relation could be well compared with and even defended in a way by Taylor's idea of self, despite the differences of approach between his theories and my own. He thought that one is self only among other selves. The fact that a language exists and is maintained only within a language community indicates this crucial feature of a self.⁶ Taylor adds, though, that this has "become an important point to make, because not only the philosophico-scientific tradition but also a powerful modern aspiration to freedom and individuality have conspired to produce an identity which seems to be a negation of this."⁷ This indeed was the starting point of my query on self.

The self-definition of a self, says Taylor, is an answer to the question who *I* am, whose original sense is found in the interchange of speakers. One can define oneself by defining where one speaks from,

> in the family tree, in social space, in the geography of social statues and functions, in my intimate relations to the ones I love, and also crucially in the space of moral and spiritual orientation within which my most important defining relations are lived out.⁸

In this context, he has, in fact, come up with a very similar notion with my *web* of pre-subjective relation. Taylor claims that a self exists only within "webs of interlocution,"⁹ in the sense that one can be a self only in relation to certain interlocutors, that is, conversation partners, and one can achieve self-definition and grasp a language of self-understanding only through the relation with them.

However, I use the term 'web' for pre-subjective relation in a different way from that of Taylor's. The pre-subjective self-in-relation that is expressed in 'our husband' is not exactly a self's way of self-definition. Rather, this use of *ouri* represents a *pseudo self-naming* that does not correspond to the actual social-familial relationship. A pre-subjective self's *web* does not define the membership, status, or place of a self in a social web of relation that is articulated in a shared language, but instead, it reveals and highlights one's being in the *world* that is full of other beings, and that precedes any social and societal relationship. A pre-subjective *web* is not restricted to the interlocutors that one communicates with, but it is much more generic; it is extended to the ones who are there, but not necessarily as the interlocutors of mine. To call everyone a familial name is a paradoxical way to extend the scope of the family and simultaneously tear down the wall of this closed group. In short, a pre-subjective *web* is literally pre-subjective, prior to a subjective self-understanding which Taylor's web is based on; it is prior logically, not chronologically.

A pre-subjective self is in this web of relation of the self as the 'we,' yet the self as an individual is not obliterated. The individuality of a self is crucial, that is why it is not only a pre-subjective 'we' but a pre-subjective 'self-in-relation.' Neisser also pointed out that an awareness of the interpersonal self is almost invariably accompanied by a simultaneous awareness of the ecological self.[10] As Taylor did, Neisser too talks about the problem that I sympathize with:

> Philosophers in the Western tradition—indeed, in many traditions—have often treated the private self as the only self worth knowing. Descartes is primarily responsible for the further claim that it is the only self we can be sure about, all other experiences being subject to error and delusion. I have argued, in contrast, that the ecological and interpersonal selves are perceived effectively and surely from the beginning of life.[11]

And in the end, he adds an essential aspect of this idea: "This argument does not dispute the value of the private self, only its epistemological priority."[12]

## 4. HUMANITY AS PRE-SUBJECTIVE WE

Although I have mentioned the telltale signs of Hegel's Eurocentrism, his idea of self and community helps us to understand the idea of pre-subjective self-in-relation that I am trying to convey—ironically, I should probably say though, because in his analysis Hegel treated China and India "as precursors of the Western world even though both continued to exist in his own day as they do in ours,"[13] which once again demonstrates the Eurocentric understanding of the world of he and his contemporaries, where the world outside their own still remains in a primitive state. Considering that Korea is very often not even considered as distinct from China, I have to say, I clearly do not approach the Korean culture and language, which this analysis of pre-subjective 'we' is based on, as that of a primitive society, as Carr illustrates, that is "relegated to the past by being regarded as leftovers from an earlier stage of humanity," where, therefore, 'we' can learn about ourselves through 'their' cultures as our precursors. Not to mention that I am never even sure where to put myself, whether 'we' or 'they,' which only leaves me with a schizophrenic state of self-definition, as Fanon also experienced and talked about.

Hegel asserts that a self-conscious self has the ability to stand on its own with its *Selbstständigkeit* (independence).[14] Here I endorse Carr's reading of Hegel, which well articulates the problem of this idea of self with the other self. Carr writes,

> Hegel may be suggesting that the self-certainty and self-centeredness of modern thought is a function of the increased "mastery and possession of nature" envisaged by Descartes and realized in the growth of science and technology. But the situation is de-stabilized when one of these confident selves encounters another one. To me the other may seem just a part of the surrounding world I must master to serve my own needs and maintain my independence. But trouble begins if he takes the same view toward me. The existence of each of us as an independent or self-standing self is challenged by the other. We are caught up in the struggle over the independence and dependence of self-consciousness.[15]

Hegel's idea of community is possible only with self-conscious, self-assertive, independent-minded individuals, in which his notion of self as "I that is We and We that is I"[16] is grounded.[17] As Carr explains, therefore, the dialectic of a community is paradoxical: "Without independent individuals there can be no genuine community; yet without a community there can be no genuinely independent individuals."[18]

Carr sees that family as a community is too close to the concept of "Universal Subject" or a "Sartrian group-in-fusion," in which the individual is obliterated rather than participating, to suit Hegel's idea of community. Even though Hegel considers family to have a crucial dialectical role in the life of an individual and a society, a family is a natural grouping that precedes everything else, rather than a social grouping that is constituted through active participation and identification of individuals.[19] An individual as a member of a family has an objective membership meaning that one does not have to consciously and deliberately identify oneself with it in order to obtain it. Once we are born into this primary relation, our belongingness to the family does not expire.

Family is an immediate example of a pre-subjective 'we' as self-in-relation. The relation in which pre-subjective self is placed in is an inevitable, necessary ontological condition that precedes all possible social groupings, even possibly prior to the formation of genuine individuality. But it is also within this group that we grow to become an independent individual, and the individuality and the self-ness of a self in pre-subjective relation is not dissolved in the we-ness. Often, even the family requires self-conscious identification and participation of the members for its maintenance, not to mention that the membership through a marital relationship is not the same as the family membership that one is born with. In Korean, there is a commonly used expression 'neighbor-cousin' which means that the neighbors who live nearby and with whom one interacts closely are better than actual family members who are sometimes far away.

But at the same time, precisely such individuals, who are self-conscious, self-assertive, and independent-minded, have the capacity to tear apart the community as well,[20] even within the boundaries of family. We reckon that as a community 'we' often stand in opposition to another group whose threat forms and maintains 'our' group.[21] An external threat often constitutes a common experience which fuses a group into a community.[22] It is common that threatened or opposed groups recognize themselves as a group instead of 'merely individuals.' The group formed by external opposition can be stabilized and survive, Carr asserts, through a story as 'our story,' which relates to collective and cultural memory. I deal with this in chapter 11, "Collective Memory: Boundary, Place, and Home."

In this context, however, Carr asks, "Do communities require external opposition in order to survive?," responding himself, on the one hand, that "history seems to suggest that they do," but, on the other hand, that it doesn't have to be so. "Humanity as such seems to be a group with which most individuals have a hard time identifying themselves," says Carr, however, we could perhaps have a community of humanity constituted by "telling a persuasive story about it."[23] That is the idea. Then who can tell such a story? It is *us*. Who else? We can self-consciously tell ourselves a story of ours as a community of humanity.

Through the action of saying '*ouri* family member,' an independent individual engages with the other, whether a member of the family or not, in the 'we' that is based on our primary relation to one another, revealing this pre-subjective relation in language. In this context, we could interpret the use of '*ouri* family member' as implying the potentiality of the realization (*Verwirklichung*) of the ideal form of a community by consciously conferring objective familial membership on both related and unrelated others—not that that's what Koreans actually mean when they say it, but that we could enlarge the dimension of our understanding of self through this phenomenon. When 'our family' overcomes the obstacle of family egoism, it definitely forms a possible story. In chapter 11, I will tell you a story of a Korean minority group in Central Asia who made their collective identity through their story of solidarity with other minority groups, through which we can have a glance at a possible story of 'being we' as humanity.

Telling this story of *ours* requires being aware of the pre-subjective we-ness through which individuals are fundamentally in relation with others and endeavoring to consciously identify with this state of self—self being both pre-subjective and subjective. One of the reasons that we have a hard time to consciously identify with humanity as our community is the same reason as for the family that we never had to identify with; it is because it is already and always was there ever since we were born. We are born into it, the community of humanity. We can make ourselves be conscious of that.

The dyad of self-other is the precondition of the 'we' for the 'I' as subject, and the 'I' and the 'Thou' have to come together to form the 'we.' But a pre-subjective 'we' is not the 'we' as 'self + other,' it is rather as 'we + we,' because the pre-subjective self is already *we* as self-in-relation, 'we + we' not as 'our we—my we' and 'their we—your we' but as *our we* to which all of us belong. The discourse of presubjectivity is an attempt to view the self as plural and the other within self with a 'better' way of dealing with the paradox of the 'we' in which self and other are separated yet in unity. By 'better' I mean the way in which (1) the identity both of a self as the 'I' and as the 'we' are not mutually exclusive but soundly preserved, so that one neither loses oneself nor others, and so that (2) the 'we' as self can place oneself (as the 'we') in a sound relation with the other 'we.' Countless we groups can interact and deal with other we groups in the light of understanding oneself as a sub-we group under the scope of the overarching concept of humanity as pre-subjective 'we.'

There have been many bad examples of the distorted we-subject that have led to leaving traumatic traces and marks in the history of mankind. One of the most regretful memories of this is unfortunately linked with one of the most influential thinkers of our time, Martin Heidegger. I will talk about this more in chapter 8, section 6 "*Das Man* in Being and Time." When we are *confused* about how to deal with self and other in the 'we,' the individual self is lost in overwhelming fear of the absence of self-understanding, and the other clashes with the self, which only results in self-destruction, because we are always *we*, neither as a Korean, Jewish, African, Francophone, black, white, female, male, heterosexual, homosexual, disabled, right-winged, left-winged, philosopher, farmer, nor everything else possible, but as a human being.

This is why it is all about understanding what it means to be human. We strive to understand it, not only scientifically and philosophically, but in life, we struggle to understand who I am, whether self-consciously or self-deceptively. In most cases of self-deceptive self-understanding, a distorted self-definition relies on the sub-group identities with which one identifies in order to find a way to define oneself. A representative and symbolic example of this phenomenon, where one loses oneself in the midst of others, we see in a crowd, which we will reflect on further in chapter 8, section 5 "Crowd." There is a good reason that the interpretation of the authentic understanding of my own existence in the fundamental ontology of *Dasein* is often practically utilized for therapeutic treatments of psychological issues. A sound existential and ontological self-understanding as an independent, individual, human being is the very ground, the key for achieving an understanding of oneself as a whole being and as the 'we.'

## NOTES

1. According to Jean Piaget's theory of cognitive developments, a self with the ability of having abstract and logical concepts, from which the sense of identity as an autonomous subject is also possible, is developed in the later phase of life rather than what we start out from as an infant (Jean Piaget, *The Origin of Intelligence in Children*, trans. Margaret Cook [New York: International University Press], 1952). However, the potential of this development should be pre-given, and the fact that a conceptual self is developed later in time after birth does not oppose the idea of a conscious self constituting one of the necessary conditions of human existence.

2. Georg Wilhelm Friedrich Hegel, *Vorlesungen über die Geschichte der Philosophie*, Bd. 20 in Werke in 20 Bänden. Red.: E. Modlenhauer und K. M. Michel. (Auf der Grundlage der »Werke« von 1832-45 neu ediert.) (Frankfurt a. M.: Suhrkamp, 1971), 314, quoted in Gerhard Gamm, *Der Deutsche Idealismus: Eine Einführung in die Philosophie von Fichte, Hegel und Schelling*, (Stuttgart: Reclam, 1997), 15–16 (my translation).

3. MacIntyre, *After Virtue*, 33.
4. MacIntyre, *After Virtue*, 33–34.
5. MacIntyre, *After Virtue*, 20.
6. Taylor, *Sources of the Self*, 35.
7. Taylor, *Sources of the Self*, 35.
8. Taylor, *Sources of the Self*, 35.
9. Taylor, *Sources of the Self*, 36.
10. Neisser, "Five Kinds," 46.
11. Neisser, "Five Kinds," 51.
12. Neisser, "Five Kinds," 51.
13. Carr points this out in his discussion on the universality of narrative self. Carr, *Time*, 182.
14. G. W. F. Hegel, *Phänomenologie des Geistes* (Frankfurt am Main: Suhrkamp, 1989), 137–145.
15. Carr, *Time*, 140.
16. Hegel, *Phänomenologie des Geistes*, 145.
17. Carr, *Time*, 143.

18. Carr, *Time*, 144.
19. Carr, *Time*, 141.
20. Carr, *Time*, 144.
21. Carr, *Time*, 158–159.
22. Carr, *Time*, 158.
23. Carr, *Time*, 159.

## Chapter 6

# Self-in-Relation and Pre-subjective We
## *Mathematical Representation*

### 1. INSIDE AND OUTSIDE: PRIMARY BOUNDARY

I imagine that the *web* in which self-in-relation is situated must look like this:

Here, I will first present a primary distinction, the starting point of understanding. It is imagined as drawn on a paper which is spatially limited; however, consider that the borders of the paper (square) do not exist and that this relation *web* extends infinitely. Furthermore, this *web* is invisible, so it looks like a void. It is invisible because the *web* of relation is an ontological precondition but epistemologically not prior to a primary distinction.

Here is one point, where I *am* here and now. But where is it?

For me to be conscious of here and now, that is, to know where I am, I need a distinction. Without a distinction, everything is identical, and one cannot distinguish this one from that one. Differentiation is the basis of knowing. In that way, there should be a beginning: a primary distinction. Here, I draw a line.

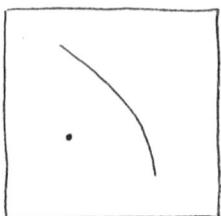

Now, we have this side, where the point is, and the other side.

The boundaries in the *web* have already been there, but the boundary is *re*created by finding myself under the distinction between inside and outside.

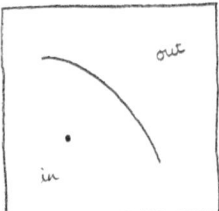

I will deal with this inside-outside distinction more precisely with a mathematical model suggested by Kauffman,[1] which he developed from an arithmetic system by Spencer-Brown. In the following sections, I will first elaborate knot logic, imaginary values, and the waveform based on the Flagg resolution by James Flagg and Kauffman,[2] then show how I utilize these in my pre-subjective self-in-relation discussion, in which I define the difference between self and other spatially.

From here, this is how Kauffman explains the primary distinction based on Spencer-Brown's *Laws of Forms*.[3]

Let's say that this is the first distinction. The inside is identified by the concavity and the outside by the convexity of the mark.[4]

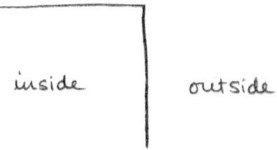

Or, we can simply drop the labels (inside, outside).

This is a shorthand for the distinction that a rectangle makes in the plane between inside and outside.

It does not change anything if the form is changed to a circle. I mark it again with 'I' referring to 'inside' and 'O' referring to 'outside.'

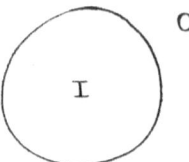

And if 'x' is the side you are on, let this mark denote the side you move to when you cross.

With this marking rule, we have the following equations that align with the circle that distinguishes inside from outside.

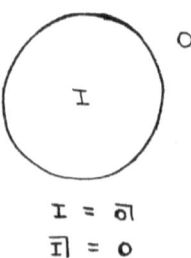

# Self-in-Relation and Pre-subjective We

This mark is an operator that indicates the crossing of the boundary, which denotes 'distinction' in the plane.

┐

This is the first distinction, which differentiates the inside on which I am from the outside. Kauffman regards this as a primitive distinction that represents the imaginary distinction between the observer and the observed. The observation is an act of a conscious subject that is the observer and the observed at the same time; this constitutes the structure of self-consciousness.[5] This is an explanation of a self-conscious subject.[6] Based on this crossing rule, I would like to present this distinction in a pre-subjective structure. The fact that this can be explained both in a subjective and pre-subjective frame implies that the two are neither mutually exclusive nor contradictory.

From here, I will show you how I use this to represent the relation between the 'I,' the 'not-I,' and the 'we.'

The side that I am on is inside, which means that the side that is inside is fluid. If I am on the side of 'I,' 'I' is inside and 'O' is outside in the previous figure. But if I am on the 'O' side, 'O' is inside and 'I' is outside. This flexibility refers to the character of this primary distinction. This distinction is not a fixed line that is pre-given. Rather, it is constantly occurring along with the change of the position of inside and outside and the crossing between them.

The side where I am on is inside as my side, and the other side that I am not on is not my side. I mark my side where I am on at this moment as 'I' and the other side where I am not on now as 'not-I' instead of the marks that represent inside 'I' and outside 'O.' This is when I am inside the circle.

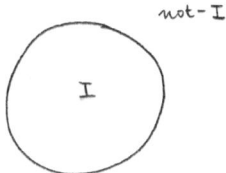

If I am on the other side, outside of the circle, it should be marked differently.

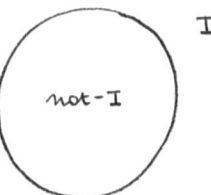

The distinction between 'I' and 'not-I' represents the relation itself. Relation is possible based on the distinction between self (I) and other (not-I). In the framework of subjectivity, regarding this crossing as the conscious act of self-observation, the 'not-I' as the observed is the objectified subject, and the unity of the observer and the observed is primitive, because they are, on the face of it, still one. But if the 'not-I' is not an objectified (othered) self, but is the other, an ontologically different other with metaphysically different properties that is not myself, this distinction represents the irreducible distinction between self and other.

When I am on the one side, I cannot be on the other side at the same time. The other cannot be on the side where I am on, because the other is not myself. 'I' is not 'not-I.'

However, the crossing between 'I' and 'not-I' (the other) puts them in relation, because the crossing that represents their relation also represents their ontological precondition as being-in-relation referring to a primary relation (unity). By having a crossing on itself, 'I' and the 'other' could be in an identical yet differentiated system which represents the self as 'we.' Through the crossing, the unity and the distinction of the 'I' and 'not-I' can be secured in a consistent structure because the crossing connects (relates) and disconnects (distinguishes).

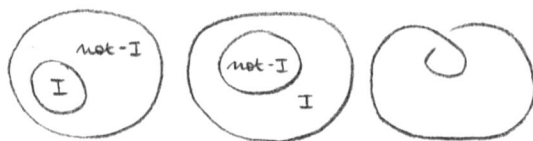

The process of boundary making by crossing reveals the relation and the distinction. I am going to explain the making of distinction and unity based on the waveform[7] model by Kauffman.

*Self-in-Relation and Pre-subjective We* 105

When 'I' is related to 'not-I,' one can think of the mutual relating between 'I' and 'not-I' as a temporal sequence between inside and outside. When this relating starts from inside, we have a waveform *a*, and if it starts from outside, we have *b*.[8]

$$a = \ldots \text{IOIOIOIOIOIOIOIO} \ldots$$

$$b = \ldots \text{OIOIOIOIOIOIOIOI} \ldots$$

Using the crossing mark, we can have the same waveforms as written below:[9]

$$a = \cdots \overline{o} | o\, \overline{o} | o\, \overline{o} | o\, \overline{o} | o\, \overline{o} | \cdots$$

$$b = \cdots \overline{I} | I\, \overline{I} | I\, \overline{I} | I\, \overline{I} | I \cdots$$

Although Kauffman characterizes the waveform as the observer's oscillation between 'I' and 'othered I,'[10] in this context, I will regard this waveform as the oscillation between 'I' and the 'other.'

$$\ldots \text{I—not-I—I—not-I—I—not-I—I—not-I} \ldots$$

Together they form a conversation and a taking of turns. Taken individually, the two waveforms are indistinguishable. When together, the phase difference suffices to tell them apart. According to Kauffman, waveforms delineate boundaries that separate imaginary spaces.[11]

$$E = \cdots \overset{z\,z\,z\,z\,z\,z\,z\,z\,z\,z}{\underset{z\,z\,z\,z\,z\,z\,z\,z\,z\,z}{ababababababa}} \cdots$$

The waveform becomes a boundary between sides labeled differently.[12]

$$\frac{z}{\overline{z}}$$

I identify this boundary as the boundary that is made by relation between inside and outside. This boundary denotes the primary distinction that represents the relation itself. It has always been there ever since I started to exist in the world, but I have to *call the other in the relation* for this relation to relate me to the other and separate me from the other at the same time.

106                    Chapter 6

I find a rich and beautiful—imaginary—representation of this boundary making process, for example, in the preludes composed by Johann Sebastian Bach.[13]

The harmony between different notes (each played by each hand) at each instant forms a waveform that creates a boundary that enables the distinction of music. The consciousness of music is possible through this distinctness of the melody created by the harmony. Before notes are played together in relation to the other notes, they don't have any distinctness as such and such a note, indistinguishable from other notes, but when they are played, they gain their distinctness as a separate note and, at the same time, in a harmonious relation to other notes, they form each instant of music that forms the melody.[14]

The boundary was formed between the two waveforms that were created by the oscillation of crossing, that is, mutually relating to the other side.

$$a = \ldots \text{IOIOIOIOIOIOIOIO} \ldots$$

$$b = \ldots \text{OIOIOIOIOIOIOIOI} \ldots$$

Kauffman and Flagg show that the waveform $a$ is not distinguishable from the other waveform $b$ when they are taken separately, because they are the same temporal sequence extending from and to infinity. Therefore, $a = b$ and $a \neq b$.

$$a = \ldots \text{I O I O I O} \ldots$$

$$b = \ldots \text{O I O I O I} \ldots$$

From here, I can tell you that, regarding the relation between self and other, because 'where I am' does not have a fixed point that designates the fixed inside or outside, the 'I' side and the 'not-I' side are ever-changing. In this regard, inside is outside, and outside is inside. There is only a temporal difference between inside and outside.

Although the starting points of these waveforms are ungraspable (because they extend from and to infinity), if the temporal difference between the starting points of the two waveforms is taken into account, 'I' on the waveform $a$ at the point $x$ meets the 'O' of the $b$ at the same point. And when the temporal difference is adjusted, 'I' on $a$ meets 'I' on $b$ at the point $x$.

$$a = \ldots\ I\ O \ldots$$
$$b = \ldots\ O\ I \ldots$$

However, they are temporal sequences with fixed points of neither beginning nor end. The difference between $a$ and $b$ can be grasped only relatively for the sake of each precise timing. In this scene, the differentiation between inside and outside exists only relatively. The side that is inside now is inside now only because I relate to the other from here where I am for the time being and make here my side (inside). However, the side that is now outside was and will be inside, and the same for the inside. In this regard, inside is not outside, but inside is outside, too. We need another model that could resolve this paradox.

The difference between the two waveforms is defined either as (1) I—other on the pre-subjective level or (2) I—othered I on the subjective level. Therefore, there are also two paradoxical situations: (1) in the self-referential consciousness of the self as subject between 'I' and the 'othered I,' and (2) in the pre-subjective self as 'we' between 'I' and the 'other.' The other in the self as 'we' is distinguished from the self ontologically, while the 'othered I' in the self as the 'I' is distinguished from the self epistemologically. In self as 'we,' the other is already in the self, therefore the self is not in a self-enclosed system. But how can the other be in the self? Self is not self anymore with the other within itself and the other is not the other anymore in the self. Between 'I' and the 'othered I,' the differentiation is imaginary, theoretically presumed, while the differentiation between 'I' and the 'other' is not imaginary, but this distinction is pre-given and irreducible. If the ontological difference between the waveforms $a$ and $b$ is not reducible, the relation between these two is the core of their unity. This is a triadic unity with 'I' (inside), 'O' (outside), and relation.

## 2. KNOT SET THEORY FOR SELF-MEMBERSHIP

Here, I will show how to resolve this paradox by applying knot set theory by Kauffman. Before I explain in detail how it works with the notion of membership in knot set theory, let me present a simple visualization of the resolving of the paradox by creating a crossing. Here, we have a ring.

This is one seamless ring without a distinction in itself. We can create a distinction by making a loop on the ring.

This loop creates a distinction between inside and outside within the ring itself.

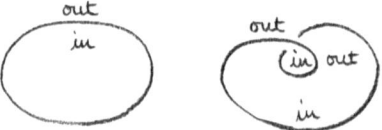

By making a loop, we have a crossing on the loop.

This twisted (differentiated identical) ring could be regarded to represent the self both as 'we' (I—other) and as 'I' (I—othered I). But if the difference is not reducible (and ontologically it is, because as long as we exist in relation, in the world, we never exist completely solely in a void), we need a structure with the unknottable third element that guarantees the distinction and relation within itself. Instead of a twisted ring, a knot that cannot be unknotted without cutting it would be more useful for this situation. I have two models for this triadic knot that we cannot unknot unless we cut it: the trefoil knot and the Borromean rings. I will now explain their mutual and self-mutual membership relations within themselves.

The crossing on the ring is crucial in this context, because on the crossing, inside becomes outside and outside becomes inside. On the crossing, the container of a set becomes a member of the set and vice versa. The membership logic on a crossing can be explained in the domain of the knot set theory.

## 3. KNOT LOGIC: LINKING AS MUTUALITY

Here, I will elaborate Kauffman's knot set theory from "Knot Logic" (1995),[15] which I apply to study the structure of the 'we' in 'our someone' in the following chapter.[16]

Let us name the three rings A, B, and C. They are woven in the way that ring A surrounds ring C, ring C surrounds ring B, and ring B surrounds ring A.

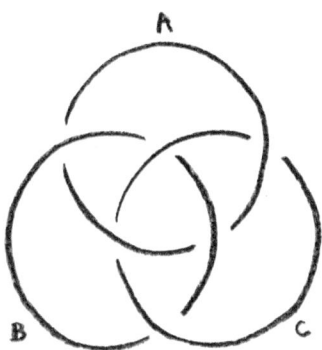

There are six crossings in this model where the three individual rings are connected and separated.

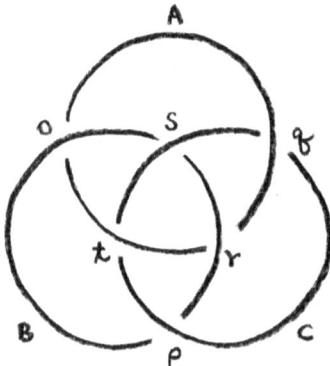

Each crossing, that is, the link between the rings, manifests the mutual relationships between the rings. Here I apply Kauffman's knot logic, which is a variant of set theory that allows mutual relationship.[17] Kauffman presents knot set theory as a diagrammatic alternative to Venn diagrams that models a nonstandard set theory and explains its relationship. A Venn diagram shows the possibility of a logical comprehension of the connective tissue in topology and geometry.

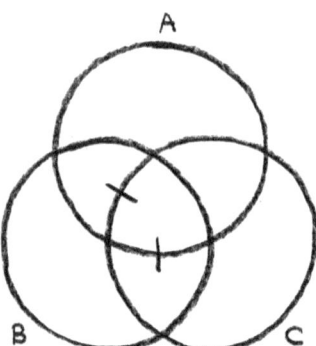

Each marker (where A intersects B and B intersects C) is placed in two regions and indicates that at least one of these regions is not empty. Therefore, some A are B and some B are C.[18] Kauffman articulates its logical connection in relation to the theory of knots and links in three-dimensional space. Let us say there are undefined objects 'a' and 'b,' and a notion of membership is denoted as 'a ∈ b,' which means 'a *belongs* to b.' It will be possible for 'a' to belong to itself or to say that 'a belongs to b' while 'b belongs to a.'[19] The notion of belongingness here is used in the context of set theory, in the sense that such and such members belong to such and such sets. Therefore, when 'a belongs to b,' 'a' as the member belongs to the set 'b,' the container.

Objects will be indicated by non-self-intersecting arcs in the plane, and a given object may correspond to a multiplicity of arcs, which will be labeled with a label corresponding to the object, whereby membership is indicated by the diagram below:[20]

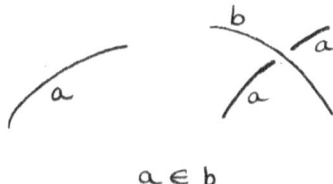

a ∈ b

Here we see that 'a belongs to b.' The arc 'b' is unbroken, while 'a' labels two arcs that meet on opposite sides of 'b,' which represents the fact that 'a passes under b' according to the convention of illustrating one arc passing behind another arc by putting a break in the arc that passes behind. This pictorial convention is important for the logic and the relationship with three-dimensional space.[21]

Kauffman shows this with the example of von Neumann construction of sets of arbitrary finite cardinality that starts with an empty set Φ = { } and building a sequence of sets $X_n$ with $X_0$ = { }, $X_1$ = {{ }}, $X_2$ = {{ },{{ }}}. By using overcrossing convention for membership, one can draw a diagram of this construction.[22]

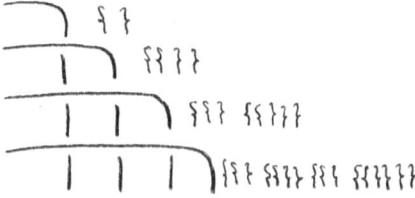

This can be applied to the Borromean rings. The three rings of the Borromean rings mutually belong together, and the crossings between the rings show their belongingness to each other. I marked the three crossings on the outer edge as 'o,' 'p,' 'q,' and the other three inside as 'r,' 's,' 't.' At the crossing 'o,' where ring A is placed under ring B, A belongs to B. At each crossing, there is a membership relationship.

The mutualities of the three rings at each crossing are as follows:

| Crossing | Belongingness |
|---|---|
| o | A ∈ B |
| p | B ∈ C |
| q | C ∈ A |
| r | A ∈ B |
| s | B ∈ C |
| t | C ∈ A |

The mutual membership relationship between different rings is, in principle, as shown below, for example, in the Borromean rings. It is simply the case that the Borromean rings consist of three rings instead of two; therefore, the mutual membership is created on six crossings instead of two.

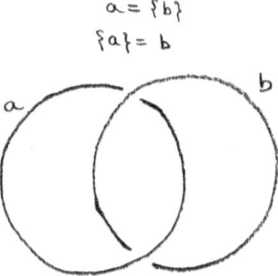

These sets are sets that are members of each other. But there are also sets that are members of themselves as well:[23]

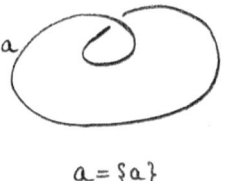

These diagrams indicate sets that may have a multiplicity of identical members:[24]

## Self-in-Relation and Pre-subjective We 113

$a = \{\ \}$
$b = \{a, a\}$

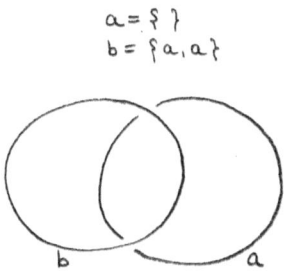

Instead of regarding the multiplicity of identical members as all equivalent to one another to condense them ({... a, a ...} = {... a ...}), Kauffman suggests another solution, in which identical members cancel in pair. Thus {... a, a ...} = {......}, which is {a, a} = { }. In diagram form, this appears like so:[25]

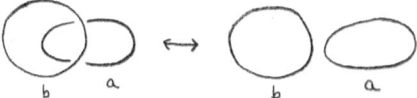

The rule of cancellation of identical members is fundamental to knot set theory, as in the second Reidemeister move:[26]

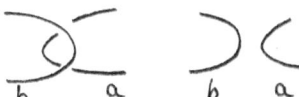

A knot consists of a single closed curve, a link may have many closed curves, and a tangle has arcs with free ends. Reidemeister proves that any knot or any link in three-dimensional space can be represented by a diagram containing only crossings of the type indicated as below.

The first Reidemeister move allows the creation or cancellation of self-membership in the corresponding knot set. But if the loop is a physical loop in a rope, "the cancellation of the loop in the first move must be paid for by a corresponding twist in the rope."[27]

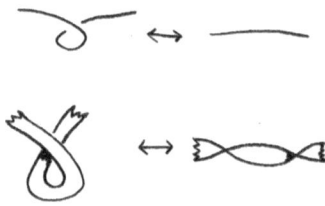

According to Kauffman, one can regard it as an *exchange* rather than an elimination or creation of the loop. If this is applied to the diagram that represents a twisted band, the self-membership is not lost as we move to the topology.[28] He claims that "*any knot set has a representative that is a member of itself, and the states of self-membership and non-self-membership are equivalent* [emphasis in original]"[29] Therefore, a radical knot set is a member of itself, if and only if it is not a member of itself.[30] This knot set gives us a way to conceptualize nonstandard sets without recourse to infinite regress through a twist in the boundary. The self-membering set is represented by a curl, where the observer on the curl itself goes from being a container to being a member (see chapter 6.2). This shows that membership becomes a *topological relationship*.[31] The same logic works in a Mobius band as well: A = −A.

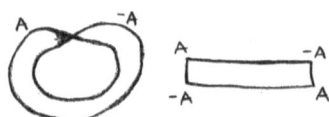

Kauffman shows that this self-membership solves Russell's paradox. Let R be the set that contains all the sets that do not include themselves. If R contains itself, R does not include itself, but if R does not include itself, R should be a member of itself. We can resolve this paradox in the domain by taking every set as a member of itself and not a member of itself.[32] One could regard this not as solving the paradoxical contradiction, but rather as resolving the contradiction.[33]

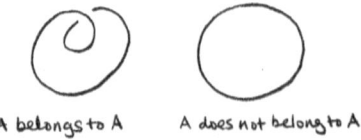

This notion of crossing is the core of understanding the mutual relation on a trefoil knot and the Borromean rings.

## 4. CROSSING AS RELATION AND THE BODILY IMAGINATION OF SPACE

We made a loop on this ring that created the distinction between inside and outside. This loop refers to relation itself. Through this loop, we have inside and outside on the same side.

If inside is self and outside is other, the distinction between and self and other is newly defined through the crossing. Self and other can be on the same side while still remaining distinct when they are in one consistent structure with a twist that differentiates and relates them. This presents the very structure of distinction and unity which signifies the relation between self and other. The reason that the primacy of the we-ness as the primitive one-ness (before distinction) should be rejected[34] is because we are embodied beings. There is an irreducible distinction between self and other.

I find Mark Wrathall's account on existential spatiality and the volatilized self, where he tries to go beyond the fixed form of embodiment that my self inhabits, quite plausible. Wrathall envisions the volatized self in the bending space in a gravitational field, where the self is not like an object in that space. It is diffused over and embodied in the whole spatial scene.[35] Regarding the unitary yet differentiated self and its fluidity in space, I can very much relate to Wrathall's analysis of volatized self. We are, however, still embodied in our own body—within this irreducible boundary of my skin. I am my body, and your body is you. My body is not really your body, even if I stand next to you and touch you. You are not inside me.

The irreducible distinction between self and other is, though, not the counterproof of the self in plurality. This pre-given, irreducible distinction points at the relation in which I am found as long as I exist. I can be in relation with the other, because the other is there. This is the primary ontological status which has to be epistemologically reflected on. The boundary making process reveals the distinction and the relation. This boundary making process is not prior to the ontological status of self-in-relation, but with a primary distinction as the starting point of understanding, the formation of the selfness begins. The distinction between inside and outside is ideational and epistemological, while the distinction between self and other is existential and phenomenological. The distinction between self and other is pre-given pre-subjectively and ontologically, but not pre-given subjectively.

However, in fact, I once was inside Thou. Everyone is once in the other in the beginning. Every single one of us was conceived in Thy body and had to be separated from the 'her,' the body of the mother—as Julia Iribarne expresses, "mother as primordial bodily one-ness."[36] Within the boundary of my skin, I perceive Thou within the boundary of Thy skin. However, not only was I once in Thou, but Thou is always in my body. Even *my* body is not really *my* body. Only 43 percent of the body's total cell count is composed of human cells, the rest are microscopic colonists.[37] These millions of tiny living organisms are not only simply there inside *my* body, but *they are my body and even my feelings*.[38] *They* make up *my* self. We are, indeed, self as we. Our being is fundamentally in relation—not only with other human beings, but all the other beings whether inside or outside of *my* boundary.

The distinction between inside and outside as self and other in imaginary space is a *bodily imagination*. If there is an observer that walks on this ring with one loop on it, the observer starts as the container (the set) and becomes the member of the set as it keeps walking, and in eventually moving on from being the member, the observer becomes the container. In other words, the observer is the observed and the observed is the observer, therefore, each one belongs to the other one, flipping constantly between the container and the member states. The observer who sees inside and outside of the twisted band *walks on the ring* to be able to see inside and outside. The metaphor of walking on a geometrical figure represents our bodily imagination of space.

Each time the one who walks on the ring walks over the crossing, the belongingness status changes. The position of the crossing is not fixed on a certain spot; instead it is here and there. Here becomes there and there becomes here constantly.

The pre-subjective bodily separation by the skin which has been always there as long as we remember—from the initial moment of consciousness—is always there in creating epistemological and existential distinction, that is, for the creation of self. Therefore, the pre-subjective self-in-relation can be differentiated from the primitive we-ness that is prior to any distinction. Yet this distinction in the pre-subjective bodily separation refers to a 'relational' one that resolves the paradox of difference and identity in oneself.

As mentioned at the beginning of this chapter, a primary relation refers to the ontological status of self-in-relation, while a primary distinction refers to the epistemological possibility of understanding. The understanding of a primary distinction means understanding how to understand, that is, understanding the principle of understanding. This understanding is theoretically prior to understanding any distinction, including the distinction between self and other. In order to understand the ontological status of the self as 'we,' we need to understand both a primary distinction and the distinction between self and other that is derived from the primary relation in which I am already placed.

In the self as 'we,' both the subjective and pre-subjective distinction exist in itself because of the ontological precondition that we *are already there* in relation and the epistemological capacity for being conscious of it. Self-in-relation is pre-subjective and reflective. Therefore, understanding the distinction in self-in-relation comes in a twofold structure: understanding (1) the distinction between the self and othered self (self-consciousness), and (2) the distinction between self and other.

I said that we need a third element between the two waveforms $a$ and $b$, the relation, for their unity. What is needed is a crossing between $a$ (I) and $b$ (not-I). This triadic structure has its distinction, unity, and relation in itself. Crossing represents the relation as both the pre-given ontological distinction and the epistemological distinction as boundary making. Self-in-relation is in the unity of this 'trinity' between I (inside), O (outside), and the crossing (relation).

The subjective (self-)consciousness that operates with the 'othered I' within itself, however, is not prior to the self-other distinction. The imagined alterity between the subjective I and the objectified I in the 'self as I' is not pre-given, and their presumed alterity could make this system fall into an infinite regress. But when the alterity is pre-given, it doesn't have to suffer from the defect of falling into infinite regress. The irreducible alterity between different rings that mutually belong to themselves on the Borromean rings represent the 'self as we' model.

## NOTES

1. Louis H. Kauffman, "Virtual Logic: The First Distinction," *Cybernetics and Human Knowing* 12, no. 4 (2005): 97–106.

2. Flagg resolution relates to the formation of waveform but I won't explain the Flagg resolution here. For detailed discussion on Flagg resolution see Louis H. Kauffman, "Time, Imaginary Value, Paradox, Sign and Space," *AIP Conference Proceedings* 627, no. 1 (August 20, 2002): 146.

3. George Spencer-Brown, *Laws of Form* (New York: The Julian Press, 1972).

4. Figures from Spencer-Brown and Kauffman.

5. See Louis H. Kauffman, "Sign and Space," in *Religious Experience and Scientific Paradigms. Proceedings of the 1982 IASWR Conference, Stony Brook* (New York: Institute of Advanced Study of World Religions, 1985), 151.

6. See Kim, "Music, Consciousness, and Knots"; Kim "Visualisation de la musique."

7. Kauffman, "Sign and Space," 151.

8. Pattern by Kauffman (Kauffman, "Sign and Space," 151–152).

9. Pattern by me.

10. Kauffman, "Sign and Space," 152.

11. Figure by Kauffman (Kauffman, "Sign and Space," 153).

12. Figure by Kauffman (Kauffman, "Sign and Space," 153).

13. J. S. Bach, *Well-Tempered Calvier, Prelude No. 2* (New York: G. Schirmer, 1893), https://www.free-scores.com/download-sheet-music.php?pdf=466.

14. See Kim, "Music, Consciousness, and Knots."

15. Louis H. Kauffman, "Knot Logic," in *Knots and Applications*, vol. 6, Series on Knots and Everything, ed. Louis Kauffman (Singapore: World Scientific, 1995), 1–110.

16. The discussion on knot logic is also in Hye Young Kim, "A Topological Analysis of Space-Time-Consciousness: Self, Self-Self, Self-Other," in *When Form Becomes Substance. Power of Gesture, Grammatical Intuition and Phenomenology of Space*, ed. Luciano Boi, Franck Jedrzejewski, and Carlos Lobo (Basel: Birkhäuser-Springer, forthcoming).

17. Kauffman, "Knot Logic."

18. Louis H. Kauffman, "Knot Logic: Logical Connection and Topological Connection," in *Mind in Mathematics: Essays on Cognition and Mathematical Method*, ed. M. Bockarova et al. (Munich: Lincom Europa, 2015), 33–57.

19. Kauffman, "Knot Logic: Logical Connection," 32.

20. Kauffman, "Knot Logic," 32–33.

21. Kauffman, "Knot Logic," 33.

22. Kauffman, "Knot Logic," 33.

23. Kauffman, "Knot Logic," 34.

24. Kauffman, "Knot Logic," 34.

25. Kauffman, "Knot Logic," 34–35.

26. Kauffman, "Knot Logic," 36.

27. Kauffman, "Knot Logic," 38.

28. Kauffman, "Knot Logic," 39.

29. Kauffman, "Knot Logic," 40.

30. Kauffman, "Knot Logic," 40.

31. Kauffman, "Knot Logic," 41.

32. Kauffman, "Knot Logic," 40.

33. "Resolving paradox" (comment from Atocha Aliseda, Professor of Philosophy at the Institute for Philosophical Research at UNAM, Mexico).

34. Brinck, Reddy, and Zahavi conclude that the I-Thou dyadic structure should be regarded as more primary than the primitive we-ness (Brinck et al., "The Primacy of the 'We'?").

35. Mark A. Wrathall, "'I' 'Here' and 'You' 'There': Heidegger on Existential Spatiality and the 'Volatilized' Self," *Yearbook for Eastern and Western Philosophy* 2017, no. 2 (2017): 234.

36. "Mutter als primordial körperliche Einheit" (my translation) (Julia V. Iribarne, *Husserls Theorie der Intersubjektivität* (Freiburg/München: Verlag Alber, 1994), 141; Edmund Husserl, *Zur Phänomenologie der Intersubjektivität. Texte aus dem Nachlass. Erster Teil: 1905–1920*, ed. Iso Kern, Husserliana 13 (Den Haag: Martinus Nijhoff, 1973), 595. I translated 'körperlich' as 'bodily' instead of 'corporeal' based on the distinction between 'Körper' and 'Leib' (Fuchs, "Zwischen Leib und Körper," 82). 'Körper' is the body that I can have and use, therefore, relates to the 'conscious I.' Irbarne's original text was written in Spanish and then translated into German, in which she did not write "Mutter als primordial leibliche Einheit," but 'körperlich.' I interpreted it as the 'unity' (Einheit) of the mother and the baby that does not refer to the primitive undifferentiated one-ness but to the unity that is based on the difference and identity. I thought that the expression 'bodily' carries this implication better than 'corporeal.'

37. James Gallagher, "More than Half Your Body is not Human," *BBC News Health*, April 10, 2018, https://www.bbc.com/news/health-43674270 (accessed April 22, 2020).

38. Ian Sample, "Gut Bacteria May Have Impact on Mental Health, Study Says," *Guardian*, February 4, 2019, https://www.theguardian.com/science/2019/feb/04/gut-bacteria-mental-health-depression-study (accessed April 22, 2020).

*Chapter 7*

# We in Diagrams

## 1. OUR HUSBAND IN DIAGRAMS

Now, let us examine 'our husband' and its relational structure in diagram form. Here we have three rings A, B, and C that represent each element of the we structure of 'our husband.'

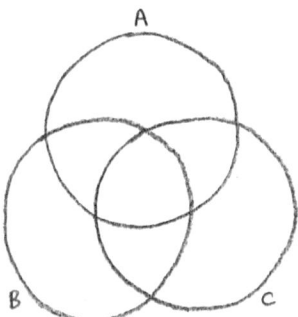

I suggest three different possible combinations of the elements A, B, and C. The first two models apply when 'our husband' is said in conversation.

1. Our husband
    A: I (self)—speaker
    B: husband (Stephen)
    C: father—listener

2. Our husband
    A: I (self)—speaker
    B: husband (Stephen)
    C: stranger—listener

The third possibility is when 'I' and 'husband' have the notion of we-ness through an action together. For example, we see the sunset (an object of a joint action) together.

3. Our husband
    A: I
    B: husband
    C: object

Now, let us start our examination with the first model. In this triadic structure of 'our husband,' there are also other possibilities of 'our someone' between these three people, and here we have a map of possible 'our someone' relationships.

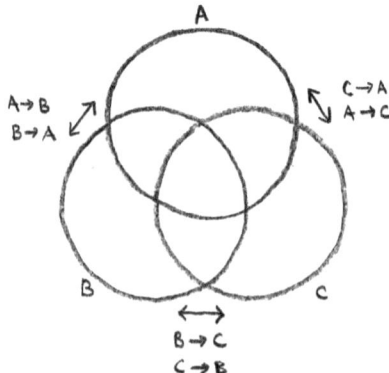

The arrows denote 'calling': 'A → B' means 'A calls B.'

$$A \to B / B \to A$$
$$B \to C / C \to B$$
$$C \to A / A \to C$$

A can call B 'our someone' and B also can for A. Therefore, the calling relationship is mutual. The double-ended arrow represents this mutuality.

Now, we see that there are three mutual relationships demonstrated through 'our someone' between A, B, and C, which I will name as α, β, and γ.

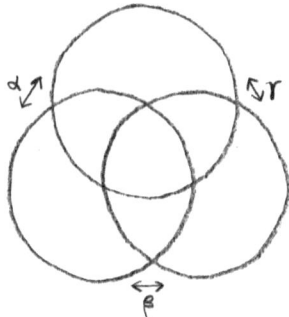

Let us see the examples of the 'our someone' for the first two cases. This is for the first model (I, husband, father).

A: I
B: husband (Stephen)
C: father

α   A → B    our husband/our Stephen (*A calls B our husband/our Stephen*)
     B → A    our wife
β   B → C    our father
     C → B    our Stephen/our son-in-law
γ   C → A    our daughter
     A → C    our father

When applied to the second model with a stranger instead of the father, we have this:

A: I
B: husband (Stephen)
C: stranger

α   A → B    our husband/our Stephen
     B → A    our wife
β   B → C    our teacher
     C → B    our Stephen
            our son-in-law (said to his father-in-law)
            our husband (said to his wife)
γ   C → A    our teacher
            our daughter (said to her father)
     A → C    our teacher

There are more variations of 'our someone,' but I did not include all of them. Here, do all three form the 'we' together, or, in other words, belong together? It seems so. This was the most significant point of the *ouri* in Korean. No matter who you are, whether related or not, whether present or not, we are all "one big happy family."[1] As mentioned briefly above, I am not quite sure about the 'happy' part, which I would like to talk more about in the end of this book. However, it does indeed show that everyone is, or can be, included in *ouri*.

This one big family represents the *web*, where all are/can be *ouri* someone: the *web* of relation. However, the 'we' here is not necessarily an *active* 'we' as a co-subject that acts on a certain thing with collective or joint intentionality. This we-ness is a latent we-state.

In this regard, the subjectivity, whether I know that I am, whether 'I' and the 'other' are the 'we,' and whether I am either pre-reflectively aware of it or reflectively conscious of it, does not have much significance. Therefore, in this particular context, it is pointless to insist on primacy of any kind, such as whether the 'we' comes first or the 'I' comes first.

## 2. OUR HUSBAND IN KNOTS

Now, I would like to apply the knot logic that I have discussed in the previous chapter to these three rings. For the membership logic of the knot set theory, we need crossings. We already have a brilliant way of making crossings on these three rings mutually related: the Borromean rings.

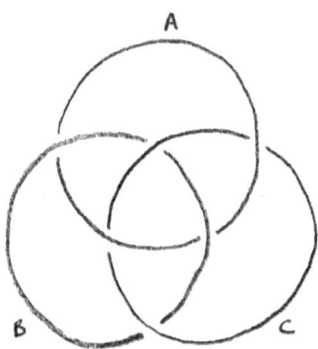

There are six crossings o, p, q, r, s, and t on these rings.

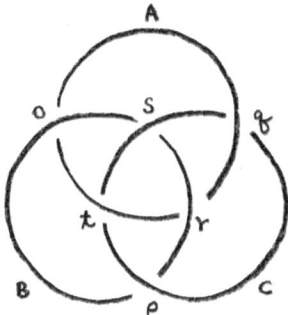

And there is a membership relationship at each crossing as follows:

| | | |
|---|---|---|
| o | A ∈ B | A belongs to B |
| p | B ∈ C | B belongs to C |
| q | C ∈ A | C belongs to A |
| r | A ∈ B | A belongs to B |
| s | B ∈ C | B belongs to C |
| t | C ∈ A | C belongs to A |

I will replace the expression 'belong to' with 'be in relation with' and apply this to the members of the 'we.'

| | | | |
|---|---|---|---|
| α | A ∈ B | o, r | I am in relation with Stephen (Stephen is in relation with me) |
| β | B ∈ C | p, s | Stephen is in relation with the father (The father is in relation with Stephen) |
| γ | C ∈ A | q, t | The father is in relation with me (I am in relation with the father) |

On each crossing the three rings meet and separate; in other words, they disconnect and unite, mutually belonging to each other. Therefore, a crossing represents where a person finds oneself in relation with another. At the same time, for that person to be able to be in relation, the person has to be an individual (not isolated) entity (each ring). Here, 'individual' does not connote the social, existential, or legal significance of a socially existing person as a contemplating subject. Rather, it simply refers to the singularity of a person.

When each A, B, and C represents each individual person, the rings in the Borromean rings show that the three are mutually interrelated. Not only in a dyadic structure between 'I' and 'Thou,' but multiple people including a third party can be mutually related all at the same time.

126                     *Chapter 7*

Self as 'we' as in 'our husband' in the structure of the Borromean rings resolves the paradox of the self-representation of self-consciousness with its trefoil knotted inner structure. I see this as a trefoil knot nestled in the center of the Borromean model on a two-dimensional plane.

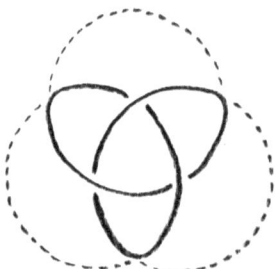

A trefoil knot is the simplest example of a nontrivial knot, which means that it is not possible to untie this knot in three dimensions without cutting it. It is one seamless line, that is, one ring.

I will name each arc of the knot as a, b, and c.

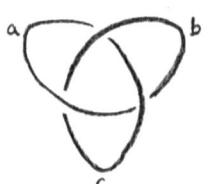

Each arc represents each person of the conversation, because each arc of this trefoil knot represents each ring of the Borromean rings.

a: I
b: husband (Stephen)
c: father (or stranger)

There are three crossings on this knot. These three crossings were marked as r, s, t on the Borromean rings.

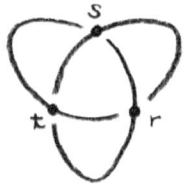

Kauffman indicates the interrelationship of the parts of the trefoil knot by describing the situation at each crossing as follows:

In this figure, c is obtained by crossing b from a. This can be described as

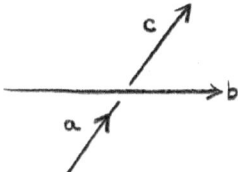

follows:

c = a ▶ b

This description is self-referential, which means that each term is defined via the other terms. This self-referential linguistic form is a description of the trefoil knot that defines the circularly interconnected spatial form.[2]

On each crossing, we have the following relationship according to Kauffman's knot logic.[3]

s   a = c ▶ b   a is obtained by crossing b from c
r   b = a ▶ c   b is obtained by crossing c from a
t   c = b ▶ a   c is obtained by crossing a from b

A trefoil knot (T) has three arcs (a, b, c) that are the parts of an identical knot, therefore the different arcs a, b, and c belong to one seamless ring: a, b, and c are identical.

This trefoil knot was nestled in the center of the Borromean rings, which is composed of three different rings interconnected. Each arc a, b, and c of this trefoil knot (T) consists of a part of each ring A, B, and C.

$$
\begin{array}{lll}
s & a = c \blacktriangleright b & B \in C \\
r & b = a \blacktriangleright c & A \in B \\
t & c = b \blacktriangleright a & C \in A
\end{array}
$$

Therefore, the arcs a, b, and c belong to one identical trefoil knot (T) and to three different rings A, B, and C, at the same time. The trefoil knot (T) belongs to the Borromean rings (A, B, C). Therefore, these arcs are same, yet different. The self-referential description through the three arcs of a trefoil knot represents the differentiation within its identical self (T). The alterity of these arcs can be obtained by the crossing rule (linking as mutuality, see chapter 6) on one identical ring, but when this knot is placed in the heart of the Borromean rings, the alterity of these arcs is given by the distinct rings.

Self as subject has the alterity of the othered self in itself through the objectification of the self.[4] The trefoil knot inside the Borromean rings represents self as 'we' that is interrelated with others in itself: self as 'we' is self-in-relation. The identity of self as an individual is embodied in the unity of a trefoil knot. The interrelatedness of self and other in the trefoil knot in the Borromean rings represents the *web*. Self is never an isolated sole entity, but is always in relation. Self is in other, other is in self: self is not solely self and other is not solely other. The knotted situation of the knot-I redefines the paradox of not-I.

The trefoil knot model represents another relational structure of 'our husband,' which is when 'our husband' is uttered or thought to oneself. I can think to myself 'what is our husband doing now?' or utter it in a monologue to myself. In this situation the listener is not another person but myself.

a: I (speaker)
b: husband
c: I (listener)

Here, 'I' as the listener is an 'othered I.' Thus we have the following:

a: I
b: other
c: othered I

As mentioned above, the arcs a, b, and c belong to a trefoil knot, which implies that not only 'I' and the 'othered I' but the 'other' also belong to this identical self-referential structure. The 'our husband' structure in the form of a trefoil knot in a monologue situation represents the self as 'we.' Perhaps, I imagine, some more plausible models for the self-as-we structure could be three trefoil knots interconnected in the Borromean structure or the Newton fractal[5] in three colors that extends infinitely within the triadic structure.

The listener of 'our husband' could be the husband himself as well.

a: I (speaker)
b: husband
c: husband (listener)

The husband (b) in 'our husband' is the othered self of the husband (c), the listener.

However, in all possible situations of saying 'our husband,' it should be assumed that 'I' is always also one of the listeners. Therefore, it should be as follows:

a: I (speaker)
b: husband
c: father, stranger, husband, I (listener)

The othered self situation is always present but also always with the other (b).

There is another triadic model in which the third person also functions as the third eye that recognizes the dyadic 'we' within triadic interactions. The triadic models that I suggest so far here with three people are different from this triad, because the third person in '*ouri* someone' models is not external to this we group. The third person in this we group is not really the third eye who is a member of another we group outside of the spoken we group. As we have examined above, if the use of '*ouri* someone' is interpreted in the framework of inclusive and exclusive we, this model of a triad with a dyad inside might fit the '*ouri* someone' as an exclusive we inside the three-person interaction.

However, the problem of applying this model to '*ouri* someone' lies in that the we group of '*ouri* someone' is not based on shared or joint action but based on an uttered we-ness. When '*ouri* someone' is clearly used as an exclusive we, the speaker cannot be the third person who is excluded from this we group. The third person outside of this we group, who recognizes the we-ness of '*ouri* someone' to which she herself does not belong, is the listener. In this case, '*ouri* someone' said to the third person is not triadic, because the listener as the external person is not included within the we-ness of '*ouri* someone.' Rather, it is 'dyad + one person,' or "triangular," as postulated by Fivaz-Depeursinge, Favez, and Frascarolo. They refer to the three-person interaction where the interaction is not only "3 together" but also the three different "2 + 1s" as "triangular."[6]

Another triadic model is the model with two people and an object. The two-person-involved triadic structure is different from the three-person triadic interactions mentioned above. It comes with an object involved that is mutually perceived by the two agents. This is the third triadic model that I suggested.

## 3. TRIAD OF SELF-OTHER-THING

The third triadic structure has a different character than the former ones, because the third element is not a person who can be both subject and object, but it is a thing that can only be an object. This object is an object of joint action or shared attention.

This is the relationship map in the case where the ring C is an object, not a person, as in the third model.

| | | | |
|---|---|---|---|
| α | $A \in B$ | o, r | I am in relation with Stephen |
| | | | (Stephen is in relation with me) |
| β | $B \in C$ | p, s | Stephen is in relation with an object |
| | | | (The object is in relation with Stephen) |
| γ | $C \in A$ | q, t | The object is in relation with me |
| | | | (I am in relation with the object) |

The object is relation both with Stephen and me. The object is there, revealed to the subject. The mutual intentionality for this object by 'Stephen' and 'I' is there.

In effect, a perceptual object has its significant place in intersubjective relation. An object that is perceivable is intrinsically intersubjective, because this object that is perceivable for me is also perceivable for others. In other words, the perceptual objects are there not only for me, but for others. As Merleau-Ponty delineates, they are intersubjectively accessible.[7]

When there is an object that is shared or at least potentially sharable with the others, those others are there not only as objects of my subjective perception, but they can be a part of my experience as other subjects who can also perceive this object that commonly appears both to me and others. In this case, the other as co-subjects co-constitutes the experience of the object. This co-subjectivity is present on this level even before a concrete empathetic encounter with another subject.

In such a situation where there is a commonly perceived object by more than one agent, Brinck distinguishes two types of sharing of attentional objects between different agents. Individual sharing consists of one person's reacting to the other person's attention, whether it be continuous or not, so that the both have the same attentional target. In this case, only one person is paying attention to the other person's attention. Mutual sharing, on the other hand, consists of two people attending to the same target and both attending to each other's attention to the target.[8]

As Falck points out, sharing of an attentional object implies causal links between attentional processes of the two agents, but for qualifying the sharing of attention, awareness of these links is not necessary.[9] He claims that the focus of the question in the studies of social interaction has moved on from a focus on the distinction between self and other to a focus on "what is shared and what is not shared." Most everyday interactions involve objects, or in the case of a conversation, the topic of the conversation to which the participants of the interaction pay their attention.

There are times when we are required to explicitly reflect on the distinction between self and other, but it is not a prerequisite for interacting, according to Falck, and is instead typically for correcting any disfluency or misunderstanding in the interactive process. Mostly, when we interact with others, we focus much more on the task at hand than the other. He concludes that the concepts of self and other emerge in our individual minds as a consequence of a social process.[10] This view, concluded from experiments in the domain of psychology, seems to provide positive empirical support for my notion of pre-subjective we that is copresent with the intersubjective we.

Although 'our someone' is possible between two agents when that someone is the listener or the speaker herself is the listener,[11] this triadic model with a shared object has a gray area for the case of '*ouri* someone,' because the mutual relationship in 'our someone' does not necessarily require a shared object of their joint action. But I find this model more useful for another phenomenon of the 'we' that I am going to deal with in chapter 9, section 2 on mutual knowledge.

## 4. PRIMARY RELATION IN PRE-SUBJECTIVE SELF

We can also have another triadic model for 'our someone' inside of the Borromean rings that represents three people in dialogue or two in monologue. At each crossing of knots, two members meet, that is, it's dyadic, but the structure of the whole thing itself is triadic that opens up room for the third party to enter. This third person is the listener from the speaker's perspective and husband from the listener's perspective. Or the third element could be interpreted as the relation itself that bonds the different individuals.

To sum up: the individuality of self and other and their relation are there necessarily together. The boundary is there, and the boundary forming process is crucial. What is primary is not the undifferentiated state, but a primary relation which can be reflected on spatially that differentiates inside from outside. These two sides are identical and different, just like the two (but one) sides on a Mobius band. The primary boundary making is the process to find self-in-relation and create relation. Relation is possible only because I am already there with the other. It is in the same way that the crossing creates separation and connection. The ontologically pre-given condition of the self-in-relation is reflected on and understood as the self as 'we.' Self as 'we' can't alone be understood in the self as 'I' system where the self as subject reflects on itself by objectifying itself, because the system of the self as subject does not have room in itself for the other who is ontologically pre-given in our being-in-relation. Pre-subjective understanding of self is understanding a primary relation of the self-in-relation and to acknowledge the pre-subjective state is to acknowledge the boundary forming process from which distinction and relation originate.

## NOTES

1. Harris, *Roadmap to Korean*, 121.
2. Kauffman, "Sign and Space," 161.
3. Kauffman, "Sign and Space," 161.

4. This model can be applied to the study of structure of consciousness and self-consciousness which I show in Hye Young Kim, "Knots and Consciousness: Knotted Models Applied to Uriah Kriegel's 'Consciousness, Permanent Self-Awareness, and Higher-Order Monitoring,'" (*4th Meeting of the CHAIN Structures of Consciousness*, Sep 2019, Sapporo, Japan. hal-02290606f: https://hal.archives-ouvertes.fr/hal-022 90606), a response to Kriegel's 'Consciousness.' In his paper, Kriegel shows that permanent self-awareness accompanies every conscious state. I present this model of consciousness in a trefoil knot form, so that we can have the inner structure of self between the observing and the observed self within the consciousness model. I attempt to prove that the paradox of self-representation of the permanent self-awareness model can be resolved through the knot logic of mutual membership.

5. https://commons.wikimedia.org/wiki/File:Newton_fractal.png.

6. Elisabeth Fivaz-Depeursinge et al., "Threesome Intersubjectivity in Infancy," in *The Structure and Development of Self-Consciousness: Interdisciplinary Perspectives*, ed. Dan Zahavi, Thor Grünbaum, and Josef Parnas, vol. 59 (Amsterdam: John Benjamins Publishing, 2004), 221–34.

7. Maurice Merleau-Ponty, *Signs*, trans. R. C. McCleary (Evanston, IL: Northwestern University Press, 1964), 23, 215, quoted in Zahavi, *Subjectivity and Selfhood*, 167; Edmund Husserl, *Die Krisis der Europäischen Wissenschaften und die Transzendentale Phänomenologie. Eine Einleitung in die Phänomenologische Philosophie* (Den Haag: Martinus Nijhoff, 1954) 468.

8. Ingar Brinck, "Attention and the Evolution of Intentional Communication," *Pragmatics & Cognition* 9, no. 2 (2001): 259–277, quoted in Andreas Falck, "From Interest Contagion to Perspective Sharing: How Social Attention Affects Children's Performance in False-Belief Tasks" (PhD Thesis, Department of Psychology, Lund University, 2016), 22.

9. Falck, "From Interest Contagion to Perspective Sharing," 23.

10. Falck, "The Social Emergence of Subjectivity," not published, with permission of the author.

11. The coagents of a joint action can be more than two people who mutually interact with each other, and multiple variations of the self-other dyad combinations are possible between more than two people as coagents.

*Chapter 8*

# Primacy of We?

This *web* of relation on the knot represents the pre-subjective self, which is self-in-relation rather than self as a subject. It is not to deny the self as a subject, but it is another variation of understanding self. Self as a subject is a self that stands in contrast to an object—on the self-reflective (or self-aware without reflection yet) epistemological level, knowing that *I* am *I*. But I don't always have to be conscious of the fact that *I* am *I* to find *myself* in relation, just as *I* can have the notion of *myself* without having the primary notion of the 'we.'

The expression 'pre-subjective we' can give an impression that it implies the primacy of the relation in the sense of the primitive we-notion that precedes the distinction between 'I' and 'Thou.' But I see the self-in-relation as pre-subjective we as different from the primary notion of the 'we' that is already internally in our head. The singularity of the self is never denied, but this singularity of self is not based on the subject-object distinction. In other words, the self does not have to objectify itself and others to obtain and maintain individuality as a single entity. The fact that the self is in relation is a strong enough condition for the self also to be able to be differentiated from the other and relate to the other. But, at the same time, the self is never out of the scope or, rather, the web of relation with the other as long as it is there (whether realizing so or not). Therefore, there is neither primacy of the singularity of the 'self' nor the plurality of the 'we.'

To further avoid confusion, I would like to take some examples with a related account on this issue and compare them with the pre-subjective we. In this regard, I will briefly discuss the following accounts: identity as community by von Foerster; collective intentionality by Searle; plural self-awareness by Schmid; Zahavi's critique on fundamental anonymity; crowd by Le Bon, Freud, Sartre, and Canetti; *das Man* by Heidegger; plural subjectivity by Carr;

and ἄλλος αὐτός and alter ego. Finally, I will compare my pre-subjective we to Bornemarks's a-subjectivity.

## 1. IDENTITY AS COMMUNITY

In his essay "On Constructing a Reality," the mathematician Heinz von Foerster suggests that the relation between 'I' and 'Thou' should be the central reference for constructing a reality instead of a solipsistic or relativistic view. He claims that in the solipsistic view, where the world is only in my imagination and the only reality is the imagining I, things get complicated if there are two organisms.[1] Imagine there is a boy with curly hair. Inside his head, there are other boys, a boy with a baseball cap, a boy with a skateboard, and so on and so forth. Inside the head of the boy with a baseball cap, again there are other people, a woman in a book, a boy dressed like a tree, a man with mustache, and so on.[2]

This curly haired boy insists that he is the sole reality, while everything appears only in his imagination. However, as von Foerster argues, this boy cannot deny that his imaginary universe is populated with apparitions that are unlike himself. Therefore, he has to admit that these apparitions may insist that they are the sole reality. In this case, their imaginary universe will be populated with only apparitions, one of which may be he himself.[3]

Von Foerster argues that the solipsistic claim falls apart when *I* invent another autonomous organism, according to the principle of relativity, which rejects a hypothesis when it does not hold for two instances together, even if it holds for each instance separately.[4] However, it is crucial that the principle of relativity is neither a logical necessity nor a proposition that can be proven to be true or false, and therefore, as he points out, one can either reject it or adopt it. If I reject it, I am the sole reality of the universe; if I adopt it, neither one of us can be the 'I' of the reality. In this context, von Foerster suggests the relation between 'I' and 'Thou' as the identity. He concludes, therefore, that reality is community.[5]

## 2. BRAIN IN A VAT

This situation is comparable to the argument of the brain in a vat by Searle.[6] According to Searle, "The brain is all we have for the purpose of representing the world to ourselves and everything we can use must be inside the brain."[7] Therefore, he argues that each of our beliefs must be possible for a being as a brain in a vat, our skull as the vat and the messages coming in by way of impacts on the nervous system.[8] Thus, all the intentionality, both individual and collective, is in the head of individuals. This means that collective intentionality is already and necessarily in the head of a single individual, even as a brain in a vat.[9]

The only option for the brain in a vat to escape this solipsism is to adopt the principle of relativity, because the brain in a vat cannot have a reality as community, because the notion of community inside the brain is primitive; in other words, it is there before the actual relation between 'I' and 'Thou,' because a brain in a vat simply cannot actually have a *real* relationship.

But at the same time, the relation between 'I' and 'Thou' as the central reference for constructing a reality on an epistemological level is still under the auspices of brain activity. The reality that I construct within my head, whether it is constructed as a community or as my sole reality, is the reality that I construct. The 'Thou' in this constructed relation is the boy with a baseball cap in the world inside the head of the boy with curly hair. Even if the boy with a baseball cap is another autonomous organism outside of me, and the boy with curly hair believes that the boy with a baseball cap is another reality and that there is a relation between him and the boy with a baseball cap, still the reality of the other boy is his belief in his head, and so is the relation that the curly haired boy created in his head. Even the I-Thou relation is trapped in the brain.

## 3. PRE-REFLECTIVE PLURAL SELF-AWARENESS

The we-ness as discussed by Hans Bernhard Schmid is not detached from embodied experiences. He talks about the "sense of us."[10] The 'we' as the "sense of us" precedes the distinction between 'I' and 'Thou.' This sense comes before your sense or my sense. It is our sense that is prior to any form of intersubjectivity or mutual recognition.[11] Schmid takes the cases of shared experiences, where the experience is neither really mine nor yours but ours, as examples that show that the subjective aspect of shared experiences is not singular but plural.[12] Schmid insists on the primacy of this plural self-awareness.

In my article "A Phenomenological Approach to the Korean 'We,'" I had the same, or at least, very similar perspective as Schmid. Toward the beginning of my investigation on the we-ness based on *ouri* in Korean, I thought that the we-ness in 'our someone' in Korean could reveal the primitive we-ness that precedes the 'I' and 'Thou.'[13] It was because I believed that the solipsism of the 'I' as the self-representing consciousness could be overcome by turning to the state of the primitive, original one-ness that is before the distinction between individuals. However, this view had a critical problem, namely that it draws too much attention to the question of the primacy of the 'we' over the individuality of each self, so that one might think that the individuality of each person and their relationship with the other individuals is underestimated, or even devalued.

In fact, Schmid speaks of the 'we' as "minds-in-relation" rather than an undifferentiated unity that involves a plurality instead of a larger scale 'I.'[14] But in the light that he argues that plural self-awareness precedes singular self-awareness,[15] that is, that there is primacy on one side instead of the other, this claim seems to mislead our discussion. What I question basically is why it isn't enough to have not only the we-ness as a collection of subjects but also the we-ness as a plural self-awareness, or pre-subjective self-relation. I don't see the point of turning our discussion into a chicken-or-the-egg-first framework. Another problem of laying the focus on the question of primacy is that this framework could give a false impression that one thing that is a priori is there at one point, but is not there anymore as the other thing is brought out. In other words, it could appear as if they were incompatible, so that we have to choose either this or that.

## 4. UNDIFFERENTIATED ANONYMITY

Zahavi warns against the threat of radical anonymity. I agree with Zahavi's account in which he insists that the fundamental anonymity prior to any distinction between self and other does not solve the problem of intersubjectivity but "dissolves it."[16] On the level of radical anonymity there is neither individuation nor selfhood. It is the state where there is no differentiation and no alterity, therefore, consequently, according to Zahavi, having no room at all for subjectivity or intersubjectivity.[17]

My first impression of *ouri* in Korean was close to the idea that the difference between self and other is a derived difference out of a common and shared, undifferentiated, anonymous life. However, the open door of *ouri* into which anybody can enter is not quite like going into a black hole where everything is sucked up and dissolved with no distinction, no order, and no structure. It is not to be *lost* in the *they*, the "undifferentiated anonymity with its latent solipsism."[18] The undifferentiated anonymity is a void where no discernment, no cognition, and no understanding is possible, therefore, not only selfhood but also relation is impossible. Rather, the *space* of *ouri* is the space of a web that consists of crossings and links.

This map of a knotted web is a bodily imagination of the connective space of self-in-relation. The countless crossings and links are to be cognized and reflected; however, they are latent relations before being *seen*.

## 5. CROWD

In reality, undifferentiated anonymity seems to appear in a crowd, where there is no individual but only collective mind. In *Psychologie des Foules*, Le Bon expounds upon the loss of self in the crowd, where individuals become anonymous and *unconsciously* follow ideas and contagious emotions neither pondering upon them nor understanding them.[19] Freud also talks about the crowd in *Massenpsychologie und Ich-Analyse* in terms of human libido driven toward a goal. Individuals unconsciously identify with other individuals in the crowd who share the same relationship to a common goal.[20] In *Critique of Dialectical Reason*, Jean-Paul Sartre speaks of the "seriality" of the crowd, by which he means "the dissolution of the series in the group-in-fusion."[21] In this state, collective feelings are fused into collective action with a distinct goal. The crowd is the collective body of collective action for collective intentionality, the shared goal. Carr also mentions the crowd in "'... so etwas wie Leiblichkeit': On Social Embodiment"[22] as the embodiment of collective acts toward a goal. In this sense, the collective action of the crowd is not only intentional but also teleological. Carr emphasizes that this goal is not mentally envisaged but incorporated in bodily movements.[23]

They commonly point at the characteristic of the crowd that is driven by a common objective.

In *Crowds and Power*, Elias Canetti differentiates the open crowd from the closed crowd. Canetti illustrates the crowd as a "mysterious and universal phenomenon" that comes about suddenly where there was nothing before.[24] In the extreme form of the spontaneous crowd, where people gathered "streaming from all sides" and formed a crowd, Canetti describes that "most of them do not know what has happened and, if questioned, have no answer; but they hurry to be there where most other people are."[25] Canetti also talks about the goal of the movements of the people, "the blackest spot where most people are gathered."[26] Apart from a few who initiated the crowd, everyone else is spontaneous and it urges growth with more and more people. An open crowd is open to everywhere, like a house with no doors, locks, and walls, as Canetti describes, and it exists until it stops growing, while the closed crowd focuses on permanence rather than unlimited growth, so it comes with boundaries, that is, limitations. Canetti compares it to a vessel into which liquid is being poured and whose capacity is known. It is exclusive, meaning that those who stand outside do not belong to this group, yet it maintains.[27] The closest example for the closed crowd could be found in a unit of soldiers in battle. In the following description from *The Warriors: Reflections on Men in Battle* by Jesse Glenn Gray, he describes some experiences of soldiers where the individual self is dissolved in the collective state of being:

> Many veterans who are honest with themselves will admit, I believe, that the experience of communal effort in battle, even under the altered conditions of modern war, has been the high point of their lives. [. . .] With the boundaries of the self expanded, they sense a kinship never known before. Their 'I' passes insensibly into a 'we,' 'my' becomes 'our,' and individual fate loses its central importance. [. . .] I believe that it is nothing less than the assurance of immortality that makes self-sacrifice at these moments so relatively easy. [. . .] I may fall, but I do not die, for that which is real in me goes forward and lives on in the comrades for whom I gave up my life.[28]

This testimony reflects what Le Bon said about heroism in the crowd, whereby individuals sacrifice their personal interests for the collective interest, and even face death for their beliefs, ideas, and ideologies.

Whether in the open crowd that is eager to expand infinitely absorbing everyone available or in the closed crowd that is controlled and selects its members, in both types of crowd, a reflecting, conscious, individual self disappears. However, it may not only be in particular situations with specific political circumstances that we dwell in the midst of an anonymous state with the others. In *Being and Time*, Heidegger delineates *das Man*, the anonymous third in which we are normally fallen and lost.

## 6. *DAS MAN* IN *BEING AND TIME*

We are, as human Dasein, absorbed in the world where we are proximately *das Man*, that is, 'they,'[29] for the most part and remain so[30] in our everydayness. Heidegger writes, *"jeder ist der Andere und Keiner ist er selber."* Everyone is the other, and no one is himself. The 'they,' which supplies the answer to the question of the 'who' of everyday Dasein, is the 'nobody' to whom every Dasein has already surrendered itself in Being-among-one-another.[31] According to Heidegger, while we are "lost in the they"[32] in our everyday life, the 'they' distracts us from standing by 'myself,' and we fail to hear our own voice. Being the 'they' among and with the other, we lose our self. The 'they,' therefore, is everyone, including 'myself,' but not necessarily 'myself.'

Paradoxically, because Heidegger's analysis of the other and being with the other in *Being and Time* does not give a fully clear account to understand what exactly the other[33] is to Dasein and how Dasein relates with the other, this vagueness of the other, who is not 'myself' as the unknown they, but also with whom Dasein is together in its everydayness, gives us a clue to understand what we would mean by saying 'one,' 'they,' *'man,' 'on,'* or 'we.'

In this state of being in the 'they,' in other words, in the we-ness, the self is lost. But even if we are lost in the midst of *das Man*, each Dasein exists as Dasein. We don't think about our death each and every day, every single moment, day and night, but that does not mean that we do not think about it at all.[34] It is not the question of whether or not. The two modes of understanding, i.e. the two modes of existing, are necessary for Dasein. Dasein as Being-in-the-world is in the world with others, as long as it exists. As long as it exists, however, it exists as an understanding self. In the context of *Being and Time*, this unreflective state is named as an inauthentic way of being, but the inauthentic way of being does neither indicate a negative, nor secondary, nor immoral way of being, rather it is as crucial as the authentic way of being. Both ways of being, when the self is lost in the 'they' ('we') and when the self is found, are fundamental to our 'self-understanding.' In *das Man*, the self is lost, but not absolutely. One can always call oneself back to oneself.

The moment that 'my' father, 'my' husband, and a stranger can be 'we' along with 'me' simply by 'being there' might be projecting this situation of 'everybody but nobody, nobody but anybody' where I don't and do belong at the same time. This might give a clue to understand the not uncommon convention of cross-using 'we,' 'you,' 'they,' and 'one' in multiple languages.

The we-ness represented here does not require any social engagement, but social interaction doesn't necessarily always mean social engagement. As experiments in cognitive sciences show, our perception is always social, and the scope of interaction goes beyond actual exchanging of contact or language.[35] For example, another person's presence, even one who is not proactively interacting with me, changes my own perception and alters my peripersonal space and the direction and the sphere of my activity.[36]

The we-ness expressed in Korean used between socially unrelated people highlights this side of the we-mode, namely that the we-mode is not what we gain as a result of the conscious pursuing of a cooperation or what individuals gather and build for a certain, common purpose, but what we are already thrown in, or what is installed in the system of our cognition that is not in any way reducible or subordinate to the I-ness. This does not mean, however, that all the cases of using 'we' always represent this mode of we-ness. There are cases where the 'we' is used as a group that is formed by individuals through their proactive and engaged actions.

Subjective perception is always intersubjective, and any intersubjective perception is necessarily accompanied with self-perception. Subjective self-perception is always grounded in one's interactive perception of the world in which one is placed, and also with one's own-othered self, through which one can come to have an awareness of the self. This is because one should be able to be aware that one is there, and this awareness is based on 'observing' one's being there. This shows the inevitable connection between subjective and intersubjective perception. In fact, it is not a brand-new argument that self-consciousness and the consciousness of others are inseparable in philosophy. Brentano and Husserl talk about this too.[37] The analogy of the bagpipe sound by Kriegel, for example, that is intentionally directed both to the bagpipe and itself, articulates that our awareness of others (objects) is always combined with our awareness of the self.[38] Husserl held the view that the personal 'I' has its origin in social life: "Personality is constituted only as the subject enters into social relations with others."[39] In this context, the 'I' is understood in a relative relation to the other, namely, the 'Thou' and the 'we,' in which the ego as a person "requires relation to a world which engages it. Therefore, I, we and the world belong together."[40] This ascribes a relative mode of being to the personal 'I.'[41] The 'we' that individuals build through social engagement is, however, a different dimension, in the sense that there are two different we-modes: one is the we-mode that is not reducible and postulated in our cognition, and the other is the we-mode that individuals form together.

Self as pre-subjective we does not—and should not—lose its individuality and personality as a whole person in the midst of a blind we-ness as anonymous whole. The notion of irreducible we-ness is not incompatible with a conscious and autonomous self. In fact, as I mentioned at the end of chapter

5, it is crucial to keep one's individuality with a conscious understanding of self in the heart of being connected to the other selves. When one loses oneself in an anonymous 'they,' one is no longer capable of being aware of one's fundamental-ontological state, that is, pre-subjective relation, which leads one to misunderstanding and misusing of the concept of being 'we' against the other, and eventually, oneself. Unfortunately, Heidegger himself showed us a miserable example of *mis*understanding of we-ness. The following is part of the open letter written by Heidegger to the students of the University of Freiburg on November 3, 1933, published on *Freiburger Studentenzeitung*:

> German Students! The National-Socialist revolution brings the full upheaval of *our* German *Dasein*. . . . The *Führer* himself and alone is the German reality and its law of today and tomorrow. Learn always deeply to know: from now on, every situation will require determination (*Entscheidung*) and every action (*Tun*) responsibility (*Verantwortung*). Heil Hitler. Martin Heidegger, Rektor.[42] (Emphasis mine)

It is a tragic irony that *Dasein* that is supposed to be *dasjenige Seiende, dem es in seinem Sein um sein Sein selbst geht* (the very entity, to whom it is about its own being itself in its being)[43] and understand its existential responsibility (*Verantwortung*) of its own being is called to lose oneself in *our Dasein* of the German nation to stand against the other and take over the responsibility that comes down from the *Führer*. This could be, in a way, considered as his personal failure as an educator,[44] but I see this as a representative example that shows the danger and toxicity of the distorted notion of we-ness that is blind both to the fundamental (pre-subjective) connectedness of our being with others and the infrangible individuality of our being within each person.

## 7. WE AS PLURAL SUBJECT

As Schmid describes, discussions about collective subjectivity have always been, however, haunted by "the specter of the group mind."[45] Modern philosophy has largely framed the problem of intersubjectivity, or alterity, in terms of the face-to-face encounter, in which the other stands over against me, in the form of I-Thou, which is due to its origins in describing a first-person *singular* experience. I am on the same page with Carr as he argues that a different way in which we relate in we-experience deserves our attention. The focus of the we-experience for Carr lies in the social activity by a collection of persons in which the members of this group do not stand in a subject-object relation. Instead each person relates to another participant in the shared experience or activity which to them is 'ours.'[46]

Carr regards the community as *"primarily* or *essentially* an intentional subject."[47] [emphases in original] Shared experiences and activities are crucial for the 'we' as plural subject to be constituted. In and through a series of experiences and actions, a plural subject is constituted by way of a reflective, narrative account of that series.[48] He says that one of the primary ways we relate to others is the participation in shared experiences and activity of the group through a membership.[49] Collective intentionality is usually referred to as we-intentionality, and the question is whether we can attribute intentionality not only to individuals but also to communities or groups of individuals.[50] If there are situations where a collective action cannot be reduced to a mere collection of individual actions, asks Carr, "then to what, exactly, are we attributing this action?"[51]

According to Carr, the we-subject as the primary form of intersubjectivity has its reality in the social experience of individuals that constitute the we-subject by identifying with it, and with the thoughts, actions, and other intentional functions they perform. This primary form of intersubjectivity is different from a face-to-face relation.[52] Among intentional experiences, there are shared emotions such as grief, outrage, and joy,[53] and the subject of these emotions is more than a collection of individuals. Carr argues, "It would be philosophically blind, or perhaps metaphysically dogmatic, to impute these emotions merely to a collection of single individuals."[54] He compares this to the metaphor of the body politic by Hobbes, where, as he puts it, "a multitude of men, are made one person, when they are by one man, or one person, represented; so that it be done with the consent of every one of that multitude in particular."[55]

In effect, the plural subject is much discussed in terms of we-agency in joint action. In joint action, at least two individuals share their attention or emotions. One of the core debates around we-agency relates to the status of self in we-agency, unlike in the case of the crowd where there is a consensual understanding that the self is lost. For example, Elisabeth Pacherie suggests a notion of "one-ness" of we-agency, which refers to the state where the boundary between self and other is blurred.[56] Pacherie quotes William McNeill's experience of "boundary loss" and "feeling they are one" during his participation in traditional communal dance and military drill: "a blurring of self-awareness and the heightening of fellow-feeling with all who share in the dance. It matches my own recollection of what close-order drill felt like."[57]

Salmela and Nagatsu, on the contrary, lay emphasis on the plurality of subjects in we-agency, that is, "a strong sense of self-other interdependence in action." They claim that "an awareness of us doing something together conceptually presupposes the awareness of self-agency."[58] The plurality of subjects, however, means more than an aggregation of individuals. There has to be a sense of we-agency such as "sharing the same fate" or "being in the same boat"⁵⁹ which is experienced through shared emotions "that accompany joint action and rationally relate to its joint goals." These emotions are to be differentiated from the emotions in the crowd that are contagious; the shared emotions in the joint action express the commitment of the individuals to the joint goal and their mutual dependence on each other.⁶⁰ Pre-subjective self-in-relation is an ontological premise of the sense of self-other interdependence in the joint action of a plural subject with a collective intentionality.

## 8. ἌΛΛΟΣ ΑΥΤΟΣ

The situation where the difference between self and other disappears does not only indicate the state of undifferentiated anonymity. There are times when there is a difference between self and other where their absolute difference disappears. Husserl talks about the situation where the other conceives of me as other just as I conceive of him as other.⁶¹ He, who is other to me, is self to himself. This moment is verbally realized when the word 'self' in Korean, *jagi*, is used to refer to the other, either the second or the third person, as well as the speaker herself. Each person is self to him or herself. This is the situation in which I observe myself under the picture of the other's observation of me. I am other to the other, and the other is self to themselves. The other, therefore, is another self, but not myself: alter ego.⁶² The distinction between self and the foreign 'I' (other) vanishes.⁶³

The undifferentiated self and other are often discussed in psychological and philosophical research in child development and pregnancy. In "The Other as Alter Ego,"⁶⁴ for example, Gail Soffer claims that at a very early stage of development, the other is "an emotive being in that it is associated with the emotive states produced in the infant by reaction and contagion." In this context, the other is not yet differentiated from the self, even if it still is the other. I have shown already that the crossing on a knot realizes this phenomenon, where self and other belong together but are separated, through visualization.

When self is 'we,' though, other is self, not only to themselves but to *myself* as well: *my* other self. In *Nicomachean Ethics*, Aristotle writes that a friend is to be regarded as ἄλλος αὐτός.⁶⁵ The literal translation into English would be 'another self.' A friend is another individual (the other), and yet *my* another self. Obviously friends whom *I* can take as *my* another self are hard to come by, and not all of our fellow human beings can be *my* friends for whom *I* can even sacrifice *my* life. However, the expression ἄλλος αὐτός illuminates the profound relation of *myself* to others. Even if it is only latent now, we all have the potential to become friends with others. Friendship does not only indicate a new relationship between people who did not know each other before. But between family members as well, friendship is an important element that binds them together. Friendship is, in fact, hard to define, but it is something that is constituted between self and other in our manner of relating to one another. The description of friendship as ἄλλος αὐτός could be read as a way of understanding our self-in-relation to others, not as an expression of exclusive devotion and loyalty to another person, but as an expression of our fundamental self-in-relation with the others, self as 'we.'

## 9. PRE-SUBJECTIVE AS A-SUBJECTIVE?

Pre-subjective is not a-subjective. The pre-subjective is not a state that comes before reflection or after reflection, before distinction or after distinction. Instead 'pre' here is used to mean 'other' or 'other than,' hence, other than the system of subjectivity. It does not mean that it denies or annuls the system of subjectivity or subjective thinking, but subjectivity doesn't have to be *the* way, the only way of understanding self. I am not calling here for a paradigm change in which language has primacy instead of subjectivity or vice versa. Subjectivity, or the basic structure of understanding self as subject, is rooted in the language that is constructed and evolved around the subject-object structure, but there are languages without this exact structure, so it is rather a call for a paradigm change in accepting diversity: the diversity of language and the diversity of perspectives.

Jonna Bornemark deals with presubjectivity and a-subjectivity in her phenomenological research on pregnancy,[66] where she points out very well the problem we have with subjectivity. She writes,

> Since Descartes, making subjectivity the starting point is supposed to be a safe haven, but one does not need to be a psychoanalyst to acknowledge that we do not know ourselves and that subjectivity is not fully transparent to itself.[67]

Thus, she attempts to investigate the limit between experiences of an already constituted subject and a-subjectivity through an analysis of the phenomena of pregnancy.[68]

Bornemark contrasts subjectivity with presubjectivity, the description of which I sympathize with. She refers to the process of subjectivity as "a closing up and an increasing fixation into one bodily perspective."[69] While the process of subjectivity radicalizes the other's alterity, presubjectivity blunts the boundaries involving the "experience of communicating vessels."[70] She insists that subjectivity and intersubjectivity emerge from presubjectivity,[71] and therefore a separation occurs between different independent entities: the sensing and the sensed ones.[72]

In this context, she regards the pre-subjective state as a-subjective, before the division between subject and object. A-subjectivity comes before self-consciousness and reflection.[73] However, she declares that presubjectivity proceeds to subjectivity, and a-subjectivity is always there in the background of subjectivity. By a-subjective life, she means an anonymous experience, and she shares her personal experience of a-subjective life:

> Once I have been so deeply under the power of a-subjective life, I realize how it is always present, how life is continually reshaped. I also realize that my subjectivity, what I understand as myself, owes everything to form-taking, a-subjective life. I am part of this a-subjective, form-taking system, partially reflecting it in a system of knowledge. Coming back from this experience I return to a 'myself,' I find again the limits and protect them in order to protect this 'us' without a strict separation between 'you' and 'me.'[74]

In this regard, she claims that we need to see the intertwinement of subjectivity and a-subjectivity.[75]

Her personal testimony is a powerful installation that supports her argument on the presence of a-subjective life, and I find it a convincing example of my theory of pre-subjective we. She distinguishes presubjectivity from a-subjectivity in the sense that she attaches presubjectivity to the fetus state and confers a-subjectivity on a pregnant woman within her already constituted subjectivity.[76] Presubjectivity is a-subjective in the sense that there is no division of subject and object yet, but presubjectivity literally means *pre*, that is, before-subjectivity, while a-subjectivity does not have the connotation of priority or posteriority of the order of the subjectivity formation. Therefore, according to the use of terminologies by Bornemark, presubjectivity cannot coexist with subjectivity due to its necessary temporal priority, while a-subjectivity and subjectivity are copresent and intertwined. In this context, the pre-subjective state refers only to the stage of development within the limited period of time in the past when we were still a fetus or a newborn. However, in my context, this *pre* does not refer to *the* beginning of my life and subjectivity but rather to the a-subjective state that is present with the subjective state. It does not necessarily indicate the temporal or chronological priority, but rather the state that is beyond the subject-object division. Temporally it could be prior, but it could be simultaneous as well with the subjective state; in other words, it does not go away afterward.

There are two problems of using the term a-subjectivity in my context instead of presubjectivity. First, I reckon that the prefix *a-* could give a strong first impression that my thesis insists on the absence of subjectivity in the we-ness at all, or that the we-ness that is discussed in this context is anti-subjectivity that denies the discussion of subjectivity at all. Second, when presubjectivity is used only to refer to the early stage of development before subjectivity is formed at all, subjectivity is regarded as being posterior in development. This could be the case, but that is neither what I would like to argue nor prove in my discussion. We can talk about a pre-subjective state before we formed subjectivity and became conscious in the very early years of our being, but none of us who are now writing, reading, and discussing are in the intrauterine or infant stage. The time of the development from pre-subjective to subjective state has already passed. The question of the beginning of my subjectivity, how everything began, has its significance only within the realm of the present. In clinical psychology, for example, the query and the interpretation of one's very first memory is not focused on whether the first memory really is the very first memory for the person, but it is important that the person believes that it is her first memory, because the focus is not on the beginning of her memory, but on the significance of the memory that she believes to be the first memory has on her current psychological state. Pre-subjective we-ness that I deal with here refers to the we-ness that we experience, conceive of, and understand for the present where we are now.

## NOTES

1. Heinz von Foerster, *Understanding Understanding: Essays on Cybernetics and Cognition* (New York: Springer, 2007), 226.
2. Von Foerster explains this with an image of a man with a bowler hat drawn by Gordon Pask. See von Foerster, *Understanding Understanding*, 226.
3. Von Foerster, *Understanding Understanding*, 226.
4. Von Foerster, *Understanding Understanding*, 226.
5. Von Foerster, *Understanding Understanding*, 226.
6. John Searle, *Intentionality: An Essay in the Philosophy of Mind* (Cambridge: Cambridge University Press, 1983).
7. Searle, *Intentionality*, 230.
8. Searle, *Intentionality*, 230.
9. Pacherie claims though that all the intentionality that is there can be in the head of individuals is one thing and that collective intentionality could be had by a single individual is another thing (Elisabeth Pacherie, "Is Collective Intentionality Really Primitive?" in *Explaining the Mental: Naturalist and Non-Naturalist Approaches to Mental Acts and Processes*, ed. Carlo Penco, Michael Beaney, and Massimiliano Vignolo [Newcastle: Cambridge Scholars Publishing, 2007], 162).
10. Hans Bernhard Schmid, *Wir-Intentionalität. Kritik des Ontologischen Individualismus und Rekonstruktion der Gemeinschaft* (Freiburg: Karl Alber, 2005), quoted in Brinck et al., "The Primacy of the 'We'?."

11. Schmid, *Wir-Intentionalität*, 138, 145, 149, 296, quoted in Brinck et al., "The Primacy of the 'We'?," 132.

12. Schmid, "Plural Self-Awareness," 9, quoted in Brinck et al., "The Primacy of the 'We'?," 132.

13. Kim, "A Phenomenological Approach to the Korean 'We.'"

14. Hans Bernhard Schmid, *Plural Action: Essays in Philosophy and Social Science* (Basel: Netherlands, 2009), 156, quoted in Brinck et al., "The Primacy of the 'We'?," 133.

15. Schmid, "Plural Self-Awareness," 23.

16. Zahavi, *Subjectivity*, 52.

17. Zahavi, *Subjectivity*, 52.

18. Zahavi, *Subjectivity*, 52.

19. Gustave Le Bon, *Psychologie des Foules* (Paris: F. Alcan, 1900).

20. Sigmund Freud, *Massenpsychologie und Ich-Analyse* (Leipzig, Wien, Zürich: Internationaler Psychoanalytischer Verlag, 1923).

21. Jean-Paul Sartre, *Critique de la Raison Dialectique: Tome I, Théorie Des Ensembles Pratiques* (Paris: Gallimard, 1960), 391, quoted in David Carr, "Intersubjectivity and Embodiment," in *Husserl's Phenomenology of Intersubjectivity: Historical Interpretations and Contemporary Applications*, ed. Frode Kjosavik, Christian Beyer, and Christel Fricke, Routledge Research in Phenomenology (Taylor & Francis, Berlin, Germany, 2018), 258.

22. David Carr, "'. . . so Etwas Wie Leiblichkeit': On Social Embodiment." *Yearbook for Eastern and Western Philosophy* 2017, no. 2 (2017): 91–103.

23. Carr, "Intersubjectivity and Embodiment," 258.

24. Elias Canetti, *Crowds and Power* (London: Macmillan, 1984), 16.

25. Canetti, *Crowds and Power*, 16.

26. Canetti, *Crowds and Power*, 16.

27. Canetti, *Crowds and Power*, 17.

28. Jesse Glenn Gray, *The Warriors: Reflections on Men in Battle* (Lincoln: University of Nebraska Press, 1999), 44–46.

29. The use of *man* in German is similar to 'one' in English and *on* in French. But, while *man* in German is the third-person singular, *on* in French refers to both the third-person singular and to the first-person plural, 'we.'

30. Heidegger, *Sein und Zeit*, 168.

31. Heidegger, *Sein und Zeit*, 165–166.

32. Heidegger, *Sein und Zeit*, 175.

33. The contemporary others. The others from the past and their relation with *Dasein* are dealt with in his analysis of tradition and historicity.

34. Kim, *Sorge und Geschichte*.

35. Gallotti and Frith, "Social Cognition in the We-Mode."

36. Gallotti and Frith, "Social Cognition in the We-Mode," 4.

37. Brentano Franz, *Psychology from an Empirical Standpoint*, ed. Linda McAlister, trans. D. B. Terrell, Linda McAlister, and Antos Rancurello (London: Routledge & Kegan Paul, 1973); Husserl, *Die Krisis*, 256; Uriah Kriegel, "Consciousness, Permanent Self-Awareness, and Higher-Order Monitoring," *Dialogue* 41, no. 3 (2002): 517–40.

38. Kriegel, *Subjective Consciousness*, 14.
39. Husserl, *Intersubjektivität. Erster Teil*, 175.
40. Husserl, *Ideen*, 319.
41. Husserl, *Ideen*, 288.
42. Bernd Martin, *Heidegger und das Dritte Reich* (Darmstadt 1989), 177, quoted in Wilhelm Schmidt-Biggemann, *Geschichte als absoluter Begriff* (Frankfurt am Main: Suhrkamp, 1991), 79 (my translation).
43. Heidegger, *Sein und Zeit*, 12 (my translation).
44. Schmidt-Biggemann, *Geschichte als absoluter Begriff*, 76–81.
45. Schmid, *Plural Action*, 32, quoted in Carr, "Intersubjectivity and Embodiment," 252. In this context, Carr points out that Hegel invented the extreme form of the idea of we-intentionality, *Geist* in the *Phenomenology of Spirit*, introducing it as the central character of the protagonist, calling it "an I that is We, a We that is I" (G. W. F. Hegel, *Phänomenologie des Geistes* [Hamburg: Felix Meiner, 1952], 40, quoted in Carr, "Intersubjectivity and Embodiment"). Here he develops a very subtle account of how the spirit (the we-subject) grows out of subjective and intersubjective experience and interaction. This notion, however, goes beyond the lives of the individuals but also "can lead not just to windy pop-philosophy and culture-speak, but also to some dangerous politics" (Carr, "Intersubjectivity and Embodiment," 252). Not only Hegel, but also the philosophers who talk about collective intentionality, according to Schmid, "think that the idea of a non-individual mind is so terribly and obviously mistaken, that there is no need for further argument," quoting Searle as denouncing such "perfectly dreadful metaphysical excrescences" (Schmid, *Plural Action*, 24 and note, quoted in Carr, "Intersubjectivity and Embodiment," 254).
46. Carr, "Intersubjectivity and Embodiment," 252.
47. Carr, "Cogitamus Ergo Sumus," 530.
48. Carr, "Cogitamus Ergo Sumus," 532.
49. Carr, "Intersubjectivity and Embodiment," 252.
50. Carr, "Intersubjectivity and Embodiment," 251.
51. Carr, "Intersubjectivity and Embodiment," 252.
52. Carr, "Intersubjectivity and Embodiment," 255.
53. Carr, "Intersubjectivity and Embodiment," 257.
54. Carr, "Intersubjectivity and Embodiment," 258.
55. Thomas Hobbes, *Leviathan* (Oxford University Press, 1996), I.16.13, quoted in Carr, "Intersubjectivity and Embodiment," 255.
56. Elisabeth Pacherie, "How Does It Feel to Act Together?" *Phenomenology and the Cognitive Sciences* 13, no. 1 (March 1, 2014), 25–46.
57. William H. McNeill, *Keeping Together in Time: Dance and Drill in Human History* (Harvard University Press, 1997), 8; Pacherie, "How Does It Feel to Act Together?" 40.
58. Mikko Salmela and Michiru Nagatsu, "How Does It Really Feel to Act Together? Shared Emotions and the Phenomenology of We-Agency," *Phenomenology and the Cognitive Sciences* 16, no. 3 (July 1, 2017): 455.
59. Raimo Tuomela, *The Philosophy of Sociality: The Shared Point of View* (Oxford University Press, 2007).

60. Salmela and Nagatsu, "How Does It Really Feel to Act Together?," 467. But they also acknowledge the distinctiveness and social relevance of the sense of unity where the boundary between self and other is not clear and deal with this as an empirical question which depends on the kind of joint actions. They see that in the case of ritualistic joint actions without proximate purpose beyond the activity, for example, the experience of boundary loss is more prevalent, but in the context of purposive joint action, experience of interdependent cooperation is more significant (Salmela and Nagatsu, "How Does It Really Feel to Act Together?," 455).

61. Edmund, *Intersubjektivität. Erster Teil*, 243.

62. Zahavi, *Subjectivity and Selfhood*, 173.

63. In "Selbst und Person der Gemeinschaft" (Husserl, *Intersubjektivität. Erster Teil*, 243–244), Husserl wrote, "es verschwindet der Unterschied zwischen Selbst und fremdem Ich, der Andere fasst mich als Fremden auf, wie ich ihn als für mich Fremden auffasse, er ist sich selbst ein 'Selbst'" (Husserl, *Intersubjektivität. Erster Teil*, 243).

64. Gail Soffer, "The Other as Alter Ego: A Genetic Approach," *Husserl Studies* 15, no. 3 (October 1, 1998): 154, quoted in Jonna Bornemark, "Life beyond Individuality: A-Subjective Experience in Pregnancy," in *Phenomenology of Pregnancy*, ed. Jonna Bornemark and Nicholas Smith (Stockholm: Södertörns högskola, 2016), 264–265.

65. Aristotle, *Nicomachean Ethics*, trans. H. Rackham, 1166a30 (Boston: Harvard University Press, 1926).

66. Bornemark, "Life Beyond Individuality."

67. Bornemark, "Life Beyond Individuality," 252.

68. Bornemark, "Life Beyond Individuality," 253.

69. Bornemark, "Life Beyond Individuality," 265.

70. Bornemark, "Life Beyond Individuality," 265.

71. Bornemark, "Life Beyond Individuality," 266.

72. Bornemark, "Life Beyond Individuality," 277.

73. Bornemark, "Life Beyond Individuality," 272.

74. Bornemark, "Life Beyond Individuality," 268.

75. Bornemark, "Life Beyond Individuality," 278.

76. Bornemark, "Life Beyond Individuality," 251.

*Chapter 9*

# Notion of Relation

### 1. I-YOU AND I-IT BY BUBER

The self-in-relation as pre-subjective we points out the plain old fact that we live in the world. This was pointed out numerous times by previous thinkers; however, as soon as the self relates to the world as a subject, the world is objectified, and this objectifying creates distance between 'I' and the world. This distance-making is different from the process of making the primary distinction, the distinction between inside and outside, where inside is outside and outside is inside at the same time. Subject is neither an object nor can an object be a subject at the same time, even if they are necessarily attached to each other.

The objectifying of the subject does not really refer to the I-Thou relation but the I-It relation following the discussion of I-Thou by Martin Buber.[1] I-It represents the subject-object relation of the self as subject. In contrast to I-It, I-Thou recognizes and builds the relation. The 'I,' in the Buberian sense of I-Thou, needs to do more than conducting a reflection as an intentional act, observing and perceiving. *I* need to say Thou. For Buber, the two primary words are the combined words I-Thou and I-It.[2] He calls the 'It' the eternal chrysalis, and the 'Thou' the eternal butterfly.[3] When *I* say Thou, the word clings to the threshold of speech, and the relation is open in the form of speech, in which 'I' can give and accept the 'Thou.'[4] I see this as a relation-making process, which is differentiated from objectifying.

The 'Thou' in this context should be differentiated from the 'Thou' in I-Thou as subject-object relation. It was *Du* in the original text in German, which already has a quite different connotation than Thou in English. From the contextual sense, Buber has the existence of the eternal Thou in mind, *Du* with the capital D, but the usual translation of *du* into English is 'you.' When

*Ich-Du* is said in German, the first impression that one gets is not what the English word 'Thou' signifies (if one is not yet familiar with the conventional translation of I-Thou). *Du* is a daily word that literally means 'you,' something that one says all the time, unlike 'Thou' in modern English, which you hear now mostly only in religious situations. In this regard as well, it seems more suitable to refer to Buber's *Ich-Du* as I-You in this context, so that it is also distinguishable from the regular I-Thou with its signification of the subject-object difference within the words.

On the contrary, when I say 'It' as is implied in the utterance of the sentence "I see the tree," it no longer speaks of a relation between 'I' and the 'tree' as I-You, but it establishes the perception of the tree as an object of human consciousness, Buber says, where the barrier between subject and object has been set up. The primary word I-It, the word of separation, has been spoken.[5] The primary word I-It can never be spoken with the whole being, but when the other primary word I-You is spoken, there is not a thing, but the speaker takes his stand in relation.[6]

Even with a tree though, according to Buber, 'I' can become bound up in relation to it instead of taking it as 'It.'[7] As Buber writes, relation is mutual. The tree is not only an impression in my head as a play of my imagination. It is bodied over against me and has something to do with me, as 'I' do with 'It,' only in a different way than with fellow human beings.[8] Human beings are, on the other hand, neither 'he' nor 'she,' bound in a specific point in space and time.[9] Buber refers to the dimension of space and time where he and she are bound as the "net of world" (Weltnetz), which, though, should be read differently than the *web* that I refer to in this context. The *web* I refer to is the *web* of relation which is flexible and changing between self and other, not the net of time and space of the world.

The man whom 'I' call 'You' is not an object of experience, but 'I' take my stand in relation to him. Relation to 'You' is direct, and it means being capable of calling the other 'You' (*Dusagenkönnen*).[10] The act of calling is not solely related to the act of calling the other 'You.' 'I' have to call myself 'I' to be able to be 'I.' In the beginning is the relation through which 'I' becomes 'I.'[11] Buber quotes a mythical saying of the Jews: "In the mother's body man knows the universe, in birth he forgets it."[12] Within the streaming of mutual life of the universe (*Allgegenseitigkeit*)[13] we live our lives, and the inborn 'You' is realized in its lived relations with those whom it meets.[14] In the poem, "Flower," by Chunsu Kim, the act of calling the other's name transforms the anonymous third-person 'he' into a flower, a gaze between 'you' and 'I.'

"when I called his (*geu-ui*) name,
He (*geu*) came to me,
and became a flower."[15]

The anonymous 'he' is written as *geu*[16] in Korean. I will discuss this word in detail in chapter 11, section 5. The word *geu* could be both the third-person singular pronoun 'he' and a demonstrative pronoun. In this context, *geu* sounds more like 'he,' but it could also be *geu* as a demonstrative pronoun that refers to the third-person who is not present or excluded from the scene or the conversation. Thus, *geu* person does not belong to the 'we.'

I have mentioned already that pre-subjective does not mean a-subjective, just as I-You and I-It go together, as Buber elaborates. They are the two primaries. We can take others, our fellow human beings in I-It relation as well, and we often, or always, do. The pre-subjective and intersubjective relation of the I-You and the subject-object relation of the I-It together form the we-ness, and the sense of *ouri* reveals the pre-subjective I-You relation in its everyday uses.

It is ironic, though, that in Korean, in everyday conversation, when you call someone 'you,' it immediately creates distance between the speaker and the listener and separates the other person from the relation. I have explained the significance of the second-person pronoun in Korean and shown some examples in chapter 3, section 2. Instead, in Korean, when you want to address the other person while also expressing your close feelings toward that person, you call this person 'self,' *jagi*. Or you don't call the other person anything. One often tries to avoid calling the listener in any form, because calling the other person will make both the speaker and the listener feel uncomfortably self-conscious of their own individual being, like an enlarged ego.

This does not, however, oppose the act of calling by Buber, because calling *Du* (you) is not an actual calling of the other person who stands in front of you, but this represents the relation-making process, or the realization (*Verwirklichung*) of relation.

The emphasis of the I-You structure by Buber lies not in 'You' but in relation. The gaze between two entities is the *calling* without voice. The act of calling 'you' by 'I' is naming the relation, through which the relation itself is (re-)created. The you in Buber's I-You is *ouri* in process, in which the self finds itself in relation. Therefore, the I-You structure is 'I-You-Relation,' which points at self-in-relation in the triad between 'I,' 'You,' and the relation between the two.

## 2. MUTUAL KNOWLEDGE: RELATIONAL ANALYSIS

Mutual knowledge refers to the fact that I know that you know that I know. In other words, there is an object of knowledge. Therefore, structurally it is always triadic: the fourth triadic model between two persons and a thing. The core of mutual knowledge is found in conversation, and reflection is the necessary condition for conversation. However, in the end of the discussion, we will see that the fundamental possibility of this intersubjective interaction lies in the primitive notion of relation which underlies the presubjectivity of the self-in-relation.

Mutual knowledge is common in our daily life. In our daily conversation, we often habitually say, "you know," before saying what we really need to say. It is not an unusual phenomenon, but we never know when this everlasting repetition of 'I know that you know that I know . . .' could—or should—end. Michael Wilby asks, how is mutual knowledge possible for cognitively limited human beings despite its infinite regress? This is the problem of how to characterize mutual knowledge without being committed to an infinite regression of mental states.[17] Wilby argues that mutual knowledge can be identified with a finite base, and in fact, it is a very simple thing.[18] First, I would like to follow how he outlines Stephen Schiffer's iterative approach to mutual knowledge.

Let's say that there is a speaker ($S$) and an audience ($A$), and they mutually know that $p$. Then we have the following:

(1) $S$ knows that $p$ / $A$ knows that $p$
(2) $S$ knows that $A$ knows that $p$ / $A$ knows that $S$ knows that $p$
(3) $S$ knows that $A$ knows that $S$ knows that $p$ / $A$ knows that $S$ knows that $A$ knows that $p$

   . . .

And this could go on ad infinitum. Schiffer suggests that we suppose that $S$ is $F$, and $F$ signifies the property of being a 'normal' conscious individual who is identical with $S$. By 'normal,' Schiffer means normal "regarding sensory faculties, reasoning capacities, etc."[19] And $A$ is $G$. $G$ is the property of being a 'normal' conscious individual who is identical with $A$. Then Schiffer proposes the following that, he insists, provides the necessary and sufficient conditions for the iteration.

"$S$ and $A$ mutually know that $p$ if there are properties $F$ and $G$ such that:

(1) $S$ is $F$
(2) $A$ is $G$
(3) Both being $F$ and being $G$ are sufficient for knowing that $p$, that $S$ is $F$, and that $A$ is $G$; i.e. $(x) (Fx \vee Gx \rightarrow Kxp \& KxFS \& KxGA)$.
(4) For any proposition $q$, if both being $F$ and $G$ are sufficient for knowing that $q$, then both being $F$ and being $G$ are sufficient for knowing that both being $F$ and being $G$ are sufficient for knowing that $q$; i.e. $(q) ((x) (Fx \vee Gx \rightarrow Kxq) \rightarrow (y) (Fy \vee Gy \rightarrow Ky(z) (Fz \rightarrow Kzq) \& Ky(w) (Gw \rightarrow Kwq))$."[20]

One of the crucial problems of Schiffer's account, as Wilby points out, refers to the fact that the property of being a normal person as "a visibly normal open-eyed, conscious person"[21] is not only underspecified to have such a central role in this account, but it is also not doing any work in the analysis, because the property of being visibly normal "does not *ipso facto* entail mutual knowledge on any subject."[22] What is important and necessary is that we are meant to suppose that $F$ and $G$ are metaphysically distinct properties,[23] and a necessary connection between these two metaphysically distinct properties is required. Wilby insists that rather than registering a metaphysical identity between the properties, it would work better if we suppose that there is a single generating property that holds upon the two individuals in question.[24] So, he supposes that $S$ and $A$ mutually know that $p$ if there is a relational property $H$ true of $S$ and $A$. Then we have the following:

(1) $S$ and $A$ are $H$.
(2) Being $H$ is sufficient for knowing that $p$, and that $S$ and $A$ are $H$.
(3) For any proposition $q$, if being $H$ is sufficient for knowing that $q$, then being $H$ is sufficient for knowing that being $H$ is sufficient for knowing that $q$.

In the first step, there is a three-place relation between $A$, $S$, and the property $H$, hence $HAS$. Then, Wilby displays these three steps as follows:

(1) $HAS$
(2) $(x)(y)(Hxy \rightarrow Kxp\ \&\ Kyp\ \&\ KxHAS\ \&\ KyHAS)$
(3) $(q)((x)(y)(Hxy \rightarrow Kxq\ \&\ Kyq) \rightarrow (z)(w)(Hzw \rightarrow Kz(x*)(y*)\ (Hx*y* \rightarrow Kx*q\ \&\ Ky*q)\ \&\ Kw(x*)(y*)\ (Hx*y* \rightarrow Kx*q\ \&\ Ky*q)))$[25]

Let me explain this: to know that $p$ $(x)$ mutually, $S$ and $A$ need to be $H$, and when $S$ and $A$ are $H$, they know that they are $H$ $(y)$. Here, instead of two separate properties $Fx$ and $Gx$, we only have a joint property $Hxy$, which saves us the problem of finding a necessary connection between distinct properties. And by adding another level of knowing to the property $Hxy$, namely, knowing that $H$ is sufficient for knowing that being $H$ is sufficient $(z)$ for knowing that $q$ $(w)$, we have $Hx*y*$ that holds $S$ and $A$ together. Wilby claims, "understood in this way, mutual knowledge is irreducible to the individual cognitive states of the individuals in question; it is something that holds of $S$ and $A$ as a pair."[26]

In this regard, I see the possibility to represent this relation within the structure of connective space of the Borromean rings. There are four points of the Borromean structure in topological space, where the fourth point represents the connectivity of the three open points. The open points are separate, as the three separate rings A, B, C in the Borromean rings, but they are connected (one) in topological space.

point 1: $S$ knows that $p$ and $S$ is $H$.
point 2: $A$ knows that $p$ and $A$ is $H$.
point 3: Being $H$ is sufficient for knowing that $p$ and that $S$ and $A$ are $H$.
point 4: Being $H$ is sufficient for knowing that being $H$ is sufficient for knowing that $q$.

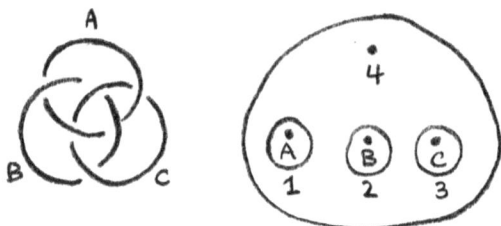

The fourth point comprises the topological boundary, the point of connection of the open points. What I would like to show, in relation to Wilby's formulation of mutual knowledge in which separate individuals stand in relation, is the necessary connection among the independent objects.

In this regard, Wilby introduces the reductive and relational analysis of joint attention by Campbell. In short, a reductive analysis does not presume a joint attention, while a relational analysis does.[27] The reformulation of Schiffer's analysis of mutual knowledge with another level of knowing, according to Wilby himself, is a relational one, because this account of mutual knowledge is "not reducible to what is known by either of the parties taken individually."[28]

This distinction between a relational and reductive analysis of mutual knowledge is relevant to our discussion of pre-subjective self as self-in-relation. The analysis of the pre-subjective self-in-relation is relational, because this state of self presumes *potential* joint attention. Wilby's description of mutual knowledge as a matter of the participants standing in a relation to each other as joint perceivers, namely, as co-subjects, rather than as objects of each other's perceptual knowledge,[29] brings us back to the question of our discussion of the 'we.' Here, it becomes clear again that the core problem of self and other lies in the problem of subject that always necessarily requires an object for reflection. Even the self-reflection of the subject is possible only when the self itself is objectified. Intersubjectivity is post-self-reflection and post-self-awareness, that is, it always stands in the structure of subject-object.

In attempts to overcome this fundamental problem of subject taking an object, Wilby talks about a "dual-subjective psychological state," which means that $S$-and-$A$ knows that $p$, where such a psychological state is not reducible or equivalent to $S$ knows that $p$ and $A$ knows that $p$. In this state of co-subjects, "the participants are in direct, unmediated cognitive contact with each other to the extent that they literally share the mental state of mutual knowledge,"[30] which could eventually lead also to a rationally coordinated action.[31] This sounds like the connected minds as expressed occasionally in daily language as 'great minds think alike.' It also seems to appeal to the notion of self as we or extended self.

Wilby clarifies that his proposal of '$x$ and $y$ mutually know that $p$' is "not to be understood as a simple conjunction of what two people know, but as a basic attitude that necessarily relates two subjects to a proposition or fact."[32] Here, mutual knowledge can be conceived of as "having not just a role to play in particular communicative and proto-communicative exchanges, but also as a driving principle behind a child's psychological development."[33] It is widely agreed in research on language development that children below the age of three are competent language users and communicators in the basic sense.[34] At this point, prominent accounts of language use and human communication face a dilemma,

> because it is assumed (a) that basic communicative situations essentially involve propositional attitude-like states of the participating agents and (b) that competent language users have the conceptual abilities to represent agents as being in such states and make folk-psychological inferences about agents so represented. These assumptions conflict with one or more robust findings in developmental psychology: that children below the age of four years do not yet possess these abilities.[35]

This implies that the young child's ability to exhibit a genuine understanding of others might require nothing more complex than "an ability to stand in an appropriately responsive relation to another."[36] From here we could assume that

> the older child's increasingly sophisticated ability to understand others—including their false beliefs—might well require not so much a 'conceptual revolution' in his understanding, but rather a honing of a skill that he has had since early infancy.[37]

If this is the case, Wilby claims, the idea of a primitive, relational notion of mutual knowledge would not be so mysterious.[38]

The point I emphasize here is that this primitive, relational notion of mutual knowledge does not disappear after the stage of early infancy. It continues to be there and function in our interaction with others even after we have developed sophisticated communicative skills. I focus on the fact that it is 'relationality' that necessarily comes with the individuality of different persons and the connection between them. Presubjectivity of self-in-relation does not deny the bodily individuality of each person. The boundary of *my* skin, that is, physical division from another, is there, even when we 'think' pre-subjectively, for example, when *I* am not aware of the other's presence in coordination in joint action or being present together. In relation, we are there together as one, but at the same time as each person.

Mutual knowledge is based on pre-subjective relation which is revealed in intersubjective interaction. The necessary interconnection of the intersubjective and pre-subjective we-notion is represented in the points that are open and closed in one structure, where the two selves connect and separate. These points represent the essence of relation. Self is in relation as a self that is different than the other but, at the same time, bound on the pre-subjective and the intersubjective level.

## 3. *GEOSIGI*: THE THING THAT YOU KNOW AND I KNOW AND I KNOW THAT YOU KNOW

*Geosigi*[39] [gaw-shee-kee] is a word that is used frequently in *Jeollado* [jaw-lado],[40] the southwest region of Korea, both as a noun and an adjective. This is a very common expression in this region, and a word which other native Korean speakers are also well aware of. This is a very oral and colloquial word. In an official context, or in documents or academic writings, this word would neither be spoken nor written. *Geosigi* refers to a thing, an object that two or more people know in common, which seems to reflect the triadic structure between subject-object-subject. This word expresses the state of mutual knowledge between speakers. In the following example, the *geosigi* that the speaker talks about is what the speaker and the listener both are believed to know, the thing that I know and you know and I know that you know.

(1) "Can I borrow *geosigi*?"
(2) "It is quite *geosigi* to hear that."
(3) "Isn't he *geosigi* from our last class?"

This word is used conveniently to indicate or refer to something that the speaker doesn't have the right word for, or can't think of the name of, or is inappropriate to say, or that the speaker simply doesn't feel like saying. It could be a thing or a replacement for a person's name. It also could be used as an adjective with an adjective ending. In (1), *geosigi* is used as a noun. The *geosigi* in (2) is used as an adjective. In (3), *geosigi* refers to the name of 'he' who is from their last class. Outside of the region where this word stems from, this word is often taken in a comical or embarrassing sense. But in this particular region, this word is used habitually to express one's feelings, opinions, thoughts, and to refer to basically anything.

What is interesting about this word is that this word can mean everything, and at the same time this word is said to let the hearer know that there is mutual knowledge between them. This is said not only between people who are related, but also complete strangers. So there are times the other has no idea, and there does not have to be a reason that they could have any mutual knowledge about anything, but it assumes that they share something, and sharing something already means that they are in relation. In English, it is similar to when we say "you know."

But there is no actual proof that both know what is being talked about, or if they are really thinking of the same thing. If a person from *Jeollado* is asked how they know what is being talked about, or whether the participants of the conversation are talking about the same thing, they would answer that they *just know*. It is the 'feeling' of knowing. These feelings, however, are not, in fact, ungraspable clouds that are floating in the air, but it is situated in concrete situations with context grounded in the awareness of the others who are there in relation: their situations, their needs, their feelings, and their backgrounds, and so on. This word is used under the precise reading of the situation, even if one is not conscious or self-conscious of this comprehension of the situation related with the others. That is how they can use the word *geosigi* without being confused. It is possible through the belief that there is mutual knowledge and that beliefs are contagious.

## NOTES

1. Martin Buber, *Ich und Du* (Stuttgart: Reclam, 1995).
2. Martin Buber, *I and Thou*, trans. Ronald Gregor Smith (Edinburgh: T. & T. Clark, 1937), 3.
3. Buber, *I and Thou*, 17.
4. Buber, *I and Thou*, 6.
5. Buber, *I and Thou*, 23.

6. Buber, *I and Thou*, 4.
7. Buber, *I and Thou*, 7.
8. Buber, *Ich und Du*, 8.
9. Buber, *Ich und Du*, 8.
10. Buber, *Ich und Du*, 17.
11. Buber, *I and Thou*, 18, 11.
12. Buber, *I and Thou*, 25.
13. Buber, *I and Thou*, 16.

14. Buber, *I and Thou*, 27. Even if we are born as a child in relation with 'You,' it is not there yet until we make an effort to establish the relation first. Buber writes,

> It is simply not the case that the child first perceives an object, then as it were, puts himself in relation with it. But the effort to establish relation comes first—the hand of the child arched out so that what is over against him may nestle under it; second is the actual relation, a saying of Thou without words, in the state preceding the word-form; the thing, like the I, is produced late, arising after the original experiences have been split under and the connected partners separated. In the beginning is relation—as category of being, readiness, grasping from, mould for the soul. It is the a priori of relation, the inborn Thou. (Buber, *I and Thou*, 27)

15. Chunsu Kim (1922–2004).
16. 그.
17. Michael Wilby, "The Simplicity of Mutual Knowledge," *Philosophical Explorations* 13, no. 2 (2010): 86–87.
18. Wilby, "The Simplicity of Mutual Knowledge," 88.
19. Wilby, "The Simplicity of Mutual Knowledge," 88.
20. Stephen Schiffer, *Meaning*, vol. 84 (Oxford: Clarendon Press, 1972), 34–35, quoted in Wilby, "The Simplicity of Mutual Knowledge," 89.
21. Schiffer, *Meaning*, 35, quoted in Wilby, "The Simplicity of Mutual Knowledge," 89.
22. Wilby, "The Simplicity of Mutual Knowledge," 90.
23. Wilby, "The Simplicity of Mutual Knowledge," 91.
24. Wilby, "The Simplicity of Mutual Knowledge," 92.
25. These proof steps are from Wilby, "The Simplicity of Mutual Knowledge," 92.
26. Wilby, "The Simplicity of Mutual Knowledge," 92.
27. John Campbell, "Joint Attention and Common Knowledge," in *Joint Attention: Communication and Other Minds* (Oxford: Oxford University Press, 2005), 288, quoted in Wilby, "The Simplicity of Mutual Knowledge," 92.
28. Wilby, "The Simplicity of Mutual Knowledge," 92.
29. Wilby, "The Simplicity of Mutual Knowledge," 93.
30. Wilby, "The Simplicity of Mutual Knowledge," 93.
31. Wilby, "The Simplicity of Mutual Knowledge," 93.
32. Wilby, "The Simplicity of Mutual Knowledge," 95.
33. Wilby, "The Simplicity of Mutual Knowledge," 96.

34. Richard Breheny, "Communication and Folk Psychology," *Mind & Language* 21, no. 1 (February 1, 2006): 74, quoted in Wilby, "The Simplicity of Mutual Knowledge," 97.
35. Wilby, "The Simplicity of Mutual Knowledge," 96.
36. Wilby, "The Simplicity of Mutual Knowledge," 97.
37. Wilby, "The Simplicity of Mutual Knowledge," 97.
38. Wilby, "The Simplicity of Mutual Knowledge," 97.
39. 거시기.
40. 전라도.

*Chapter 10*

# Feelings and Corporeality

## 1. CONTAGION

Falck, Brinck, and Lindgren claim that beliefs are contagious. When we follow others' attentional direction without reflection, we tend to focus on the same information that the others focus on. This happens "automatically" without necessarily reflecting on the fact that we are doing so.[1] In this regard, Falck argues that contagion is a powerful means of explaining the phenomenon of shared beliefs regardless of whether or not we reflect on the fact that the beliefs are shared or not. According to Falck, contagion-based sharing is noncognitive, meaning that we do not reflect on how the sharing comes to be possible, even if the shared information itself is cognized. Sharing information is cognitively lean, even though there are others who intermittently attract attention. In the account of contagion-based sharing, there is no need to meta-represent the beliefs of others in order to share those beliefs.[2]

Max Scheler describes the characteristic of contagion as the situation where there is a complete lack of mutual understanding because the one in the situation is "quite unconscious of the contagion to which he succumbs."[3] In other words, contagion is characterized through "foreign emotion" of the other in that it is not reciprocally understood.[4] In this situation, the feeling is shared through imitating bodily movements, that is, mimesis through corporeal resonance, not through aligned feeling.[5] Canetti describes contagion as the force that grows the crowd,[6] and Hilge Landweer takes an example of a fleeing herd from Canetti as an opportunity to discuss corporeal interaction. The increase of energy through the synchronization of direction and movement is one of the three characteristics of fleeing masses. Landweer points out that this means "synchronization of *corporeal* direction and movement."[7] From here, Landweer further discusses emotional contagion and shared

## 2. FEELINGS: BODILY SELF

Legrand takes the subject as constitutively bodily.[8] She claims that self-as-subject should be differentiated from self-as-object, and that bodily reflection is possible, such as self-touching as self-perception, that is, embodied reflection.[9] According to Legrand, the experience of self-as-subject involves the experience of self as oriented toward intentional objects from one's first-person perspective and the experience of self as in contact with intentional objects through one's bodily feelings. She explains that subjectivity and intentionality are co-constitutive of the bodily self. The physical body can be taken as an intentional object and be experienced as expressing its subjectivity through bodily dimensions.[10] In this context, bodily feelings play the important role of stretching the subject's intention to the world beyond its own bodily boundaries. Goldie explains that bodily feelings can tell you things not just about your own body and emotions, but also about other parts of the world beyond the surface of your body and that which comes into physical contact with it.[11] Slaby also argues that bodily sensations are crucial carriers of world-directed intentionality, which are intentionally directed feelings, not just at one's body and its physiological changes, but at the world beyond the body.[12] Thus, bodily self-consciousness, namely, bodily subjectivity, goes beyond one's skin boundary,[13] says Legrand.

The others in this world, though, are objects of *my* intentionality, including *my* own self-as-object. As Merleau-Ponty said, the other's gaze transforms *me* into an object when *I* am touched by your gaze.[14] Likewise, you become you as an object to *my* perception when *I* perceive you. Within this framework, the others have to be *believed* to be other subjects who also take *me* as the object of their perception. Here, we could fall back into the problem of solipsism, where the world is a constructed reality like the community in the head of the boy with curly hair (chapter 8, section 1). Neither *my* bodily feelings nor *my* self as both subject and object and *my* realization of it can provide any ontological basis for the subjectivity of others. This was the problem in the context of mutual knowledge. Mutual knowledge is possible only between two metaphysically different individuals who are both supposed to be, in the framework of subject-object, subjects. The knowledge of mutual knowledge is the object of both agents. Thus, through this shared object, I can assume the other's subjective consciousness. Or simply, as in the example that Legrand suggests, it is cold, not only for *me*, but it is to the others as well. Through communication, *I* can obtain the information that the other also feels the same as *I* do. It is cold for *us*. Husserl also talked about the 'collective mind' (*Gemeingeist*) that comes about through communicative acts.[15] In the situation of joint action, however, such as when two people use a two-handed saw, neither verbal communication nor conscious coordination is necessary to make the one identical, shared saw function.

## 3. EMOTIONAL CONTAGION, SHARED FEELINGS, INTERCORPOREALITY

Being cognitive and having senses necessarily require a body which interacts with the environment in which it is embodied.[16] We are bodily beings who are connected with the world through corporeal interaction. Landweer claims that "it is not the subject that 'communicates,' but instead it is the corporeal directions of contraction and expansion that interact with the particular directions of movement or corporeal tendencies of the person we face."[17] Landweer adopts the two forms of corporeal interaction from Schmitz and re-terms them as "unipolar" and "bipolar."[18] She elaborates that in bipolar corporeal interaction, there are always two initiators that determine the corporeal directions as two individuals in a corporeal relation, while in the unipolar corporeal interaction, it is initiated and directed by one pole from outside.[19] She argues that unipolar corporeal interaction is at the basis of all types of shared feeling.[20]

Her hypothesis is that shared feelings and mass emotion are possible through the process of corporeal interaction. In this regard, she talks about the "affectedness" of a feeling, because feelings affect us corporeally, meaning that they "intervene in our individual corporeal dynamic of contraction and expansion and change it."[21] In short, therefore, affectedness means having a feeling, but she differentiates feeling from being affected by it. Being affected by a feeling indicates the feeling of the feeling.[22] When more than one person shares feelings, they are affected by one and the same feeling, because the shared feeling is "not what they would each themselves feel personally."[23] She explains that they have their own affectedness as their own corporeal feeling "for themselves" that exists twice, but the feeling is singular. This is the situation where different people are affected by the same feeling together and feel their shared affectedness. Therefore, she regards shared feeling as unipolar corporeal interaction.[24] Those who are interacting reciprocally with shared feelings have to perceive each other corporeally, but do not necessarily turn their attention toward each other directly. Shared feelings do not require explicit consciousness, but a peripheral, reciprocal registering of each other is necessary.[25]

Corporeal attunement is fundamental and indispensable in our everyday life. Landweer takes an example of two people trying to pass each other in a tight passageway. In their interaction, they both accommodate their corporeal directions to each other and coordinate their glances and movements.[26] We can see this intercorporeality easily, as Landweer also describes, in the case of well-attuned cooperation in shared manual labor, such as two skilled people using a two-handed saw together, or in the case of playing sports, or playing and creating music together.[27]

Christian Meyer and Ulrich von Wedelstaedt explain intercorporeality in terms of Merleau-Ponty's 'carnal phenomenology.'[28] They emphasize the fact that

> even after we have learned as infants to distinguish between ourselves (our own bodies) and the world (including the bodies of others), we are still able and even fated to continue experiencing corporeal 'we-ness' when we share the same sensory and physical space.[29]

Intercorporeality is observed in many social activities, but Sheets-Johnstone finds the basis of the "sense of living self" in "animacy and motility."[30] This property enables all forms of "primordial intercorporeality in which the boundaries of kinesthetic subjectivity blur."[31] Schmitz, Landweer, Trevarthen, Meyer and von Wedelstaedt, and many others talk about the social importance of reciprocal rhythm and resonance that bring about intuitive and internal corporeal interaction and inter-coordination.[32] Rhythm is allied with bodily processes.[33] In such "mutual incorporation,"[34] or "solidary encorporation,"[35] the normal awareness of "me and the world," and "ego and alter" collapses "into a single, unified, and harmonic action,"[36] which Hunter and Csikszentmihalyi describe as flow of unified sensation of motion.[37] Meyer and von Wedelstaedt write that the their three approaches of 'intercorporeality,' 'interkinesthesia,' and 'enaction' share "a rejection of intellectualist and representationalist accounts of intersubjectivity" and insist that our lived and living bodies can become extended to be "intertwined with artifacts, objects, materials and environmental conditions as well as other bodies,"[38] which would prevent a conceptual and ontological reduction of self to an isolated individual body.[39]

Tomasello expounds on the evolution of the skills of action imitation, joint intention, and joint attention in the context of human collaborative activity. He claims that skills for understanding individual intentionality gave an adaptive advantage to primate individuals in the context of competition, and human communicative conventions arose in situations with joint goals based on the human skills of role reversal imitation and cooperative motives.[40] Likewise, Chris Frith also emphasizes the crucial role of mimicry in terms of his analysis of irreducible we-intentionality. In social interaction, mimicry is a pervasive behavior whereby we spontaneously copy the other's behavioral mannerisms such as postures, gestures, facial expressions, emotions, and languages.[41] Primitive emotional contagion is "the tendency to automatically mimic and synchronize facial expressions, vocalizations, postures, and movements with those of another person and, consequently, to converge emotionally."[42]

Facial expressions have a major part in social interactions among these nonverbal signals,[43] but not only facial expressions of emotion are processed rapidly without awareness. Gaze direction in corporeal interaction is also another important facial cue when we observe the behavior of others. It has been known that direct gaze and eye contact have a strong impact on the capacity for intersubjective behavior in young infants.[44] Frith says that this ability enables us to discover what people are looking at, which could reveal the information of their interests and intentions.[45] In fact, we are very sensitive to eye gaze and its direction and can specify the target of the gaze quite accurately.[46] As Reddy describes, gaze in corporeal interaction among two or more people affects each other and their personal feelings:

> Someone smiles at you and you feel pleased. The feeling which infuses you is not separable from (and cannot be understood separately form) the smile of the other person; your feeling includes the other person's.[47]

In this corporeal interaction, your feeling is not anymore only your feeling, but there is shared affectedness between you and the other, yet you don't have to necessarily be conscious of this interaction.

The reason that mimicry is so pervasive in our daily life is because mirroring behavior has many advantages. For example, in the case of speech, mirroring enhances alignment of the communicants. What is interesting, though, is that these effects occur—probably only—when the person is not conscious of the imitation.[48] Subjective consciousness alone does not seem to provide a convincing account for an explanation of self in the case of nonverbal social interactions such as corporeal interaction, shared feelings, and emotional contagion.

In her discussion on corporeal communication and interaction, Landweer writes that "it is not the subject that consciously communicates,"[49] but it is the corporeal directions of movements and interactions between different agents that communicate.[50] This is a process that takes place "below the threshold of consciousness."[51] However, I find it very important to note that she also points out that "small children learn most forms of unipolar corporeal interaction by practicing them repeatedly," and particularly complex forms of cooperation such as joint handwork, playing music in an orchestra, or playing sports in a team can be accomplished in the process of intentional solidary incorporation. However, for the development of complex forms based on joint intentions, intuitive solidary incorporation is an important prerequisite.[52] This substantiates my argument that self is in relation both pre-subjectively and intersubjectively.

The incorporated feelings shared between selves-in-relation through unreflected but physically well-attuned interactions embody the pre-subjective state, where self, other, and their relation exist but are not reflected in the subject-object framework. Intersubjective interaction in such a state is not consciously coordinated, but the two selves affected by the shared feeling interconnect and interact. This unipolar feeling is fundamentally based on the feeling of being-in-relation which is pre-subjective.

## 4. INVOLVEMENT, RELATIONSHIP, AND TO FEEL WITH: EMPATHY BY HELLER

We are self-in-relation situated in pre-subjective we; however, this doesn't mean that we are a-subjective or a-reflective. Rather, we are both: pre-subjective and intersubjective. We need to be consciously conscious of this fundamental relation that we are placed in and affected by. It is crucial for us to pay attention to our relations with others and feel with them in order to keep the relational web in shape. We are given life, and we have it without having had to ask for it or build it ourselves, but that does not mean we cannot undo it. Whether we keep it or not, we can decide. It is the same with the web; whether to keep it or not, we can decide—at least, to some extent.

In an interview with the German television show Monitor from *Das Erste*,[53] shortly before elections in Germany, as she was asked what her thoughts were on the far-right political party, *Alternative für Deutschland*, the so-called *AfD*, who regards the commemorative culture of Holocaust as *lächerlich und lästig* (ridiculous and irritating), Ágnes Heller said that "it is a dreadful phenomenon of forgetting of the past, which is the survived and re-experienced racism" and she continues that the biggest danger is *Gleichgültigkeit*, indifference, that is, the scariest threat is that we are *not conscious* of the threat; the biggest danger is to not see the danger. *Gleichgültigkeit*, she elaborates, means that one neither wants to (*will nicht*) know where they live nor wants to realize what our own past was like. At the end of the interview she says that the only thing that she could say is *gebt Acht*, give attention. This is the core of what I would like to talk about concerning "to feel with."

There are number of prominent studies on empathy, which I won't repeat here. What I would like to talk about here is what it means to *feel with*, *Mitgefühl*, based on an unpublished manuscript "Über die Verschiedenheit der Ästhetischen, Reflektierten, und Ethischen Empathie" by Heller.[54] The reason I want to talk about this particular 'feeling' is found in the end of Heller's *A Theory of Feelings*.[55] The title of the epilogue of this book reads "On Human Suffering." For the finale of her theory of feelings, Heller chose to speak about human suffering. Not hope, not love, but she talks about pain and suffering. Why? What does she want to talk about? What made her want to write a theory of feelings in the first place? My reading of this book started from the epilogue, with this curiosity. That is where, I believe, the heart of her theory of feelings lies, which is that we have to be conscious of the suffering of others, and have to learn how to feel—how to empathize. In the world now, where seven out of ten children are undernourished, 70.8 million people are forcibly displaced, and 25.9 million are refugees, Heller's theory is telling us what we should not miss in order to survive as human beings.[56] This is deeply connected to why I initially wanted to ponder upon we-ness and question it thoroughly again.

"To feel means to be involved in something" is the key phrase of Heller's theory of feelings, which is how her book *A Theory of Feelings* starts and ends. This involvement could be "positive or negative, active or reactive, direct and indirect." In any case, it means the subject is involved with something, which could be "anything: another human being, a concept, myself, a process, a problem, a situation, another feeling, another involvement,"[57] in any way, either this or that way.

This person, who is a feeling being, is standing in the center of their own world as being-in-the-world, but not in the sense of egocentrism or social isolation. This world of being-in-the-world is more than just a place of being: human existence *happens* (*geschieht*) as being-in-the-world itself. As this existence happens, so does the world, in which the subject exists with other beings and things. We are involved with these beings and things in this or that way, as far as we exist as being-in-the-world. As long as we exist in this world as human beings, we 'care' about our own being, our own world, our own past and future, and we ask the meaning of our own existence: existing as 'being in the world' is, therefore, a temporal understanding process. Existing itself already presupposes 'being involved' with my own being, even if one didn't 'want to' be involved with any other beings or things. As long as we exist, we understand, we feel, we are involved: that is the 'way of being' of human existence.

What does it mean, though, when we say that we understand as we exist? We understand our own time, our world, and therefore our existence. This is a temporal happening (*Geschehen*) that happens (*geschieht*) in the present. We understand ourselves in this process. But how? This *Geschehen* which is each person's own *Geschichte* (story) can be understood when it is told (*erzählt*), because a story can be understood only when it is told.[58] Heller also remarks that "our autographical memories, our subjective identity, consist of various stories (narratives) that we tell for ourselves about our own past. These narratives contain cheerful and sad emotional experiences that one re-experiences in autobiographical narratives."[59] She points out, though, that this "re-experience" does not imply that one feels the exact same joy or sadness of the time of the original experience. It is rather a kind of *Mitgefühl*, that is, empathy: *feeling with* ourselves about what we have experienced, gained and lost.

Here what is significant about this *feeling with* my own self lies in fact that my experienced *feeling with myself* in memories is not the same as the feeling at the original moment of the experience. It is because the situation now is different, and the understanding of the former situation and the conceptual comprehension can change as well. As Heller says in the interview with *Das Erste*, that is why we can invent new tragedies, such as a new experience of racism, even if history doesn't repeat itself and we don't have to repeat the history.

We can postulate that this *Mitgefühl* with my past is "empirically universal" for all human beings because "there is no human being without autographical memories" and the "the story that one tells about oneself, at least in a psychologically not troubled person, is never feelingless, neither fully nor at all indifferent (*gleichgültig*)."[60] However, this doesn't mean that *feeling with others*, which Heller refers to as empathy, is present in all exemplars of homo sapiens, because empathy, she claims, is neither affect nor instinct, such as courage, sadness or joyfulness. Rather, empathy is an emotion that is situated in a concrete situation, and a concrete "trigger" (*Auslöser*) is required to arouse these feelings. The triggers of emotions are dependent on the situation, and, therefore, are concrete and specific to different circumstances, and not only the situation but also the judgment of other people holds good for an aspect of the triggers of my feelings. At the point where the trigger and the evaluation of our feeling codetermine, we cannot talk about either affects or instincts, but only emotions. Emotions are not what we are born with. Heller argues that they are not "natural," because one cannot inherit them. It is hard to say that one is born with "aggression or sympathy," just as we cannot say that we are born with emotions as such "grief, pleasure, wanderlust, angst, enthusiasm, hate"[61] and so on and so forth. Her stance here is clearly distinguished from that of Rousseau or Hobbes, who believe that empathy is human nature. Empathy as an emotion[62] is always relevant to situations and concepts, because emotions are situated. This includes being historically situated. Therefore, "the structure of emotions and the way one actually deals with them," as well as the "emotional concepts"[63] themselves, are historically situated. Historical, because they are involved with our memories of the past.

What we remember and what we forget, however, we can choose. Remembering and forgetting are always selective,[64] which Heller regards as a fundamental point. It is up to us what to choose to remember and what to forget; this is indeed a substantial moment for understanding empathy as an emotion. It is not naturally given as a certain disposition, but we are to decide; we must make a choice for our action of feeling. We have to 'want' to or 'not want' to be aware of certain situations, phenomena, our past, and others. Thus, we have to learn how to feel.

What does it mean to "learn how to feel?" Don't we already feel certain feelings even before we learn how to talk? The expression of feelings seems rather naturally given and something we are born with, rather than educated about. Heller also agrees with the fact that "feelings as biological signals are not learned,"[65] but she says that,

> the process of their differentiation is tied to learning. First of all, we must learn what it is we feel, inasmuch as we "cannot help ourselves" without such knowledge, since we are not beings guided by instinct. The identification of feelings often goes together with the understanding or interpretation of feelings.[66]

To learn how to feel means, therefore, to learn how to understand the feelings.

As I have mentioned above, the understanding of one's own self is to understand one's own history (*Geschichte*): to understand means to understand the past of one's own, and to understand what to remember and what to forget. It is to learn how to be conscious of one's own situation and history, to contemplate on it, to reflect it on my current situation, and therefore, to know where I am situated now and through which I can be aware and conscious of the other.

In French, the words, consciousness (*Bewußtsein*) and conscience (*Gewissen*) are not distinguished, they are the same: *la conscience*. In "Five Approaches to the Phenomenon of Shame,"[67] Heller defines shame as an innate feeling, but conscience as an emotional type of feeling involving cognition. The words "conscience," "*constientia*," "*Gewissen*" indicate that the role played by knowledge in the constitution of this feeling is intimately connected to the activity of a reflective self-consciousness.[68] Being conscious is to know, to be reflective, and especially to have conscience—which always includes the others in my understanding. To understand my history is never only to understand my isolated history, but this history always *happens* with the history of others, because we are after all in the world as being-in-the-world.

However, "our self is always and inescapably particular," remarks Heller, because "we receive *ready-made* certain given particularities along with our genetic code, the *dumb species character*."[69] We opt to, therefore, be particularist. We can, though, choose to be an individual rather than particularist. According to Heller, the difference between particularist and individual behavior is constituted in the relationship to the feeling.[70] What does it mean to be an individual? Heller defines this concept of an individual in light of one's relation to the world and to oneself:

> The person relating individually to the world (and to himself) is characterized by distance both to himself and to the world. The individual is the one who selects from the system of customs of his environment on the basis of values chosen by himself. And he selects likewise individually (again, on the basis of his chosen value system) from among his own particularities, from among the constituents of his psychological character, preferring (opting) some and repressing or eliminating the symptoms of others on the basis of the choice of values. Of course, the condition of the formation of the individual relationship is that there must be a way to choose from the values.[71]

Whether a person becomes a particularist or an individual personality is entirely up to one's "moral and intellectual character,"[72] and developing a moral and intellectual character and becoming an individual are mutually dependent. Heller distinguishes three layers of human character, which are the psychological, the moral, and the intellectual. Initially, the psychological character begins to develop at birth. The moral character begins to develop from the acquisition of language. Finally, the intellectual character begins to develop together with the moral character and perhaps never stops developing. It is an interesting point that "the moral and intellectual character can assume different relations to one's own psychological character, thereby distancing oneself from oneself."[73] According to Heller, "the emotional character is already a result of such a distancing of the moral and intellectual character from the psychological character or the lack thereof," and functions as "an evaluating concept."[74]

As one might assume, it is not an easy task to relate oneself to the world individually. While it is difficult to become an individual, however, the good news is that it becomes ever easier to remain an individual once one becomes one. For example, as Heller writes, "to respond to expressions of frankness with love, to reject flattery with contempt, to love those whom we love for their own sake, etc., all this requires an effort at the beginning, but eventually becomes increasingly *natural* [emphasis in original]."[75]

In spite of that, the majority of people are rather particularist with regard to their actions, and even the majority of individuals remain individuals only in the tendency of their actions. It is not a fixed acquisition that we once gain and remains for good, rather we experience "day in and day out collisions between individual and particularist feelings between the particularist and the individual relationship to the emotions." Heller refers to these as "emotional habits."[76] She explains that both emotional character and emotional personality are feeling habits, because "all those feeling habits to which we can apply the categories of Good and Bad are included into the category of emotional personality."[77]

To learn how to feel is to learn how to be conscious, how to contemplate, how to be reflective, and, therefore, how to understand. However, if this feeling does not turn into an emotional habit, "it is always forgettable," maybe for good.[78] To learn how to feel, therefore, should be the process of habitually learning how to feel. We have to learn how to feel, not only to be involved in the given situations, but also to learn how to 'relate' myself, especially to 'others.'

We live, act, and remember always from the point of view of the evaluated situation that we are in now, and while emotions are empirically universal to human beings, empathy is "another thing," says Heller. She distinguishes three different types of empathy and explicates the similarities and differences between them: aesthetic, reflected and ethical empathies. We can feel empathy for someone who has nothing to do with us, for example, for the protagonist of an opera, whose life ends in tragedy. Heller calls this feeling an aesthetic empathy. An empathy, on the other hand, can be also ethically and/or practically and/or reflectively dealt with. Heller doesn't put them under a particular hierarchal structure between practical-ethical, aesthetical, aesthetical-ethical, or reflective-ethical empathies. They all are not inborn, but they all play a certain role in our life. However, she does say that there are "historical differences" between them: the aesthetical and reflective empathies were present in all groups and cultures of mankind as a resisting force against aggression and violence, but ethical empathy, even if not born in our time, has at least become significant.[79]

Now we have to learn how to help the other, whether they belong to us or not, insists Heller at the end of her empathy paper. Empathy now has to be more than just reflective and aesthetical. These two are still needed to support moral and empathetic development, but what matters is that we not only feel with the other, but also feel to help them, which could be motivated by empathy.[80] We can learn this and habituate it as well. This process of learning feelings, especially emotions, is "a process of fitting together."[81] This is the way to fight the hate, aggression, and fear against the others.[82] This is, therefore, not to be moral for the sake of being moral, but, as Heller claims, it is to survive and exist as human beings in the era where "humanity is no longer an abstract idea, but a problem."[83] To become an individual depends on "whether humankind can become a constitutive idea, a problem for the individual."[84]

So now, why does Heller talk about pain and suffering? Already in the middle of her book, Heller writes, that "it is in the course of suffering that King Lear learns to feel something he had never felt as a king: empathy with other sufferers."[85] Pain is reflective and characterizes human relationships in all of their forms, therefore it could give us signals when something is wrong in a relationship: the signal to "help yourself and help others."[86] Meanwhile suffering just "falls on us" and does not depend on our intentions, decisions, and our choices. It is only passive. Then how could King Lear learn empathy? Heller reveals the secret: when suffering is converted to our pain, we can learn how to feel. This is a crucial point, because "as social beings we are not unavoidably subjected to suffering."[87] So, we ought to pay attention, be conscious and understand *to help myself and others*, because we are, after all, self-in-relation.

## NOTES

1. Cecilia Heyes, "Submentalizing: I Am Not Really Reading Your Mind," *Perspectives on Psychological Science* 9, no. 2 (March 1, 2014), 131–143, quoted in Andreas Falck et al., "Interest Contagion in Violation-of-Expectation-Based False-Belief Tasks," *Frontiers in Psychology* 5 (2014), 1–5.
2. Andreas Falck, "Contagion-Based Mechanisms in Verbal and Non-Verbal False-Belief Tasks" (n.d.). with permission of the author.
3. Scheler, *The Nature of Sympathy*, 113–114.
4. Scheler, *The Nature of Sympathy*, 12.
5. Hilge Landweer, "Mass Emotion and Shared Feelings," *Yearbook for Eastern and Western Philosophy* 2017, no. 2 (2017): 113.
6. Canetti, *Crowds and Power*, 77.
7. Landweer, "Mass Emotion and Shared Feelings," 110.
8. Dorothée Legrand, "Phenomenological Dimensions of Bodily Self-Consciousness," in *The Oxford Handbook of the Self*, ed. Shaun Gallagher (Oxford: Oxford University Press, 2011), 208.
9. Legrand, "Phenomenological Dimensions," 224.
10. Legrand, "Phenomenological Dimensions," 225–226.
11. Peter Goldie, "Emotions, Feelings and Intentionality," *Phenomenology and the Cognitive Sciences* 1, no. 3 (September 1, 2002): 238, quoted in Legrand, "Phenomenological Dimensions," 221.
12. Jan Slaby, "Affective Intentionality and the Feeling Body," *Phenomenology and the Cognitive Sciences* 7, no. 4 (December 1, 2008): 434, quoted in Legrand, "Phenomenological Dimensions," 221.
13. Legrand, "Phenomenological Dimensions," 218.
14. Maurice Merleau-Ponty, *Phenomenology of Perception*, trans. C. Smith (New York: Routledge, 2013), quoted in Legrand, "Phenomenological Dimensions," 220.
15. Iribarne, *Husserls Theorie Der Intersubjektivität*, 189; Husserl, *Zur Phänomenologie der Intersubjektivität* 165ff, 192ff.
16. Richard Menary, "Introduction. What Is Radical Enactivism?," in *Radical Enactivism: Intentionality, Phenomenology and Narrative.*, ed. Richard Menary, vol. 2 (Amsterdam: John Benjamins Publishing, 2006), 2, quoted in Christian Meyer

and Ulrich von Wedelstaedt, "Intercorporeality, Interkinesthesia, and Enaction: New Perspectives on Moving Bodies in Interaction," in *Moving Bodies in Interaction–Interacting Bodies in Motion: Intercorporeality, Interkinesthesia, and Enaction in Sports*, ed. Christian Meyer and Ulrich von Wedelstaedt, vol. 8 (Amsterdam: John Benjamins Publishing, 2017), 6.

17. Landweer, "Mass Emotion and Shared Feelings," 106–107.

18. Hermann Schmitz, *Der Leib* (Berlin/Boston: DeGruyter, 2011), quoted in Landweer, "Mass Emotion and Shared Feelings"; Hilge Landweer, "Choreographies With and Without a Choreographer. Intuitive and Intentional Corporeal Interactions," in *Touching and to Be Touched. Kinesthesia and Empathy in Dance and Movement*, ed. Gabriele Brandstetter, Gerko Egert, and Sabine Zubarik (Berlin/New York: DeGruyter, 2013).

19. Landweer, "Mass Emotion and Shared Feelings,' 109.

20. Landweer, "Mass Emotion and Shared Feelings," 110.

21. Landweer, "Mass Emotion and Shared Feelings," 108.

22. Landweer, "Mass Emotion and Shared Feelings," 108.

23. Landweer, "Mass Emotion and Shared Feelings," 111.

24. Landweer, "Mass Emotion and Shared Feelings," 111.

25. Landweer, "Mass Emotion and Shared Feelings," 112

26. Landweer, "Mass Emotion and Shared Feelings," 107; Landweer, "Choreographies With and Without a Choreographer," 137.

27. Landweer, "Mass Emotion and Shared Feelings," 108; Landweer, "Choreographies With and Without a Choreographer," 139.

28. Merleau-Ponty, *Phenomenology of Perception*; Merleau-Ponty, *Signs*; Maurice Merleau-Ponty, *The Visible and the Invisible*, trans. A. Lingis (Evanston, IL: Northwestern University Press, 1968), quoted in Meyer and von Wedelstaedt, "Intercorporeality, Interkinesthesia, and Enaction."

29. Meyer and von Wedelstaedt, "Intercorporeality, Interkinesthesia, and Enaction," 3–4.

30. Maxine Sheets-Johnstone, "Animation: The Fundamental, Essential, and Properly Descriptive Concept," *Continental Philosophy Review* 42, no. 3 (August 1, 2009), quoted in Meyer and von Wedelstaedt, "Intercorporeality, Interkinesthesia, and Enaction," 6.

31. Meyer and von Wedelstaedt, "Intercorporeality, Interkinesthesia, and Enaction," 6.

32. Hermann Schmitz, *Der Unerschöpfliche Gegenstand. Grundzüge der Philosophie* (Bonn: Bouvier, 1990), 152, quoted in Landweer, "Choreographies With and Without a Choreographer," 133, 144; Colwyn Trevarthen, "The Self Born in Intersubjectivity: The Psychology of an Infant Communicating," in *The Perceived Self: Ecological and Interpersonal Sources of Self-Knowledge*, Emory Symposia in Cognition, 5, ed. Ulric Neisser (Cambridge: Cambridge University Press, 1993), 126, quoted in Meyer and von Wedelstaedt, 'Intercorporeality, Interkinesthesia, and Enaction,' 9.

33. Kenneth Burke, *Counter-Statement*, vol. 143 (University of California Press, 1968), 140–141, quoted in Meyer and von Wedelstaedt, "Intercorporeality, Interkinesthesia, and Enaction," 9.

34. Thomas Fuchs and Hanne de Jaegher, "Enactive Intersubjectivity: Participatory Sense-Making and Mutual Incorporation," *Phenomenology and the Cognitive Sciences* 8, no. 4 (December 1, 2009): 465, quoted in Meyer and von Wedelstaedt, "Intercorporeality, Interkinesthesia, and Enaction," 10.

35. Landweer, "Choreographies With and Without a Choreographer," 137–138.

36. Jeremy Hunter and Mihaly Csikszentmihalyi, "The Phenomenology of Body-Mind: The Contrasting Cases of Flow in Sports and Contemplation," *Anthropology of Consciousness* 11, no. 3–4 (September 1, 2000): 14, quoted in Meyer and von Wedelstaedt, "Intercorporeality, Interkinesthesia, and Enaction," 11.

37. Hunter and Csikszentmihalyi, "The Phenomenology of Body-Mind," 14, quoted in Meyer and von Wedelstaedt, "Intercorporeality, Interkinesthesia, and Enaction," 11.

38. Meyer and von Wedelstaedt, "Intercorporeality, Interkinesthesia, and Enaction," 11.

39. Tom Froese and Thomas Fuchs, "The Extended Body: A Case Study in the Neurophenomenology of Social Interaction," *Phenomenology and the Cognitive Sciences* 11, no. 2 (June 1, 2012): 214, quoted in Meyer and von Wedelstaedt, "Intercorporeality, Interkinesthesia, and Enaction," 11.

40. Michael Tomasello, *Origins of Human Communication* (Cambridge, MA: MIT Press, 2010), 339–340, quoted in Meyer, *Culture, Practice, and the Body*, 314.

41. Tanya L. Chartrand and Rick van Baaren, "Human Mimicry," *Advances in Experimental Social Psychology*. Vol. 41 (Cambridge, MA: Academic Press, 2009): 219–274; Yin Wang and Antonia Hamilton, "Social Top-down Response Modulation (STORM): A Model of the Control of Mimicry in Social Interaction," *Frontiers in Human Neuroscience* 6 (2012), 1–10.

42. Elaine Hatfield et al., "Primitive Emotional Contagion," *Review of Personality and Social Psychology* 14 (1992): 151–77; Matt Iacobini et al., "Emotional Contagion in Interactive Art," in *Proceedings of the International Conference on Kansei Engineering and Emotion Research, Paris, France*, 2010.

43. Ralph Adolphs, "Social Cognition and the Human Brain," *Trends in Cognitive Sciences* 3, no. 12 (1999): 469–79; Beatrice de Gelder, "Why Bodies? Twelve Reasons for Including Bodily Expressions in Affective Neuroscience," *Philosophical Transactions of the Royal Society B: Biological Sciences* 364, no. 1535 (2009): 3475–84.

44. Ingar Brinck, "The Role of Intersubjectivity in the Development of Intentional Communication," *The Shared Mind: Perspectives on Intersubjectivity*, ed. Jordan Zlatev, Timothy P. Racine, Chris Sinha, and Esa Itkonen (Amsterdam: John Benjamins Publishing Company, 2008): 118–21.

45. Chris Frith, "Role of Facial Expressions in Social Interactions," *Philosophical Transactions of the Royal Society B: Biological Sciences* 364, no. 1535 (December 12, 2009): 3453–58.

46. S. M. Anstis et al., "The Perception of Where a Face or Television 'Portrait' is Looking," *The American Journal of Psychology* 82, no. 4 (1969): 474–489.

47. V. Reddy, *How Infants Know Minds* (Cambridge, MA: Harvard University Press, 2008).

48. Jessica L. Lakin and Tanya L. Chartrand, "Using Nonconscious Behavioral Mimicry to Create Affiliation and Rapport," *Psychological Science* 14, no. 4 (July 1, 2003): 334–39.

49. Landweer, "Choreographies With and Without a Choreographer," 137.

50. She explicates these directions of movements relating to the notion of "Bewegungssuggestionen" ("suggestions of movements" by Schmitz). (Landweer, "Choreographies With and Without a Choreographer," 137; Schmitz, *Der Unerschöfpliche Gegenstand*, 140–151, 282–284, quoted in Landweer, "Mass Emotion and Shared Feelings," 207.).

51. Landweer, "Choreographies With and Without a Choreographer," 137.

52. Landweer, "Choreographies With and Without a Choreographer," 158.

53. September 15, 2017.

54. Ágnes Heller, "Über die Verschiedenheit der Ästhetischen, Reflektierten, und Ethischen Empathie" (unpublished). with permission of the author.

55. Ágnes Heller, *A Theory of Feelings* (Lanham, MD: Lexington Books, 2009).

56. http://www.unhcr.org/figures-at-a-glance.html. I have started quoting this number since I started my research on intersubjectivity and the we-ness a few years ago. I had to update the number every year because each year the number has been increasing. When I initially prepared this chapter and presented at the conference "Agnes Heller's Theory of Emotions in Context" at the Etvös Lorand University, Budapest, Hungary in 2017 (November 16–17, 2017) under the title of "Involvement, Relationship, and Feelings," the number was 65.6 million for the number of the forcibly displaced and 22.5 million for the refugees.

57. Heller, *A Theory of Feelings*, 11.

58. Kim, *Sorge und Geschichte*.

59. Heller, "Empathie" (my translation).

60. Heller, "Empathie" (my translation).

61. Heller, "Empathie."

62. Heller distinguishes feelings from emotions in *A Theory of Feelings*, but not so strictly. I also use these terms freely to refer to empathy as a feeling or an emotion in this context.

63. Heller, *A Theory of Feelings*, 168.

64. Heller, "Empathie."

65. Heller, *A Theory of Feelings*, 105.

66. Heller, *A Theory of Feelings*, 106.

67. Ágnes Heller, "Five Approaches to the Phenomenon of Shame," *Social Research: An International Quarterly* 70, no. 4 (2003): 1015–30.

68. Ágnes Heller, "Five Approaches," 2012.

69. Heller, *A Theory of Feelings*, 143.

70. Heller, *A Theory of Feelings*, 143.

71. Heller, *A Theory of Feelings*, 145.

72. Heller, *A Theory of Feelings*, 160.

73. Heller, *A Theory of Feelings*, 160.

74. Heller, *A Theory of Feelings*, 160.

75. Heller, *A Theory of Feelings*, 157.

76. Heller, *A Theory of Feelings*, 157.

77. Heller, *A Theory of Feelings*, 94.

78. Heller, *A Theory of Feelings*, 136.

79. Heller, "Empathie."

80. Heller, "Empathie."
81. Heller, *A Theory of Feelings*, 143.
82. Heller, "Empathie."
83. Heller, *A Theory of Feelings*, 224.
84. Heller, *A Theory of Feelings*, 224.
85. Heller, *A Theory of Feelings*, 96.
86. Heller, *A Theory of Feelings*, 224.
87. Heller, *A Theory of Feelings*, 224.

*Chapter 11*

# Collective Memory
## *Boundary, Place, and Home*

### 1. COLLECTIVE IDENTITY AND CULTURAL MEMORY OF THE KORYO SARAM

There is yet another aspect of the we-ness: collective identity that comes together with cultural memory attached to geographical dynamics and transmitted history. Here, I will talk about collective identity and the cultural history of communities by telling a story—or history—of a certain group whose status was and is so insignificant in world history that they had no other option than playing the role of the other in the global picture of the world. It is the story of the Koryo Saram in Central Asia.[1] It is a story of the Koreans who were not included in the history of *ouri* of Korea, 'one big happy family,' but these marginalized Koreans made their own cosmopolitan 'one big family' with the other marginalized others.

Koryo Saram (고려사람, Корё сарам) refers to the Koreans who had lived in Primorsky Kray (Приморский край), the maritime province of Wondong, and who were deported by the Soviet Union between 1937 and 1939 to Central Asia. The word *saram* literally means 'person' or 'people' in Korean. Therefore, Koryo Saram refers to the people who came from *Koryo*, that is, Korea. It was around 1869 that they started crossing the Tumen River on the border of Korea and Russia, and their numbers increased after the Japanese colonization of Korea from 1910 to 1945. Presumably around 180,000 to 200,000 of them were deported by Stalin under the pretense of searching out and eliminating "Japanese spies" in the eastern part of the Soviet Union.[2]

The majority of these people took up residence in Uzbekistan and Kazakhstan, but could not return to Korea even after Japan's surrender at the end of the Second World War in 1945. Korea regained its independence but was shortly after divided into two states: the North under the Soviet Union and the South under the United States. In 1950, the Korean War broke out, and this incomplete war left the Korean peninsula broken into two pieces until the present day. As these two Koreas have been caught in this state of complete separation after the war, South Korea became an island without borders that touch the Eurasian continent. On this peninsula in East Asia, therefore, there are now two isolated islands under the shade of the ideologies of the Cold War. South Korea is, as a result, situated in a state where there are no borders that one can cross on foot. This borderless situation leads South Korea to a state of blockage where nobody is free to leave or enter unless they cross the sea. This ironic situation has isolated South Korea with invisible borders: this place, therefore, becomes the place for no other. Neither can one can reach the other nor can the other reach this place without overcoming the depth of the sea that surrounds this island.

In this vortex of history, the stories of the Koryo Saram have become dim in the memories of Koreans. The history of "the Korean diaspora in Eurasia"[3] is a fraction of the forgotten memories of Korea, the memories that connect Korea to the open place, the continent, their past and their future: a forgotten time and space. It was in the 1990s, as the Soviet Union collapsed, that the Koryo Saram faced another crisis: they were driven out, especially in Uzbekistan where "the authoritarian post-Soviet government confiscated assets and imposed the Uzbek language."[4] Some of them came *back* to South Korea. There are now some thousands of the Koryo Saram living in South Korea, largely in the city of Ansan. When they came *back*, however, they could not enter South Korea as Koreans, but they reside in Korea as the other, not only in the sense of their national status, but also in the sense of their social, cultural, psychological, and historical distance from the *normative* Korean society. Koryo Saram, thus, now refers to the Korean people in Central Asia who originally came from Korea but became 'the other' in Korea.

The history of the Koryo Saram begins with their collective experience of mass deportation to Kazakhstan in 1937. The year 1937 is the "time code that constructs the primal scene of the Koryo people in Central Asia."[5] This time has been "stigmatized as the time of state violence of forced migration," which Soyoung Kim calls "the origin of their pain,"[6] or rather "time-coding of pain" as "time-coded collective suffering."[7] The Koryo Saram could survive this time of suffering thanks to help from the local Kazakh people. Their experience of survival with the Kazakhs led them later to offer their help to the Chechens who were forced to migrate to Kazakhstan between 1943 and 1944,[8] through which "Kazakhs, Koryo people, and Chechen people formed a community that emerged after a catastrophe," which is time-coded in their collective memory.[9] Soyoung[10] points out that under these circumstances, the Koryo people experienced a "multiplicity of race and culture":[11] Their sense of solidarity with other ethnic groups such as Kazakhs and Chechen people came from their experience of exchanging support with others after their own migration.[12]

This collective memory of the Koryo Saram turned into the cultural memory of subsequent generations, which in turn constituted their identity as the Koryo Saram. The survival of the identity of the Koryo Saram was possible through this cultural memory, because, as Heller elaborates, "the presence or absence, the very life or decay of a people, does not depend on the biological survival of an ethnic group, but on the survival of shared cultural memory."[13] A cultural memory, however, could not be established by the state by force.[14] When cultural memory is reinforced by a nation, ethnicity, and religion, or any of the three, it could serve as a rather "potent weapon"[15] whereby mythology is replaced by ideology.[16] The cultural memory of the cosmopolitan subaltern groups in Central Asia can be distinguished from the policy on minorities by a federal state such as the Soviet Union. This was "Central Asian internationalism embodied by peasants, workers, and nomads" through their cultural memories shared together in solidarity.[17]

As Heller points out, places are crucial for cultural memory. Whether it be mythological or historical, places must remain concrete and distinct.[18] The collective and cultural memory of the Koryo Saram is grounded in Wondong and then in Central Asia. Their memory of survival and coexistence with others in Central Asia is revived and re-lived in new places where they now reside, such as, for example, Ansan, South Korea. Ansan is a place where the Koryo Saram could take up and maintain the cultural memory of the Koryo Saram of the past in Central Asia. They actualize the internationalism of the subaltern groups in Central Asia in the late 1930s in present-day Ansan: now with other subaltern groups of varied historical and cultural backgrounds, such as the people from South Asia and China instead of Kazakhs, Chechens, or Russians.

We constantly constitute our identity through remembering. This is the process of remembering in the sense of "re-member-ing,"[19] not simply remembering as members of groups, but instead constituting groups. This reveals the core of the cultural memory of the Koryo Saram and their *identity* as Koryo Saram. There is no identity without shared memory,[20] argues Heller, but "every generation experiences the past as its present."[21] Assmann explains that cultural memory *always* relates its knowledge to an actual present situation.[22] There are two modes of cultural memory: one is the "mode of potentiality" (*Modus der Potentialität*) and the other is the "mode of actuality" (*Modus der Aktualität*).[23] The former functions as an archive, providing the whole picture, while the latter refreshes the memories and makes them available in the present.[24] It has been soundly demonstrated by multiple political historians of memory that contemporary circumstances provide the cues for certain images of the past.[25]

Soyoung proclaims, however, that "from the perspective of Korean culture (that centers around South Korea)," the identity and cultural memory of the Koryo Saram mingled with the Kazakhs, Chechens, Jews, and Russians in Central Asia "makes one reconsider the articulations of the network of language, race, geography, ethnicity, and nation as well as the apparatuses and arrangements of homogenization and anti-homogenization."[26] She compares the history of forced migration of the Koryo Saram and other minority groups in Central Asia to the *History of Madness* by Foucault,[27] in terms of exclusion.[28] I endorse this interpretation: the collective and cultural memory of minority groups in Central Asia relates to the history of exclusion, violence, and oppression upon the other by the power, that is, *the subject*. The solidarity of the subaltern groups in Central Asia and their memories of solidarity, however, transformed their memory of suffering into the making of a history of coexistence: a history of creating a new place for identities of the oppressed, the minorities as who they are, but at the same time, also for new forms of cosmopolitanism where the world is happening with diverse poles and axes.

## 2. BORDER, PLACE, AND WORLD

Places are the space of our life and our memory. As mentioned earlier, places make identities. Place refers to a particular portion of space. It could mean not only area, position, environment, but also situation or occasion. Out of infinite void, what creates space is the borders (boundaries), because borders enable differentiation and distinction. Borders make the identical different and the infinite finite. Borders are the beginning of knowledge, because borders define objects by differentiating one thing from another thing. Space is created with borders. The process of dividing and *closing* is the geometrical foundation of space. Place, on the other hand, is the process of *opening* of the space with a meaning. When a certain meaning is given to a certain portion of space, it becomes a place. One of the lexical definitions of place is "home."[29] What gives a place a meaning is the memory that the place represents. Where history is remembered, history is happening; it becomes the place for someone. Place is the world where one's life happens. Borders are, therefore, paradoxical: borders close and differentiate, but this differentiation opens understanding. The beginning of knowing is knowing the difference between this and that. To know oneself, one should differentiate the knowing self from the known. To know this place, one should distinguish this place from that place. We cannot understand without borders, but these borders do not limit understanding. We separate and connect on the borders. Borders let us know who we are, and we make the borders.

## 3. COSMOPOLITANISM

As a representative space of *co-lives* of multiple subaltern groups, Central Asia could serve as a prototype for an alternative frame for understanding solidarities and a new form of internationalism apart from that of globalization. Soyoung remarks that in the works of Lavrenti Son, a second-generation Koryo Saram film director, one can sense that the affective sentiment of *han* [han],[30] roughly interpreted as sorrow, oppression, unavenged injustice, or isolation, of the Koryo Saram is transposed to a sense of gratitude and feeling of requital for the kindness of the people who hosted them, such as Kazakhs and Russians, hospitality in the case of the Chechen migration to Central Asia, and solidarity.

Among the films of Lavrenti, Soyoung pays special attention to a short documentary film entitled "Koryo Saram." In this short documentary film, Song interviews people near Ushtobe who are not ethnically Koryo but speak the Koryo language.[31] These people from Ukraine, Kazakhstan, Russia, and with Kurdish origin who speak Koryo share their linguistic performativity thanks to the remaining influence of the history of forced migration.[32] The Koryo Saram, many of whom were experienced farmers, emerged as the leaders of the Kolkhoz (колхо́з),[33] and the people who worked with them came to speak the Koryo language through their experiences at the Sovkhoz (совхо́з)[34] or even through adoption.[35] They are, however, not only ethnically neither Koryo, nor Korean, nor people of *Joseon* [jo-sun],[36] but they have also not experienced life in "the sovereign territories of South or North Korea."[37]

These non-Koryo Korean speaking people in Kazakhstan do not fit into the general picture of "being Korean."[38] This peculiar case shows a different spectrum of cosmopolitanism than the stereotype of metropolitan cosmopolitanism in today's globalized world. For example, the multilingual performativity of a Kurdish woman in the film *Koryo Saram* who speaks five languages, Kurdish, Russian, Koryo (Korean), Kazakh, and Georgian, is different from that of the "usual" combination of the Euro-American languages such as English, German, French, Italian, Spanish, and so on[39] according to our metropolitan globalization standards. Soyoung calls this "subaltern cosmopolitanism." Gratale uses the term cosmopolitanism similarly to Ulf Hannerz, who describes it as "an orientation, a willingness to engage with the other."[40] The cosmopolitan connection of the minority groups in Central Asia seems to fit this description better than the cosmopolitanism of the internationalized world, where a girl in Tashkent buys an Elsa backpack after watching *Frozen*.

## 4. PLACE OF THE OTHER

Ansan is now best known as the 'multi-cultural' city in Korea. This 'colorful' city of many cultures is also the city of factory complexes into which migrant labor forces flow. A good number of migrant workers in Korea come from South Asia, and their skin color is often darker than that of Koreans. They are often viewed and treated as the 'colored' with all the negative connotation that comes with the idea of 'colored' in Korean society: Ansan is colorful, and colored. Among them, however, are also the Koryo Saram and Korean Chinese,[41] Koreans who returned to Korea as the other. This city, filled with these *colorful* people, is one of the most open places of South Korea, "putatively a homogenous and monolingual nation,"[42] where people believe that they belong to this 'one big happy family,' whatever the idea of this family may be. Ansan is where different people with different backgrounds, languages, cultures, and histories gather and settle. It is a new home for the other.

At the same time, though, this place is also among the most isolated and separated places in Korea, forming the 'slum' or the 'colored' area, where 'the others' are permitted to stay temporarily. This place is where these third 'they' made their home, but to which they cannot return as they wish once they leave. The un-returnability of this place represents the state of the borderless Korea as an un-open space. The Koryo Saram made their home in Ansan where they moved along with their memories and history from Central Asia, which Soyoung refers to as "the process of transposing homes."[43]

Ansan is a weird place; on the one hand, it is the most open, in the sense that it has the highest population of the 'needed' but 'unwanted,' the 'outcast,' but is at the same time the most excluded and isolated place, where these people are always there as the other in Korean society. It is home for them, but also home for nobody at the same time. Everyone seems to feel *un-homey* (Unheimlichkeit—Un-zuhause) here: the feeling of being isolated, being alone. The twist of this *un-homey-ness* lies, however, in that this feeling is the "primordial phenomenon" that opens up the possibility for an authentic understanding of being in the state of angst.[44] The cultural memory of the Koryo Saram was not included within the boundaries of the *ouri* of normative Korean society, but they bring their memory and their history from Central Asia to Ansan. The geographical and political borders between 'we' and 'not-we' are demolished in the place where they made their homes. In their places they meet other worlds: they connect with the others whom they embraced in their 'we' and who also embraced them mutually. They have a "plurality of spaces"[45] within their open boundaries of the 'we.'

The history and the collective identity of the Koryo Saram is a good representation of the we group that is formed by an external opposition then stabilized and survived through their story as 'our story,' as Carr explained in the context of his theory of historical narrative and the 'we' (see chapter 5, section 3). The history of deportation and oppression by an external force initiated their we-ness as the Koryo Saram, but the significance of the stabilization and the survival of this group lies in their history and memory of solidarity with the others. I find this a convincing and truthful story of the 'we,' the pre-subjective we as humanity. In the end, it is *us* who tells *our* story.

## 5. MULTIPLE WE'S AND THE OUTSIDER: *OURIDEUL* AND *GEU*

In Korean, there is another expression for parties excluded from the 'we.' To point at a person, you can say 'this person' or 'that person' as in many languages, but there is a third demonstrative pronoun in Korean which is *geu* [ge].[46] This is hard to translate into English because there is no matching term. This particular demonstrative pronoun refers to someone or something that does not belong to the 'we.' In this sense, the 'we' itself as a whole can be opposed to the one who does not belong to it, which is neither you, nor she, nor he, nor they, nor this, nor that.

This reveals another whole dimension of the 'we.' This 'not-in-the-we-belonging' person can be taken as an object in contrast to the all, who belong to the 'we.' The 'we' stands in contrast to someone who is neither this person, nor that person, nor she/he/it, nor they, but to someone who does not belong to this 'we' at all by existing in a separate time and space. This distance is, however, not only spatiotemporal, but also emotional and psychological, referring to someone I do not know (*wissen aber nicht kennen*). Even a stranger, however, at the same time, if she/he is present with me in the conversation, could belong to the 'we,' because by being there, that person is no longer another object in contrast to the 'we.'

A stranger and my father are not the same 'he,' but they can be included in the 'we,' in which I, my father, the stranger, and the third person, who is referred to in the conversation, belong together in the 'we.' This belonging together does not, however, necessarily entail a social or psychological bond between different individuals. In this 'we,' these three individuals' memories are neither necessarily shared nor do their individual time-consciousnesses overlap to construct a common, shared timeline, but they nevertheless belong together.

Who gets to become *geu* and who decides it? Sometimes it is a given. We surely don't know everyone, and the person who we don't know but talk about is naturally *geu*. Also, if the person who the speaker talks about is not present at the site of conversation, that person is referred to as *geu*, because of the actual physical distance, but the people whom we know, are close to, or even family members can become *geu*, as how Korea made the Koryo Saram *geu* people. It depends on how you feel about that person. For example, in the following sentence *geu* person could be (1) a person whom the speaker doesn't know or is not close to, (2) the person who is not there with the speaker and the listener, or (3) someone the speaker knows well and is close to, but with whom the speaker is probably not necessarily happy with at the time of speaking.

"Why did *geu* person do that?"

Therefore, this *geu* person here could be a complete stranger and the husband of the speaker at the same time. The emotional relation of the speaker to the person that is spoken of is flexible. In other words, who belongs to us and who doesn't is not always necessarily a question of the place of my birth, the people with whom I am blood-related, the culture with which I identify, the color of my skin, the people whom I work with, and so on and so forth. We all belong to *ouri*, technically, no matter what. After all, we belong to the human race, as the writer Toni Morrison says, the only race.

But there are also multiple different groups of 'we.' They appear and disappear, even in one conversation; this 'we,' that 'we,' my 'we,' your 'we,' our 'we,' there can be a number of different layers of the 'we.' There are we's. The variety and the plurality of the 'we' is undoubtably there, and it is not a problem. It is not the diversity of the 'we' that causes the problem, but it is how we 'feel about' the other we's. Here, it is important to note that there is a fundamental difference between not-we and not-I. Not-I is a necessary part of the 'I.' For 'I' to call itself 'I,' it has to have not-I in itself. However, it is not the case for the 'we.' Not-we is not the necessary condition for the formation and maintenance of the 'we.' Not-we is not in the 'we,' it is against the 'we.' This is why not-we is used as one of the most convenient and effective sources of political propaganda.

We is already a plural pronoun, therefore it is bizarre to make it 'more plural.' However, in Korean, *ouri* can be pluralized again by adding the plural suffix *deul* [del]. *Ourideul* literally means we's, the plural of the 'we.' The pluralized 'we' is used, in most cases, simply as 'we.' It is neither strange nor changes the meaning if one replaces *ourideul* with *ouri*.

"Don't worry, *ourideul* will help."
"Don't worry, *ouri* will help."

In this sense, *ourideul* in place of *ouri* is a superfluous expression, but it is not an uncommon expression. It is a daily word that is used quite often both in written and spoken form. The National Institute of Korean Language also explains that *ourideul* is a surplus expression but not grammatically wrong.[47] The Korea University Korean Dictionary, however, differentiates *ourideul* from *ouri* in the sense that the group *ourideul* indicates is more specific and individual than that of the *ouri*. It is defined that *ourideul* refers to the speaker and the people who are around or the group which the speaker belongs to.[48] For example, the *notre* (our) of the title of the ballet *Notre Faust* is translated as *ourideul* in Korean. The boundary of the 'we' group in *ouri* is vague and fluidic, but the boundary of *ourideul* feels clearer and more firm. I assume that it might be related to the character of the word *ouri*, that it has the strong connotation of the 'one big family.' Namely, even if it is plural, *ouri* gives an impression of the unity, or feeling of 'one-ness.' It is as if each person in *ouri* is taken as self-in-relation rather than as a single person, so to emphasize the plurality of the members of the group, the suffix *deul* has to be added. In the same sense, *neohi* [naw-hee],[49] the second-person plural and *jeohi*, another first-personal plural, are used with *deul* as well, such as *neohideul* and *jeohideul*.

The contradiction between 'I' and 'Thou' sticks out more clearly between *ourideul* (plural first-person plural) and *neohideul* (plural second-person plural) than in the case of *ouri*. That is probably why it is more common to say *ouri* for, for example, country or home. In the case of husband, it means something other than 'my husband.' If the speaker says *ourideul* for 'our husband,' it means the husband whom 'we' have in common. *Ourideul* has a clearer feeling of 'this group' compared to *ouri*. Each one of us has a number of groups of *ourideul*, the specific groups to which I belong, but to which not everyone can belong. The expression *deul* brings out the fact that there are multiple selves in the group, rather than that there are multiple groups. Each member of the we group, therefore, seems to have a stronger feeling of identification or membership with the group and the other members of the group, when the group is referred to as *ourideul* instead of *ouri*. It is ironic that the double plurality of *ouri* seems to highlight the self-ness within the more distinct and more closed boundary.

## 6. THE FEELING OF SAYING *OURI*: BEING AT HOME

When one says *ouri* in Korean, the impression that one gets is that it is more than to indicate this, that, or my someone or something. For example, one can simply say 'husband' to refer to her/his husband without 'our,' which is also grammatically correct and common in Korean. If you say "husband wants to go for a walk," everyone knows that you are talking about your husband. But then why do they say 'our husband' in Korean? Even when one thinks to themself, as a native Korean speaker (not talking to anyone else), one can still refer to my husband as 'our husband' in Korean. In this sense, this 'our' is not to indicate a particular husband, either 'my,' 'our,' or 'not my husband,' but 'our husband' is the same as 'husband' that comes with the feeling of being connected.

What then is the immediate impression or mental image that a person could have when saying 'our husband'? For example, one could reflect upon the image that comes up when saying 'pencil.' One pictures a pencil that he/she can hold and use to write. When I say 'our husband' in Korean, for instance, the very first thing that comes to my mind is a door to a house which is my home. This is not the door of the actual house where I have grown up or now live, but it is a symbolic door of home, home not as a specific place, but home where I belong. The expression 'our someone' of one's family that comes with the projection of a door to home can be represented in the Chinese characters that mean 'home' or 'house,' which are 宇 [oo][50] and 宙[51] [joo]. When these two characters are combined together, they form one word that means 'the cosmos,' 'the universe,' 'space.' This door seems to be this space of 'our' that opens up whenever someone needs to enter to be home 'with me.' But this 'with me' also doesn't feel like 'I' am already there waiting for others to enter, but the space behind this door seems like where we all are, who 'I' refer to as 'our,' including myself.

It probably was not a coincidence that I have this picture though. The Chinese character for door is 門 [moon],[52] which is the word for door in Korean as well. This was the imaginary door that was envisioned as I was trying to 'see' how it felt to say *ouri* someone' in Korean. The Chinese words for the 'I' and the 'we' are 我 [wo][53] and 我們 [wo-men]. And, in the word that refers to the 'we,' you see the 門. It may be a revelation of the cultural imprinting that I was neither aware nor conscious of, or an awakening of a blurred trace of my personal memory that originates from my childhood education experience. Whatever the case may be, I have the feeling of *ouri* as being in a house with this door that could be opened for anyone. I am not in an undifferentiated unity, but also do not exist as a sole subject. This house (with a roof) is not unlimited, but also not limited only to my kin or myself. It is worth noting that in forming collective identity based on cultural memory, the notion of home attached to a place played a crucial role. Home is an actual place with which 'I' and 'we' can identify, and a place that can be transposed. It is a certain, particular place distinct from everywhere else, but it could be everywhere.

Home as a place represents the characteristic of embodiment of self in spatiality. We as bodily selves stand in relation with others beyond our bodily boundaries. Each individual person is there standing in the open τόπος (place, topos), yet in necessary relation (as topological boundaries) with others. Home could be regarded as primitive, in the sense that most of us are born into a home, but it is not always the case. We all need home, but we leave home and lose home too. The absence of home does not mean not having a place to put your head down and store your things, but it means to be separated from relation, standing outside of the sphere of the *web*. Having to leave home is the fundamental cause of existential anxiety. Anxiety is, after all, the feeling of *un-homey-ness*. For every single one of us living in the world where leaving home is considered to be a necessary procedure, it may not come as a surprise that anxiety is placed in the core of our existence. But home is not a fixed property that cannot be created again or changed. It is a dynamic and open space within the boundary of connection. And this boundary is constantly in formation.

## NOTES

1. Part of this section appears in Hye Young Kim, "The Place of Worlding: Central Asia—Korea. Subaltern Cosmopolitanism." In *Worlding Asia: Asian/Pacific/Planetary Convergences*. Durham, NC: Duke University Press, forthcoming.
2. Soyoung Kim, "Towards a Technology of the Dead: Kim Soyoung on Her 'Exile' Documentary Trilogy," *Senses of Cinema* 78 (2016), https://www.sensesofcinema.com/2016/feature-articles/kim-soyoung-exile-trilogy/.
3. Kim, "Towards a Technology of the Dead."
4. Kim, "Towards a Technology of the Dead."
5. Soyoung Kim, "Subaltern Cosmopolitanism: World and Cinema beyond Empire," *Hwanghae Review*, no. 89 (December 2015), 79.
6. Kim, "Subaltern Cosmopolitanism," 79.
7. Kim, "Subaltern Cosmopolitanism," 79.
8. Kim, "Subaltern Cosmopolitanism," 80.
9. Kim, "Subaltern Cosmopolitanism," 79.
10. Soyoung is the first name of Soyoung Kim. However, instead of using her last name, Kim, I will quote her under her first name to avoid confusion and distinguish the different authors with the same family name. There are multiple authors with the family name Kim who are cited in this book. In Korea, most names consist of three syllables, the first name with two syllables and the family name with one syllable. When they are cited in Korean academic writing, the full name including the first and family name is used as one word. For example, "KimHyeYoung."
11. Kim, 'Subaltern Cosmopolitanism,' 80.
12. Kim, "Subaltern Cosmopolitanism," 81.
13. Ágnes Heller, "A Tentative Answer to the Question: Has Civil Society Cultural Memory?" *Social Research* 68, no. 4 (2001): 1032.
14. Heller, "A Tentative Answer," 1033.
15. Heller, "A Tentative Answer," 1033.
16. Heller, "A Tentative Answer," 1033.

17. Kim, "Subaltern Cosmopolitanism," 82.
18. Heller, "A Tentative Answer," 1032.
19. Jeffrey K. Olick, "Collective Memory: The Two Cultures," *Sociological Theory* 17, no. 3 (November 1, 1999): 342.
20. Heller, "A Tentative Answer," 1038.
21. Heller, "A Tentative Answer," 1032.
22. Jan Assmann, "Kollektives Gedächtnis und Kulturelle Identität," in *Kultur und Gedächtnis*, ed. Jan Assmann and Tonio Hölscher (Frankfurt am Main: Suhrkamp, 1988), 13.
23. In the sense of "being up-to-date" or "currentness."
24. Assmann, "Kollektives Gedächtnis," 13.
25. Olick, "Collective Memory," 341.
26. Kim, "Subaltern Cosmopolitanism," 79.
27. Michel Foucault, *History of Madness*, trans. Jean Khalfa and Jonathan Murphy (New York: Routledge, 2006).
28. Kim, "Subaltern Cosmopolitanism," 79-80.
29. "Place," in *Cambridge Dictionary*, accessed July 28, 2018, https://dictionary.cambridge.org/dictionary/english/place.
30. 한.
31. Kim, "Subaltern Cosmopolitanism," 81.
32. Kim, "Subaltern Cosmopolitanism," 80.
33. Kolkhoz refers to the collective farms of the U.S.S.R. formed by combining small individual farms together in a cooperative structure. Kolkhoz is considered as an intermediate stage in the transition to the ideal of state farming, for example, Sovkhoz.
34. Sovkhoz is the "state-operated agricultural estate in the U.S.S.R. organized according to industrial principles for specialized large-scale production. Workers were paid wages but might also cultivate personal garden plots. Its form developed from the few private estates taken over in their entirety by the state in the original Soviet expropriations" (https://www.britannica.com).
35. Kim, "Subaltern Cosmopolitanism," 78-81.
36. 조선 朝鮮.
37. Kim, "Subaltern Cosmopolitanism," 79.
38. Kim, "Subaltern Cosmopolitanism," 80.
39. Kim, "Subaltern Cosmopolitanism," 78.
40. Joseph Michael Gratale, "Geographies of Cultural Globalisation and Cosmopolitanism of the Future," in *The Psychology and Politics of the Collective: Groups, Crowds and Mass Identifications*, ed. Ruth Parkin-Gounelas (New York/London: Routledge, 2012), 147.
41. Joseonjok [jo-sun-jok] 조선족 朝鮮族.
42. Kim, "Towards a Technology of the Dead."
43. Kim, "Subaltern Cosmopolitanism," 86.
44. Heidegger, *Sein und Zeit*, 184–191.

45. Filip Mattens, "From the Origin of Spatiality to a Variety of Spaces," in *The Oxford Handbook of the History of Phenomenology*, ed. Dan Zahavi (Oxford: Oxford University Press, 2018), 566.

46. 그. The discussion on *geu* is also found in Kim, "A Phenomenological Approach to the Korean 'We.'"

47. *National Institute of Korean Language*, n.d., https://www.korean.go.kr/front/mcfaq/mcfaqView.do?mn_id=217&mcfaq_seq=3777.

48. *Korea University Korean Dictionary*, n.d., https://ko.dict.naver.com/#/entry/koko/ae7b653022ae417eaf272337bf530e85.

49. 너희.

50. 우 (pronunciation in Korean).

51. 주.

52. 문.

53. Pronunciation in Chinese.

*Chapter 12*

# Epilogue
## *Violence of the We*

How do Koreans *really* feel about the expression *ouri*? Obviously, it depends on whom you are talking to. However, the immediate reaction from the Korean people around me, when they heard about my project on *ouri*, was mostly negative. It is complicated, but one of the reasons was its association with nationalism. Although '*ouri* mom' is probably the most frequently used *ouri* expression in the context of daily conversation, many Koreans, when they are asked to give an example of *ouri*, would first associate this word with '*ouri* country' or '*ouri* people.' Regardless of whether everyone is in agreement or not, Korea is still under the shadow of military culture, much of which has been passed down from the time of colonization and maintained under a series of dictator leaders, and which is often disguised as the Confucian tradition of community. William McNeill's description below is a quite accurate illustration from an outsider's viewpoint.

> In China, Korea, and Japan, however, calisthenics and other forms of mass movement in unison continue to flourish with the uninhibited support of political and economic leaders, despite (or even because of) past associations with Japan's imperial ambitions. Schools, factories, political parties, and, in Japan, religious sects all rely on rhythmic movement in unison to establish and confirm collective solidarity among those who participate. Confucian family discipline and a traditional reliance on formal education as a practical path to personal and family advancement do much to explain the striking economic growth of these countries since World War II. But in all probability, muscular bonding also contributes to their success, by creating and enhancing social cohesion and willing cooperation at all levels of society.[1]

He speaks of economic growth and of the positive sides of this community culture in China, Korea, and Japan, but this description entails many more stories in it that are, in fact, not so positive. The expressions '*ouri* country' and '*ouri* anything' that is related to the nation in Korean cause complex feelings for the majority of Koreans. They feel self-defensive of their '*ouri* country' and '*ouri* people' due to the memory of colonization, but at the same time, the *ouri* culture is accompanied by feelings of fear and displeasure rooted in the suppression of individual freedom and character. It was only in 1945 that Korea regained their sovereignty after almost forty years of colonization. The military-style culture that is still present in all levels of schooling, for example, is among the latent traces of colonization. Korea is a rapidly changing society, and the traces seem to be evaporating faster and faster with every new generation. However, even in the 1990s, for example, a huge number of schools in Korea strictly controlled the appearance of their students. Students already wore the same school uniform, but they were required to have the same hair style, the same kind of shoes, the same color of socks, and so on. If someone dared to break the rule of being the same, whoever and whatever was sticking out was cut off. Physical punishment was the norm in the field of education for treating misbehaving students, which to a large extent implied that they didn't act like everyone else.

Korea is, after all, a country that is still technically at war. The end of Korean War was never declared; it was only a cease-fire. South and North Korea are '*ouri* people' but not '*ouri* nation,' yet sharing '*ouri* culture, language, and history.' They are one and the most feared other for each other at the same time. In 1969, mandatory military education in high school and college started in South Korea under the name of self-defense against North Korea. By 1988, they stopped teaching the military class in college and in high school, but it disappeared completely only in 1997. In the military, what is most important is obedience to authority in order to keep corporate order, hold the group together, and maintain high efficiency. About two years of military service is still mandatory for all males in South Korea, which means the majority of working men in this society have been trained in the military.

It is a fact that the propaganda for patriotism is at the core of any military setting all over the world. The boundary between patriotism and nationalism is blurred. Anxiety in the never-ending state of war empowers the justification of nationalism. Who belongs to us and who doesn't becomes an important question, not only within the boundary of the military, but everywhere. Everyone judges and is judged consciously and unconsciously to discover who belongs to us and who doesn't. The easiest way to track down a non-member is to check their identity: identity in a fragmentary, one-dimensional sense, namely whether they are identical with everyone else. This identity is not bound with necessary difference. There is no room for difference in this group. The worst part of the situation is that the ones who are already in this group do not even realize anymore what is happening or what is being done for this group to be maintained as a closed crowd. This is the situation where people become blind and numb to the ordinary violence that is justified under the name of holding the insiders together and keeping outsiders out. When ordinary violence becomes the norm of the society, collective anxiety invades and occupies the individual space. There is no space for individuality and therefore, humanity.

Korea, though, is not the only society in this everlasting collective anxiety state. The consistent rise of nationalism and racism on a global scale is rooted in contagious, collective anxiety and fed by the faceless fear of the masses. Countless journeys and fights to find, to protect, to steal, to expand, and to make home are everywhere. We all need to be at home, but home is not the boundary for securing a place for incubating fear of the other. When home becomes a closed fortress built up with 'family egoism,' this distorted community seems to cause an even more severe isolation of individuals. According to the World Health Organization, the suicide rate in South Korea is the tenth highest in the world and the highest among OECD countries as of 2019, with a significantly high rate of suicide among the elderly and young students. What a brutal irony of the country of *ouri*, the 'one big happy family.' Home is space with open boundaries where we separate and connect. Home is where we make ourselves home. It is all about *how we make ourselves feel about ourselves*.

## NOTE

1. McNeill, William H. *Keeping Together in Time: Dance and Drill in Human History* (Cambridge, MA: Harvard University Press, 1995), 151–152.

# Bibliography

Adams, Nikki and Thomas J. Conners. "Imposters and Their Implications for Third-Person Feature Specification." *Linguistics*, forthcoming. https://doi.org/10.1515/ling-2020-0047.
Adolphs, Ralph. "Social Cognition and the Human Brain." *Trends in Cognitive Sciences* 3, no. 12 (1999): 469–79. https://doi.org/10.1016/S1364-6613(99)01399-6.
Agha, Asif. *Language and Social Relations*. Vol. 24. Cambridge: Cambridge University Press, 2006.
Anstis, S. M., J. W. Mayhew, and Tania Morley. "The Perception of Where a Face or Television 'Portrait' is Looking." *The American Journal of Psychology* 82, no. 4 (1969): 474–489.
Anton, John P. "On the Meaning of Kategoria in Aristotle's Categories." In *Essays in Ancient Greek Philosophy V: Aristotle's Ontology*, edited by Anthony Preus and John P. Anton. New York: SUNY Press, 1992.
Apelt, Otto. "Die Kategorien des Aristoteles." In *Beiträge zur Geschichte der Griechischen Philosophie*, edited by Otto Apelt. Leipzig: Meiner, 1891.
Arendt, Hannah. *Essays in Understanding 1930–1954: Formation, Exile and Totalitarianism*. New York: Schocken, 1994.
Aristotle. *Nicomachean Ethics*. Translated by H. Rackham. Boston: Harvard University Press, 1926.
———. *Categories, De Interpretatione*. Translated by Jinseong Kim. Seoul: E J Books, 2005.
Assmann, Jan. "Kollektives Gedächtnis und Kulturelle Identität." In *Kultur und Gedächtnis*, edited by Jan Assmann and Tonio Hölscher. Frankfurt am Main: Suhrkamp, 1988.
Bach, J. S. *Well-Tempered Calvier, Prelude No.2*. New York: G. Schirmer, 1893. https://www.free-scores.com/download-sheet-music.php?pdf=466.
Bäck, Allan. *Aristotle's Theory of Predication*. Vol. 84. Leiden: Brill, 2000.
Bermúdez, José Luis. *The Paradox of Self-Consciousness*. Cambridge, MA: The MIT Press, 1998.

Bernasconi, Robert. "Must We Avoid Speaking of Religion? The Truths of Religions." *Research in Phenomenology* 39, no. 2 (2009): 204–223.
Bonitz, Hermann. *Über die Kategorien des Aristoteles*. Vol. 10. Vienna: Braumüller in Komm, 1853.
Bornemark, Jonna. "Life beyond Individuality: A-Subjective Experience in Pregnancy." In *Phenomenology of Pregnancy*, edited by Jonna Bornemark and Nicholas Smith. Stockholm: Södertörns Högskola, 2016.
Brentano, Franz. *Psychology from an Empirical Standpoint*. Edited by Linda McAlister. Translated by D. B. Terrell, Linda McAlister, and Antos Rancurello. London: Routledge & Kegan Paul, 1973.
Brinck, Ingar. "The Role of Intersubjectivity in the Development of Intentional Communication." In *The Shared Mind: Perspectives on Intersubjectivity*, edited by Jordan Zlatev, Timothy P. Racine, Chris Sinha, and Esa Itkonen. Amsterdam: John Benjamins Publishing Company, 2008: 115–140.
Brinck, Ingar, Vasudevi Reddy, and Dan Zahavi. "The Primacy of the 'We'?." In *Embodiment, Enaction, and Culture: Investigating the Constitution of the Shared World*, edited by Christoph Durt, Thomas Fuchs, and Christian Tewes. Cambridge, MA: MIT, 2017.
Buber, Martin. *I and Thou*. Translated by Ronald Gregor Smith. Edinburgh: T. & T. Clark, 1937.
——. *Ich und Du*. Stuttgart: Reclam, 1995.
Cambridge Dictionary, s.v. "place." accessed July 28, 2018. https://dictionary.cambridge.org/dictionary/english/place.
Canetti, Elias. *Crowds and Power*. London: Macmillan, 1984.
Carr, David. "Cogitamus Ergo Sumus: The Intentionality of the First-Person Plural." *The Monist* 69, no. 4 (1986): 521–33
——. *Time, Narrative, and History*. Bloomington: Indiana University Press, 1991.
——. *Experience and History. Phenomenological Perspectives on the Historical World*. Oxford: Oxford University Press, 2014.
——. "'… so Etwas Wie Leiblichkeit.': On Social Embodiment." *Yearbook for Eastern and Western Philosophy* 2017, no. 2 (2017): 91–103.
——. "Intersubjectivity and Embodiment." In *Husserl's Phenomenology of Intersubjectivity: Historical Interpretations and Contemporary Applications*, edited by Frode Kjosavik, Christian Beyer, and Christel Frick. Routledge Research in Phenomenology. New York: Taylor & Francis, 2018: 249–62.
Chartrand, Tanya L., and Rick van Baaren. "Human Mimicry." In *Advances in Experimental Social Psychology*. Vol. 41. Cambridge, MA: Academic Press, 2009: 219–74. https://doi.org/10.1016/S0065-2601(08)00405-X.
Choi, Jaehoon. "Jussive Subjects as Imposters." *Linguistics*, no. 74 (2016): 3–24.
Cysouw, Michael. "Inclusive/Exclusive Distinction in Independent Pronouns." *The World Atlas of Language Structures Online*. Munich: Max Planck Digital Library. http://Wals.Info/Chapter/39, 2008.
Dabashi, Hamid. "Can Non-Europeans Think? What Happens with Thinkers Who Operate Outside the European Philosophical 'Pedigree'?" *Al-Jazeera*. Accessed

November 20, 2017. http://www.aljazeera.com/indepth/opinion/2013/01/201311 4142638797542.html.
Damasio, Antonio. *The Feelings of What Happens*. New York: Mariner Books, 2000.
van Dijk, Teun A. "Introduction: Dialogue as Discourse and Interaction." In *Handbook of Discourse Analysis*, Vol. 3, edited by Teun A. van Dijk. Cambridge, MA: Academic Press, 1985.
Dennett, Daniel, *Consciousness Explained*. New York: Back Bay Books, 1991.
Einstein, Albert. *Relativity: The Special and General Theory*. Translated by Robert W. Lawson. London: Methuen & Co., 1920.
Falck, Andreas. "From Interest Contagion to Perspective Sharing: How Social Attention Affects Children's Performance in False-Belief Tasks." PhD Thesis, Department of Psychology, Lund University, 2016.
———. "Contagion-Based Mechanisms in Verbal and Non-Verbal False-Belief Tasks." n.d.
———. "The Social Emergence of Subjectivity." n.d.
Falck, Andreas, Ingar Brinck, and Magnus Lindgren. "Interest Contagion in Violation-of-Expectation-Based False-Belief Tasks." *Frontiers in Psychology* 5 (2014): 23. https://doi.org/10.3389/fpsyg.2014.00023.
Fanon, Franz, *Black Skin, White Masks*. Translated by Charles Lam Markmann. New York: Grove Press, 1968.
Fishman, Joshua A. "The Sociology of Language." In *Language and Social Context : Selected Readings*, edited by Pier Paolo Giglioli. Harmondsworth: Penguin Books, 1990.
Fivaz-Depeursinge, Elisabeth, Nicolas Favez, and France Frascarolo. "Threesome Intersubjectivity in Infancy." In *The Structure and Development of Self-Consciousness: Interdisciplinary Perspectives*, edited by Dan Zahavi, Thor Grünbaum, and Josef Parnas. Amsterdam: John Benjamins Publishing, 2004: 221–34.
Foer, Jonathan Safran. "Why We Must Cut out Meat and Dairy before Dinner to Save the Planet." *The Guardian*, September 28, 2019. https://www.theguardian.com/books/2019/sep/28/meat-of-the-matter-the-inconvenient-truth-about-what-we-eat.
von Foerster, Heinz. *Understanding Understanding: Essays on Cybernetics and Cognition*. New York: Springer, 2007.
Foucault, Michel. *History of Madness*. Translated by Jean Khalfa and Jonathan Murphy. New York: Routledge, 2006.
Freud, Sigmund. *Massenpsychologie und Ich-Analyse*. Leipzig, Wien, Zürich: Internationaler Psychoanalytischer Verlag, 1923.
Frith, Chris. "Role of Facial Expressions in Social Interactions." *Philosophical Transactions of the Royal Society B: Biological Sciences* 364, no. 1535 (December 12, 2009): 3453–58.
Fuchs, Thomas. "Zwischen Leib und Körper." In *Leib und Leben. Perspektiven für eine neue Kultur der Körperlichkeit*, edited by Martin Hähnel and Marcus Knaup. Darmstadt: WBG, 2013: 82–93.
Gallagher, James. "More than half your body is not human." *BBC News Health*, April 10, 2018. https://www.bbc.com/news/health-43674270 (accessed April 22, 2020).

Gallagher, Shaun. "Philosophical Conceptions of the Self: Implications for Cognitive Science." *Trends in Cognitive Science* 4, no. 1 (2000): 14–21.
Gallotti, Mattia, and Chris D. Frith. "Social Cognition in the We-Mode." *Trends in Cognitive Sciences* 17, no. 4 (2013): 160–65. https://doi.org/10.1016/j.tics.2013.02.002.
Gamm, Gerhard. *Der Deutsche Idealismus: Eine Einführung in die Philosophie von Fichte, Hegel und Schelling.* Stuttgart: Reclam, 1997.
Gazzinga, Michael S. *The Mind's Past*, Berkeley and Los Angeles: University of California Press, 1998.
de Gelder, Beatrice. "Why Bodies? Twelve Reasons for Including Bodily Expressions in Affective Neuroscience." *Philosophical Transactions of the Royal Society B: Biological Sciences* 364, no. 1535 (2009): 3475–84. https://doi.org/10.1098/rstb.2009.0190.
Giglioli, Pier Paolo. *Language and Social Context: Selected Readings.* Harmondsworth: Penguin Books, 1990.
Goldie, Peter. *The Mess Inside, Narrative, Emotion, and the Mind.* Oxford: Oxford University Press, 2012.
Gratale, Joseph Michael. "Geographies of Cultural Globalisation and Cosmopolitanism of the Future." In *The Psychology and Politics of the Collective: Groups, Crowds and Mass Identifications*, edited by Ruth Parkin-Gounelas. New York/London: Routledge, 2012: 136–51.
Gray, Jesse Glenn. *The Warriors: Reflections on Men in Battle.* Lincoln: University of Nebraska Press, 1999.
Gumperz, John J. "The Speech Community." In *Language and Social Context: Selected Readings*, edited by Pier Paolo Giglioli. Harmondsworth: Penguin Books, 1990.
Han, Chung-Hye, and Dennis Ryan Storoshenko. "Semantic Binding of Long-Distance Anaphor Caki in Korean." *Language* 88, no. 4 (2012): 764–90.
Harris, Richard. *Roadmap to Korean: Everything You Ever Wanted to Know about the Language.* 2nd Edition. Seoul: Hollym, 2005.
Hatfield, Elaine, John T. Cacioppo, and Richard L. Rapson. "Primitive Emotional Contagion." *Review of Personality and Social Psychology* 14 (1992): 151–77.
Hegel, G.W.F. *Phänomenologie des Geistes.* Frankfurt am Main: Suhrkamp, 1989.
Heidegger, Martin. *Sein und Zeit.* Tübingen: Max Niemeyer Verlag, 2006.
———. *Was Ist Metaphysik.* Frankfurt am Main: Vittorio Klostermann, 2007.
Held, Klaus. *Lebendige Gegewart. Die Frage nach der Seinsweise des transzendentalen Ich bei Edmund Husserl. Entwickelt am Leitfaden der Zeitproblematik,* Den Haag: Martinus Nijhoff, 1966.
Heller, Ágnes. "A Tentative Answer to the Question: Has Civil Society Cultural Memory?" *Social Research* 68, no. 4 (2001): 1031–40.
———. "Five Approaches to the Phenomenon of Shame." *Social Research: An International Quarterly* 70, no. 4 (2003): 1015–30.
———. *A Theory of Feelings.* Lexington Books, 2009.
———. "Über die Verschiedenheit der Ästhetischen, Reflektierten, und Ethischen Empathie." n.d.

Hoy, David C. "History, Historicity, and Historiography in Being and Time." In *Heidegger and Modern Philosophy*, edited by Michael Murray. New Haven and London: Yale University Press, 1978: 329–354.
Hume, David. *A Treatise of Human Nature*. Oxford: Clarendon Press, 1888.
Husserl, Edmund. *Ideen zu einer reinen Phänomenologie und phänomenologischen Philosophie. Zweites Buch. Phänomenologische Untersuchungen zur Konstitution*. Den Haag: Martinus Nijhoff, 1952.
———. *Die Krisis der Europäischen Wissenschaften und die Transzendentale Phänomenologie. Eine Einleitung in die Phänomenologische Philosophie*. Den Haag: Martinus Nijhoff, 1954.
———. *Ideen zu einer reinen Phänomenologie und phänomenologischen Philosophie. Erstes Buch. Allgemeine Einführung in die reine Phänomenologie*. Den Haag: Martinus Nijhoff, 1973.
———. *Zur Phänomenologie der Intersubjektivität. Texte aus dem Nachlass. Erster Teil: 1905–1920*, Vol. 13, edited by Iso Kern. Husserliana. Den Haag: Martinus Nijhoff, 1973.
———. *Zur Phänomenologie der Intersubjektivität: Texte aus dem Nachlass Zweiter Teil: 1921–1928*. Vol. 14. Den Haag: Martinus Nijhoff, 1973.
Iacobini, Matt, Tina Gonsalves, Nadia Bianchi-Berthouze, and Chris Frith. "Emotional Contagion in Interactive Art." In *Proceedings of the International Conference on Kansei Engineering and Emotion Research, Paris, France*, 2010.
Iribarne, Julia V. *Husserls Theorie der Intersubjektivität*. Freiburg/München: Verlag Alber, 1994.
Jeong, Kyeong-Ouk. "The Use of the First Person Plural Possessive Pronoun Woorie in Korean Language." *Journal of Korean Language Education* 16, no. 3 (2005): 405–22.
Kauffman, Louis H.. "Sign and Space." In *Religious Experience and Scientific Paradigms. Proceedings of the 1982 IASWR Conference, Stony Brook*. New York: Institute of Advanced Study of World Religions, 1985: 118–64.
———. "Knot Logic." In *Knots and Applications*, Series on Knots and Everything, Volume 6, edited by Louis Kauffman. Singapore: World Scientific, 1995: 1–110. https://doi.org/10.1142/9789812796189_0001.
———. "Time, Imaginary Value, Paradox, Sign and Space." *AIP Conference Proceedings* 627, no. 1 (August 20, 2002): 146–59. https://doi.org/10.1063/1.1503680.
———. "Virtual Logic: The First Distinction." *Cybernetics and Human Knowing* 12, no. 4 (2005): 97.
———. "Categorical Pairs and the Indicative Shift." *Applied Mathematics and Computation* 218, no. 16 (2012): 7989–8004. https://doi.org/10.1016/j.amc.2012.01.042.
———. "Knot Logic: Logical Connection and Topological Connection." In *Mind in Mathematics: Essays on Cognition and Mathematical Method* (Interdisciplinary Studies on the Nature of Mathematics 3), edited by M. Bockarova, M. Danesi, D. Martinovic, and R. Nunez. Munich: Lincom Europa, 2015: 33–57.
Kim, Chunsu. *Flower, He Came to Me and Became a Flower*. Seoul: Siinsaenggak, 2013.

Kim, Hye Young. "Care and History: Phenomenology of Dasein in the Framework of Martin Heidegger's Being and Time." *Existentia* XXIV FASC.1-2 (2014): 57–68.

———. *Sorge und Geschichte: Phänomenologische Untersuchung im Anschluss an Heidegger*. Duncker und Humblot, 2015.

———. "A Phenomenological Approach to the Korean "We": A Study in Social Intentionality." *Frontiers of Philosophy in China* 12, no. 4 (2017): 612–632.

———. "Knots and Consciousness: Knotted Models Applied to Uriah Kriegel's "Consciousness, Permanent Self-Awareness, and Higher-Order Monitoring"." *4th Meeting of the CHAIN Structures of Consciousness, Sep 2019*, Sapporo, Japan. hal-02290606f. https://hal.archives-ouvertes.fr/hal-02290606.

———. "A Topological Analysis of Space-Time-Consciousness: Self, Self-Self, Self-Other." In *When Form Becomes Substance. Power of Gesture, Grammatical Intuition and Phenomenology of Space*, edited by Luciano Boi, Franck Jedrzejewski, and Carlos Lobo. Basel: Birkhäuser-Springer, forthcoming.

———. "The Place of Worlding: Central Asia – Korea. Subaltern Cosmopolitanism." In *Worlding Asia: Asian/Pacific/Planetary Convergences*. Durham, NC: Duke University Press, forthcoming.

———. "Music, Consciousness, and Knots: Visualization of Music." In *Ecrire comme composer : le rôle des diagrammes*, edited by Franck Jedrzejewski, Antonia Soulez, Carlos Lobo. Sampzon, France: Delatour, forthcoming.

———. "« Visualisation de la musique dans l'espace » : pour une compréhension de la spatialité et de la temporalité de la musique." *Intentio*, forthcoming.

Kim, Lan. "A Note on Imposter Expressions in Korean." *Linguistics*, no. 71 (2015): 139–60.

Kim, Soyoung. "Subaltern Cosmopolitanism: World and Cinema beyond Empire." *Hwanghae Review*, no. 89 (December 2015): 67–87.

———. "Towards a Technology of the Dead: Kim Soyoung on Her 'Exile' Documentary Trilogy." *Senses of Cinema* 78 (2016). http://sensesofcinema.com/2016/feature-articles/kim-soyoung-exile-trilogy/.

Korea University Korean Dictionary, s.v. "ourideul," accessed March 31, 2019, https://ko.dict.naver.com/#/entry/koko/ae7b653022ae417eaf272337bf530e85.

Kriegel, Uriah. "Consciousness, Permanent Self-Awareness, and Higher-Order Monitoring." *Dialogue* 41, no. 3 (2002): 517–40. https://doi.org/10.1017/S0012217300005242.

———. "Consciousness as Intransitive Self-Consciousness: Two Views and an Argument." *Canadian Journal of Philosophy*, 33, no. 1 (March 2003): 103–132.

———. *Subjective Consciousness: A Self-Representational Theory*. Oxford: Oxford University Press, 2009.

Lakin, Jessica L. and Tanya L. Chartrand. "Using Nonconscious Behavioral Mimicry to Create Affiliation and Rapport." *Psychological Science* 14, no. 4 (July 1, 2003): 334–39. https://doi.org/10.1111/1467-9280.14481.

Landweer, Hilge. "Choreographies With and Without a Choreographer. Intuitive and Intentional Corporeal Interactions." In *Touching and to Be Touched. Kinesthesia and Empathy in Dance and Movement*, edited by Gabriele Brandstetter, Gerko Egert, and Sabine Zubarik. Berlin/New York: DeGruyter, 2013: 131–59.

———. "Mass Emotion and Shared Feelings." *Yearbook for Eastern and Western Philosophy* 2017, no. 2 (2017): 104–17.
Le Bon, Gustave. *Psychologie des Foules*. Paris: F. Alcan, 1900.
Legrand, Dorothée. "Phenomenological Dimensions of Bodily Self-Consciousness." In *The Oxford Handbook of the Self*, edited by Shaun Gallagher. Oxford: Oxford University Press, 2011.
MacIntyre, Alasdair. *After Virtue. A Study in Moral Theory*. Notre Dame, IN: University of Notre Dame Press, 2007.
Marcel, Gabriel. *Être et Avoir*. Paris: Fernand Aubier, 1935.
———. *Being and Having*. Translated by Katharine Farrer. Westminster: Dacre Press, 1949.
Mattens, Filip. "Introducing Terms. Philosophical Vocabulary, Neologism and the Temporal Aspect of Meaning." In *Meaning and Language: Phenomenological Perspectives,* Vol. 187, edited by Filip Mattens. Dordrecht: Springer Science & Business Media, 2010.
———. "From the Origin of Spatiality to a Variety of Spaces." In *The Oxford Handbook of the History of Phenomenology*, edited by Dan Zahavi. Oxford: Oxford University Press, 2018. https://www.oxfordhandbooks.com/view/10.1093/oxfordhb/9780198755340.001.0001/oxfordhb-9780198755340-e-38.
McNeill, William H. *Keeping Together in Time: Dance and Drill in Human History*. Boston: Harvard University Press, 1997.
Merleau-Ponty, Maurice. *Phénoménologie de la Perception*. Paris: Gallimard, 1945.
Meyer, Christian and Ulrich von Wedelstaedt. "Intercorporeality, Interkinesthesia, and Enaction: New Perspectives on Moving Bodies in Interaction." In *Moving Bodies in Interaction–Interacting Bodies in Motion: Intercorporeality, Interkinesthesia, and Enaction in Sports*, Vol. 8, edited by Christian Meyer and Ulrich von Wedelstaedt. Amsterdam: John Benjamins Publishing, 2017.
National Institute of Korean Language. *The Dictionary of the National Institute of Korean Language*. https://stdict.korean.go.kr/search/searchView.do.
Neisser, Ulric. "Five Kinds of Self-Knowledge." *Philosophical Psychology* 1, no. 1 (1988): 35–59.
Niranjana, Tejaswini. "Alternative Frames? Questions for Comparative Research in the Third World." *Inter-Asia Cultural Studies* 1, no. 1 (January 1, 2000): 97–108. https://doi.org/10.1080/146493700361024.
Olick, Jeffrey K. "Collective Memory: The Two Cultures." *Sociological Theory* 17, no. 3 (November 1, 1999): 333–48. https://doi.org/10.1111/0735-2751.00083.
Pacherie, Elisabeth. "Is Collective Intentionality Really Primitive?" In *Explaining the Mental: Naturalist and Non-Naturalist Approaches to Mental Acts and Processes*, edited by Carlo Penco, Michael Beaney, and Massimiliano Vignolo. Newcastle: Cambridge Scholars Publishing, 2007.
———. "How Does It Feel to Act Together?" *Phenomenology and the Cognitive Sciences* 13, no. 1 (March 1, 2014): 25–46. https://doi.org/10.1007/s11097-013-9329-8.
Parmentier, Richard J. *Signs in Society: Studies in Semiotic Anthropology*. Bloomington: Indiana University Press, 1994.

Pellencin, Elisa, Maria Paola Paladino, Bruno Herbelin, and Andrea Serino. "Social Perception of Others Shapes One's Own Multisensory Peripersonal Space." *Cortex* 104 (2018): 163–79. https://doi.org/10.1016/j.cortex.2017.08.033.

Piaget, Jean. *The Origin of Intelligence in Children*, trans. Margaret Cook, New York: International University Press: 1952.

Reddy, Vasudevi. *How Infants Know Minds*. Boston: Harvard University Press, 2008.

Ricoeur, Paul. *Temps et récit*, tome I. Paris: Seuil, 1983.

———. *Soi-même comme un autre*. Paris: Seuil, 1990.

———. *Oneself as Another*. Translated by Kathleen Blamey. Chicago and London: University of Chicago Press, 1992.

Salmela, Mikko, and Michiru Nagatsu. "How Does It Really Feel to Act Together? Shared Emotions and the Phenomenology of We-Agency." *Phenomenology and the Cognitive Sciences* 16, no. 3 (July 1, 2017): 449–70. https://doi.org/10.1007/s11097-016-9465-z.

Sample, Ian. "Gut Bacteria May Have Impact on Mental Health, Study Says." *Guardian*, February 4, 2019. https://www.theguardian.com/science/2019/feb/04/gut-bacteria-mental-health-depression-study (accessed April 22, 2020).

Sandiford, Mark. *Qallunaat!: Why White People Are Funny*. ONF/NFB, 2006. http://www.nfb.ca/film/qallunaat_why_white_people_are_funny/?fbclid=IwAR3x_a0M8taD1RStt59Z-weMTmWMUB2syQQpRU7prHLfDGkhgJo_-1xpSck.

Sartre, Jean-Paul, *Being and Nothingness*. Translated by Hazel E. Barnes. New York: Washington Square Press, 1992.

———. *La Transcendance de l'Ego*, Paris: Librairie Philosophique J. Vrin, 2012.

Schechtman, Marya. "The Narrative Self." In *The Oxford Handbook of the Self*, edited by Shaun Gallagher. Oxford: Oxford University Press, 2011.

Scheler, Max. *The Nature of Sympathy*. Translated by Peter Heath. New York: Routledge, 2017.

Schmid, Hans Bernhard. "Plural Self-Awareness." *Phenomenology and the Cognitive Sciences* 13, no. 1 (March 1, 2014): 7–24. https://doi.org/10.1007/s11097-013-9317-z.

Schmidt-Biggemann, Wilhelm. *Apokalypse und Philologie*. Göttingen: V&R Unipress, 2007.

———. *Geschichte als absoluter Begriff*. Frankfurt am Main: Suhrkamp, 1991.

Searle, John. *Intentionality: An Essay in the Philosophy of Mind*. Cambridge: Cambridge University Press, 1983.

———. *The Construction of Social Reality*. New York: Simon and Schuster, 1995.

Shoemaker, Sydney. *The First-person Perspective and Other Essays*. Cambridge: Cambridge University Press, 1996.

———. *Identity, Cause, and Mind*. Oxford: Oxford University Press, 2003.

Spencer-Brown, George. *Laws of Form*. New York: The Julian Press, 1972.

Stern, Daniel. *The Interpersonal World of the Infant. A View from Psychoanalysis and Development Psychology*. London: Karnac Books, 1998

Strawson, Galen. *Real Materialism and Other Essays*. Oxford: Oxford University Press, 2008.

―――. *Selves. An Essay in Revisionary Metaphysics*. Oxford: Oxford University Press, 2009.

―――. "The Minimal Subject." In *The Oxford Handbook of the Self*, edited by Shaun Gallagher. Oxford: Oxford University Press, 2011.

Taylor, Charles. *Sources of the Self. The Making of the Modern Identity*. Cambridge, MA: Harvard University Press, 1989.

Thompson, Evan. *Mind in Life. Biology, Phenomenology, and the Sciences of Mind*. Cambridge, MA: The Belknap Press of Harvard University Press, 2007.

Trevarthen, Colwyn. "Communication and Cooperation in Early Infancy. A Description of Primary Intersubjectivity." In *Before Speech: The Beginning of Human Communication*, edited by M. Bullowa. London: Cambridge University Press, 1979: 321–347.

Tuomela, Raimo. *The Philosophy of Sociality: The Shared Point of View*. Oxford: Oxford University Press, 2007.

Vogeley, Kai and Shaun Gallagher. "Self in the Brain." In *The Oxford Handbook of the Self*, edited by Shaun Gallagher. Oxford: Oxford University Press, 2011: 111–36.

Wang, Yin and Antonia Hamilton. "Social Top-down Response Modulation (STORM): A Model of the Control of Mimicry in Social Interaction." *Frontiers in Human Neuroscience* 6 (2012). https://doi.org/10.3389/fnhum.2012.00153.

Wilby, Michael. "The Simplicity of Mutual Knowledge." *Philosophical Explorations* 13, no. 2 (2010): 83–100.

Wittgenstein, Ludwig. *Philosophical Remarks*, edited by Rush Rhees. Translated by Raymond Hargreaves and Roger White. Oxford: Basil Balckwell, 1998.

―――. *Preliminary Studies for the "Philosophical Investigations." Generally known as The Blue and Brown Books*. Oxford: Blackwell Publishing, 2007.

Wrathall, Mark A. "'I' 'Here' and 'You' 'There': Heidegger on Existential Spatiality and the 'Volatilized' Self." *Yearbook for Eastern and Western Philosophy* 2017, no. 2 (2017): 223–34.

Yanabu, Akira. *History of the Birth of Translated Words in Modern Japan (Honyakugo Seiritsu Jijyo)*. Translated by Ok-Hee Kim. Seoul: Maeumsanchaek, 2001.

Zahavi, Dan. *Subjectivity and Selfhood: Investigating the First-Person Perspective*. Cambridge, MA: MIT Press, 2008.

―――. "Unity of Consciousness." In *The Oxford Handbook of the Self*, edited by Shaun Gallagher. Oxford: Oxford University Press, 2011.

―――. "The Experiential Self: Objections and Clarifications" *Self, No Self? Perspectives from Analytic, Phenomenological, and Indian Traditions*, edited by Mark Siderits, Evan Thompson, and Dan Zahavi. Oxford: Oxford University Press, 2011.

Zanuttini, Raffaella, Miok Pak, and Paul Portner. "A Syntactic Analysis of Interpretive Restrictions on Imperative, Promissive, and Exhortative Subjects." *Natural Language & Linguistic Theory* 30, no. 4 (November 1, 2012): 1231–74. https://doi.org/10.1007/s11049-012-9176-2.

# Index

*abeonim*, 53
affectedness, 167, 169
ἄλλος αὐτός, 145–46
*Allgegenseitigkeit*, 154
alter ego, 145
alterity, 62–64, 117, 128, 138, 143, 146
anaphor, 51
anonymity, 76, 138–39, 145
Aristotle, 11, 56, 145
a-subjective, 89, 146–47, 155, 170
atemporality, 68
Austronesian language, 40
autonomous, 19, 69, 78, 89, 96n1, 136–37, 142
autonomy, 78, 89
*avoir*, 55–57

being-in-relation, 104, 132, 170
belong, 1, 9, 21–22, 27, 29–34, 37–42, 55, 90, 91, 95, 111–12, 116–17, 124–25, 128–30, 140–42, 145, 155, 175, 186–90, 196
belongingness, 31, 35–36, 93, 111–12, 116
Bermúdez, José Luis, 68–69
Bernasconi, Robert, 7
*Besinnung*, 48n69, 71
binding theorical status, 51
bipolar, 167

bodily self, 166, 190
Bornemark, Jonna, 136, 146–47
Borromean rings, 109, 111–12, 115, 117, 124–28, 132, 157–58
boundary, 99, 101, 103–6, 114–16, 132, 144, 151n60, 158, 160, 166, 189, 191, 197; boundary making, 104, 115, 117, 132
brain in a vat, 136–37
Brentano, Franz, 142
Brinck, Ingar, 19, 76, 119n34, 131, 165
Buber, Martin, 153–55, 162n14
*bun*, 36

Canetti, Elias, 140, 165
carnal phenomenology, 168
Carr, David, 2, 48n69, 70–72, 74, 77, 83–84n119, 91, 93–94, 139, 143–44, 150n45, 187
Cartesian, 2, 69
categories, 11–12
Central Asia, 94, 181–86
China, 92, 195, 196
classical anthropology, 4
closed crowd, 140, 197
clusivity, 20, 22, 27, 29–36, 38–41, 130, 140
coagent, 133
*cogito ergo sum*, 2, 55, 57, 65, 69, 78

coherence of life, 71–72
collective anxiety, 197
collective memory, 181–84
collective mind, 139, 167
communication, 3, 8–9, 76, 159, 166–67, 169
community, 21, 43, 48n69, 73–74, 91–95, 136–37, 144, 182, 195–97
conceptual self, 68, 96n1
consciousness, 61, 63, 68–69, 75–76, 87–88, 106, 116, 133n4, 142, 167, 173; human consciousness, 72, 154; time-consciousness, 70, 187
contagion, 145, 165–66, 169
corporeal attunement, 168
corporeal interaction, 165–69
cosmopolitanism, 184–85
crossing, 103–6, 108–13, 115–17, 124–25, 127–28, 132, 138–39, 145
crowd, 139–40, 144–45, 165, 197
cultural memory, 10, 181, 183–84, 186

*Dasein*, 13, 77, 83–84, 96, 141, 143, 149
*Das Man*, 84, 135, 141
Descartes, René, 2, 92–93, 146
differentiation, 54, 63, 75–77, 87–88, 100, 103–4, 107, 115, 117, 119, 128, 132, 138–39, 145, 173, 184
Dilthey, Wilhelm, 71, 74, 91
Dunnett, Daniel, 72
dyad, 76, 95, 119n34, 125, 130, 132, 133n11

εἶναι, 11, 13, 56
emotional contagion, 165–67, 169
empathy, 1–2, 51, 170, 172–73, 175–76, 179
epistemological, 5, 33, 84, 88, 92, 100, 107, 115–17, 135, 137
epistemologically, 88, 100, 107, 115
epistemological priority, 88, 92
epistemology, 82
*Erzähler*, 72, 77
ethnography, 8, 33

*être*, 55, 57
Eurocentrism, 92
exclusive we, 30–34, 40–41, 130
extended I, 38–39, 43–44
extended self, 37, 42–44, 68, 72, 159

Falck, Andreas, 131, 165
family egoism, 94, 197
Fanon, Franz, 5, 93
Fichte, Johann Gottlieb, 64, 89
first-person phenomenon, 61
first-person plural, 39, 149, 189
first-person singular, 19, 24, 39, 41–42
Flagg resolution, 101, 118n2
von Foerster, Heinz, 135–36, 148n2
Foucault, Michel, 184
Freud, Sigmund, 135, 139
Frith, Chris, 3, 15n6, 168–69

*gaein*, 54
Gallagher, Shaun, 70, 73, 75
Gallotti, Mattia, 3, 15n6
gaze, 154–55, 166, 169
*Gemeingeist*, 167
*geosigi*, 160–61
*Geschehen*, 72, 171
*Geschichte*, 72, 171, 173
*Geschichtlichkeit*, 71
*geu*, 154–55, 187–88
*geudae*, 52
Gray, Jesse Glenn, 140

Habermas, Jürgen, 76
*Hangeul*, xi–xii
Hegel, G.W.F., 74, 89, 92–93, 150n45
Heidegger, Martin, 55, 71, 83–84n119, 91, 95, 141, 143
Heller, Agnes, 170–76, 183
history, 1, 5–6, 13, 15, 21, 30, 48n69, 55, 72, 74–75, 83n119, 89, 94–95, 172–73, 181–82, 184–87, 196
home, 42–43, 184, 186, 189–91, 197
honorific, 26, 31, 39–41, 52–54
humanity, 92–95, 187
Hume, David, 69

Husserl, Edmund, 142, 145, 167

'I', 2, 14, 19, 38–39, 42, 44, 50–53, 57–58, 62–68, 70, 76–77, 88, 95, 103–8, 122, 124–25, 129, 131–32, 135–37, 140, 142, 145, 153–55, 188–90
I, the subject, 64
*Ich-Du*, 154
*ida*, 11, 55–56
identity, 9, 30, 32, 43, 67, 68, 72, 74, 88, 91, 95, 96n1, 117, 119n36, 128, 135–36, 172, 183–84, 196; collective identity, 94, 181, 187, 190
inclusive we, 31, 33–34, 40
incorporated feelings, 170
incorporation, 139, 168, 170
independence, 93
indexical, 50
individual, 65, 74–76, 84n127, 87, 90–96, 125, 128, 131, 137, 139–40, 144–45, 150n252, 155–57, 167–68, 173–75, 187, 189–90, 196–97
individuality, 23, 54, 91, 92, 94, 132, 135, 138, 142–43, 160, 197
Indo-European language, 4, 77, 78, 90
intentionality, 3, 4, 62, 76, 87, 131, 137, 139, 144, 145, 150n45, 166, 168–69
interaction, 4, 8, 38, 73, 130–31, 142, 150n45, 156, 160, 167–70
interconnected, 127–29
interconnection, 160
intercorporeality, 167–68
interpersonal self, 73
interrelated, 125, 128
intersubjective, 1–2, 131, 142, 150n45, 155–56, 160, 169–70
intersubjectivity, 1–2, 14, 73, 76, 137–38, 143, 144, 146, 158, 168
intrinsically intersubjective, 131
introspection, 65
involvement, 170–71
*ipséité*, 74
Iribarne, Julia, 116
I-Thou, 38, 39, 76, 119n34, 137, 143, 153–54

I-You, 50, 153–55
I-You-Relation, 155

*jagi*, 14, 49–52, 54, 58n13, 64, 67, 145, 155
*jagi jasin*, 49
*jane*, 52
Japan, 13, 35, 47n53, 50, 51, 54, 181, 195–96
*jeo*, 39–41
*jeohi*, 26–27, 39–42, 47n58, 189
*jeohideul*, 189
joint action, 3, 31, 38, 122, 130, 132, 133n11, 144–45, 151n60, 160, 167
*jonjae*, 11–13
*juche*, 54

Kauffman, Louis, 50, 101, 103–7, 109–11, 113–14, 127
Kim, Chunsu, 154
Kim, Soyoung, 182, 184–86
knot, 109, 113–15, 126–29, 133n4, 135, 145
knot-I, 128
knot logic, 101, 109–10, 124, 127, 133n4
knot set theory, 89, 107–10, 113, 124
*Körper*, 55, 119n36
Koryo Saram, 181–88
Kriegel, Uriah, 63, 68, 69, 133n4, 142

Landweer, Hilge, 165–69
Le Bon, Gustave, 139–40
Legrand, Dorothée, 166
*Leib*, 55, 119n36
linguistics, xi, 4, 21, 51, 78, 90
linking, 109

Mach, Ernst, 44n2, 44n3
MacIntyre, Alasdair, 72, 74, 90–91
Malagasy, 7, 10, 62, 79, 90
Marcel, Gabriel, 55, 57
McCune-Reischauer System of Romanization (M-R), xi
McNeill, William H., 144, 195

means-end, 71
medio-passive subject, 75
membership, 30–33, 37, 42, 89–94, 108–111, 114, 124, 133, 144, 189; self-membership, 107, 114, 109
membership relation, 109
membership relationship, 33, 112, 125
Merleau-Ponty, Maurice, 55, 57, 131, 166, 168
meta-name, 21
metaphysical, 4, 33, 54, 68, 88, 150n45, 157
metaphysically, 78, 104, 144, 157, 166
metaphysics, 55
middle voice, 77–78
mimicry, 168–69
minimal subject, 67–68
*Mitgefühl*, 170, 172
Mobius band, 114
Morrison, Toni, 188
M-R. *See* McCune-Reischauer System of Romanization (M-R)
multipolarity, 51
mutual: knowledge, 38, 155–61, 166; membership, 109, 112, 133; relationship, 110, 132; self-mutual, 109
mutuality, 122, 128

*na*, 39–40
narrative, 48n69, 67, 70–75, 144, 187
narrative self, 48n69, 71–73, 91, 96n13
Neisser, Ulric, 68, 72–73, 92
*neo*, 39–40, 50, 52–54
*neohi*, 40, 189
*neohideul*, 189
von Neumann construction, 111
Newton fractal, 129
*nim*, 36
nonconceptual self-consciousness, 68–69
nonreflective, 68–69; nonreflective self-consciousness, 69
North Korea, xi, 185, 196
nosism, 42–44

nosistic, 29, 44
not-I, 103–6, 117, 128, 188
not-we, 188

objectified I, 117
objectified self, 61, 64–65
*omeonim*, 53
one big happy family, 21, 36, 124, 181, 186, 197
ontological, 54, 70, 88, 96, 115–17, 143, 145, 166; condition, 93; difference, 107; precondition, 100, 104, 117; priority, 69
ontologically, 44, 68, 70, 78, 104, 107, 109, 116, 132
ontologically pre-given, 132
ontology, 13, 96
open crowd, 140
othered I, 105, 107–8, 117, 129
othered self, 104, 117, 128–29, 142
otherness, 57, 74, 78
our husband, 19, 26–28, 30, 32–37, 39, 43–44, 90–91, 121, 126, 128–29, 189–90
*ourideul*, 187–89
*ouri* husband, 20, 22, 26, 36, 44, 87
*ouri* someone, 21, 124, 130, 132, 190
our someone, 20, 26, 28–29, 33, 35–36, 109, 122–24, 131–32, 137, 190

Pacherie, Elisabeth, 144, 148n9
pan-meta-name, 51
paradox, 51, 69, 78–79, 79n6, 95, 107–8, 114, 117, 117n33, 126, 128, 133n4
paradoxical, 78, 92, 107, 114, 184
Piaget, Jean, 96n1
plural first-person plural, 189
*pluralis excellectiae*, 42
*pluralis majestatis*, 42
*pluralis modestiae*, 43
plurality of spaces, 187
plural second-person plural, 189
plural subject, 4, 74, 143–45
pre-reflective, 62–64, 68–69; cogito, 69; consciousness, 87; experience, 87;

Index                                                                213

plural self-awareness, 137; subject, 87
pre-subjective, 1, 3, 87, 89, 95, 107, 117, 143, 146, 148, 155, 160, 170; bodily separation, 116–17; distinction, 117; I-You relation, 155; relation, 87, 89, 91, 94, 117, 143; self, 87, 90–93, 95, 107, 132, 135, 158; selfhood, 44; self-in-relation, 44, 78, 89–92, 101, 145, 158, 160; self-relation, 138, 160; state, 87–88, 132, 147–48, 170; structure, 103; understanding, 132; we, 13–14, 92–93, 95, 99, 131, 135–36, 142, 147, 153, 170, 187; web, 92; we-ness, 89, 95, 148; we-notion, 160
pre-subjectively, 116
primary boundary, 99, 132
primary distinction, 88–89, 99–101, 103, 105, 116–17, 153
primary relation, 65, 88, 93–94, 104, 117, 132
primordial phenomenon, 186
private self, 68, 92
pro-drop language, 90
psychology, 2, 3, 131, 148, 159

*Qallunaat*, 5–6
Qawasqar, 42

Reddy, Vasudevi, 19, 76, 169
Revised Romanization System (RR), xi
Ricoeur, Paul, 7, 72, 74
RR. *See* Revised Romanization System (RR)

Sartre, Jean-Paul, 63, 69, 76, 135, 139
Schechtman, Marya, 74
Scheler, Max, 76, 165
Schmid, Hans Bernhard, 63, 135, 137–38, 143
Searle, John, 76, 135–36, 150n252
second-person plural, 40, 189
second-person singular, 14, 39, 49, 52, 55

*Sein und Zeit*, 77
*Selbstbestimmung*, 78, 89
*Selbstständigkeit*, 93
*Selbstvollzug*, 71
self-agency, 144
self as we, 87–88, 116, 129, 159
self-awareness, 61–63, 69; permanent self-awareness, 133n4; plural self-awareness, 135, 137–38; post-self-awareness, 159; pre-reflective self-awareness, 63, 137
self-consciousness, 61–63, 69, 93, 103, 117, 126; bodily self-consciousness, 166; intransitive self-consciousness, 69; nonconceptual self-consciousness, 68, 69; nonreflective self-consciousness, 69; pre-reflective self-consciousness, 69; primitive self-consciousness, 69; reflective self-consciousness, 173; subjective self-consciousness, 3
self-definition, 72–73, 91, 93, 95
selfhood, 1, 58, 68, 72, 138; pre-subjective selfhood, 44
self-in-relation, 87, 93, 95, 99, 116–17, 128, 132, 135, 139, 146, 153, 155–56, 158, 160, 170, 176, 189
self-naming, 91
self-reference, 63, 65
self-referential, 65, 67, 107, 127–29
self-reflection, 62–63, 158; post-self-reflection, 159
self-representing, 65
self-understanding, 4, 64, 73, 78, 84n119, 91–92, 95–96, 141
selves-in-relation, 170
*seonsaengnim*, 53
shared feelings, 166–67, 169
shift, 50
Shoemaker, Sydney, 64–65
*Sinn*, 71–72, 77
social cognition, 2–3
Soffer, Gail, 145
*soi-même*, 74
South Korea, 182–84, 186, 196–97

Spencer-Brown, George, 101
story, 7, 10, 15, 72–74, 77–78, 94–95, 171–72, 181, 187
storyteller, 71, 77
storytelling, 78
Strawson, Galen, 65, 67–68
subject-object, 52, 67–68, 77, 80n9, 89–90, 135, 143, 146, 147, 153–55, 159–60, 166, 170
subjective consciousness, 166, 169
subject of action, 71
subject of experience, 67–69

Taylor, Charles, 73, 77, 91–92
Temporality, 67, 70–72, 74
third-person singular, 14, 49, 54, 155
τί ἐστι, 11, 56, 65
to be, 10–13, 55–57
to have, 55–57
τόδε τι, 11, 56, 65
τόπος, 190
topological space, 157–58
trefoil knot, 109, 115, 126–29, 133
Trevarthen, Colwyn, 73, 168
triad, 130, 133, 155
trinity, 117

*Übereinstimmung*, 77
unconscious, 165

unconsciously, 139, 196
un-homey, 6, 186
un-homey-ness, 186, 191
unipolar, 167, 169–70

Venn diagram, 110
Vogeley, Kai, 75
void, 88, 99, 109, 138, 184

waveform, 101, 105–7
we, 1–4, 6–9, 13–15, 19–21, 25, 27–33, 35–39, 41–44, 48, 53, 76–77, 87–88, 92–95, 107–9, 119, 124, 126, 128, 130, 132, 135, 137–38, 141–44, 186–90
web, 37, 88, 91–92, 99, 101, 124, 128, 135, 138–39, 154, 170, 191
webs of interlocution, 91
von Wedelstaedt, Ulrich, 168, 177
we-intentionality, 144, 150, 169
we-ness, 1, 14–15, 29, 33, 37–39, 77, 88–89, 91, 94, 115, 117, 119n34, 122, 124, 130, 137–38, 141–43, 147–48, 168, 171, 176n56, 181, 187
Wilby, Michael, 156–60
Wittgenstein, Ludwig, 64–66
*woorie*, 21, 45n9

Zahavi, Dan, 19, 61–63, 68, 76, 138

# About the Author

**Hye Young Kim** is an associate researcher at the Husserl Archive at l'Ecole Normale Superieure in Paris, France. She is the author of *Sorge und Geschichte: Phänomenologische Untersuchung im Anschluss an Heidegger* (2015, Berlin).

www.ingramcontent.com/pod-product-compliance
Lightning Source LLC
Chambersburg PA
CBHW050904300426
44111CB00010B/1373